SKILL

SKILL

A top-producing agent's guide to earning unlimited income

BY DAVID GREENE

BiggerPockets®
PUBLISHING
Denver, Colorado

Praise for
SOLD

"As the person who brought David into real estate sales, I've watched his growth in this area from zero to hero. David's explanations and systems for how to become a top-producing agent are unquestionably effective. I can't think of a better person to write a book this needed in the industry."

—David Osborn, *New York Times* best-selling author of *Wealth Can't Wait* and *Bidding to Buy*

"David opens up his entire playbook here and doesn't leave anything out. A must-have for any agent who takes their business seriously."

—Aaron Amuchastegui, host of *Real Estate Rockstars* podcast and author of *Bidding to Buy*

"I wish this book had existed when I was selling real estate! David has done a fantastic job of breaking down what it takes to be successful into simple, easy-to-follow steps that help agents master their craft and become top producers. I love this book!"

—Pat Hiban, former No. 1 agent for both Keller Williams and RE/MAX, *New York Times* best-selling author of *6 Steps to 7 Figures*

Skill: A Top-Producing Agent's Guide to Earning Unlimited Income
David Greene

Published by BiggerPockets Publishing LLC, Denver, CO
Copyright © 2022 by David Greene
All Rights Reserved.

Publisher's Cataloging-in-Publication Data

Names: Greene, David, 1974-, author.
Title: Skill: a top-producing agent's guide to earning unlimited income / by David Greene.
Series: Top-Producing Real Estate Agent
Description: Denver, CO: BiggerPockets Publishing, 2022.
Identifiers: LCCN: 2020941714 | ISBN: 9781947200371 (paperback) | 9781947200388 (ebook)
Subjects: LCSH Real estate agents. | Real estate business. | Success in business. | Selling. | BISAC BUSINESS & ECONOMICS / Real Estate / Buying & Selling Homes | BUSINESS & ECONOMICS / Real Estate / General | BUSINESS & ECONOMICS / Sales & Selling / General
Classification: LCC HD1382 .G74 2022 | DDC 333.33068--dc23

Printed on recycled paper in the United States of America
10 9 8 7 6 5 4 3 2 — 1

Dedication

To **Tim Rhode**, for being my first mentor, believing in me, and introducing me to top-level real estate sales production.

To **David Osborn**, for the doors you helped open and the blueprints you shared.

To **Daniel Del Real**, for being the best example of the perfect Realtor I've found.

To **Gary Keller** and **Jay Papasan**, for setting the tone for what a great book should look like.

To **Krista Keller**, for helping me build this.

To **Kyle Renke**, for being the lion/guinea pig of this content!

TABLE OF CONTENTS

INTRODUCTION 14

CHAPTER ONE
TOP-PRODUCER TRAITS. 17
What Is a Top Producer?. 17
Reverse Engineering Success 18
Top-Producer Qualities. 19
Your Standards Determine Your Success. 26
Top-Producer Standards 28
Raising Your Standards with Clients 32
Raising Your Standards in Negotiating 33
Raising Your Standards in Communication 34

CHAPTER TWO
FUNNEL PROGRESSION (TOOL ONE): FINDING PEOPLE 37
Sales Funnel 39
Keys to Successful Lead Generation 40
Goal of the Contact 42
Sample Phone Call Script 47

CHAPTER THREE

FUNNEL PROGRESSION (TOOL TWO): CONVERTING CLIENTS............................50
Improve Your Close Rate through Preparation..................53

CHAPTER FOUR

FUNNEL PROGRESSION (TOOL THREE): THE PSYCHOLOGY NEEDED TO GET IN CONTRACT...........................72
Psychological Concepts to Help Your Business.................75
The Trusted Guide...79
The "Big Why"..81
Going Three Levels Deep..................................85
The Pendulum of Fear and Greed 87
FOMO..89

CHAPTER FIVE

FUNNEL PROGRESSION (TOOL FOUR): THE KNOWLEDGE TO CLOSE THE DEAL..........93
Practical Knowledge Application: Anticipating
    Problems Before They Occur 95
Buyer's Remorse 102
Strategies for Listing Agents 104
What Top-Producing Agents Do 110
Completing the Closing Circuit 115

CHAPTER SIX
COMMON PROBLEMS WITH EACH TOOL........ 120
Common Problems with Lead Generation 121
Common Problems with Appointments/Presentations......... 125
Common Problems with Psychology 130
Common Problems with Knowledge......................... 132

CHAPTER SEVEN
STRATEGIC PLANNING 135
Empowerment through Planning............................ 135
The Importance of Vision................................. 136
Reverse Engineering 136
GPS 1:3:5 137
4-1-1.. 139
33 Touches... 140
Daily Plan... 141
Lead versus Lag Measures................................. 142
PLAN.. 144
Hourglass Theory 145

CHAPTER EIGHT
SOCIAL MEDIA................................. 151
Stats on Social Media Usage 152
Social Media Content 153
Using Social Media as a CRM.............................. 160
Marketing Listings 161
Triggering Interest...................................... 164
Finding Balance 169

CHAPTER NINE

FINDING HELP 172

Ways to Scale 174
When You'll Need Help 177
How to Find Help 183
Win–Win Propositions 188
How to Ensure Mutual Growth 192
Path to Progress. 194

CHAPTER TEN

LISTING LIKE A PRO 202

The Skills You'll Need. 204
Determining List Price 207
The Listing Process 213
Nailing the Presentation. 219
Focus on Listings 227

CHAPTER ELEVEN

THE BUY/SELL COMBO 230

Why You Want Both Sides 231
The Buy/Sell Pitch 232
Running the Numbers 235
The Roadmap 239
The Four Methods of the Buy/Sell Combo. 242
Synergy 245
Finding Clients for the Buy/Sell Combo 246

CHAPTER TWELVE
NEGOTIATION STRATEGIES 249
The Power of Tension 250
The Tension Formula 251
Agents Creating Win–Win Solutions 253
Getting Your Point Across Effectively 256
Baseline Adjustment 257
Using the Spectrum 258
The Triangle Theory 260
Prizing 263
The Tier System 267

CHAPTER THIRTEEN
UNDERSTANDING FINANCING 270
How the Mortgage Market Works 272
Different Loan Products 276
Preapproval Process 278
Explaining the Costs of Borrowing to Your Clients 280
Foreclosure Process 283
Common Pitfalls 285
Finance Hacks 291

CHAPTER FOURTEEN
WORKING WITH INVESTORS 299
Why Work with Investors 300
What Investors Want: ONFIRE Agents 301
The Language of Investors 304
Running the Numbers 309
House Hacking 312

Pitfalls of Working with Investors 315
Leveraging Your Real Estate Investment Knowledge
    to Close More Deals 319
Build Your Wealth through Real Estate Ownership 320

CHAPTER FIFTEEN

MOMENTUM 324
Progression Models. 325
Domino Theory 327
Rules of Momentum 328
Vicious and Virtuous Cycles. 332
Flows and Cycles 333
Skill Set Bleed-Over and Momentum 335
Momentum and Business Growth. 337
Investing in Real Estate to Improve Your Business 337
Buyer/Listing Skill Set Bleed-Over 338

CONCLUSION 343

INTRODUCTION

I wrote the first book in this series, *SOLD*, with the new agent in mind. I still distinctly remember how it felt to be a new agent. It was a ridiculous cocktail of excitement, ambition, nerves, fear, confusion, frustration, and helplessness. I had a lack of direction paired with the drive to create an experience unlike any other. My desire to help other agents avoid that mess drove me to write the first book and provide some clarity.

In this book, I'm speaking to those who undertook that journey and are ready for the next leg. *SKILL* is, in my opinion, a much better book, with much better content, and will lead Realtors to a much better life. While not being broke is good, being wealthy and having more than one needs is much, much better. *SKILL* takes the steps of *SOLD* and shows you how to climb the ladder to where the top producers earn their fruit.

Put simply, there's not much point in becoming a Realtor if you're not going to do it well.

Agents give up weekends, nights, normal work hours, and oftentimes their sanity to help others build wealth. Isn't that a crazy concept? Clients will complain that commissions are too high, but the amount of wealth your client accumulates because you help them buy real estate makes commissions pale in comparison.

Good agents who accomplish their clients' goals deserve to be compensated well. Great agents need to be compensated even better. It's my belief that agents who deliver excellence deserve the financial fruits of their work.

SKILL was written to help you become a great agent. This book breaks down into detail every aspect of this job you wish someone showed you (but no one did). My goal is to make you feel like you're looking over the shoulders of top producers on how they conduct their tasks and speak with their clients. It's no surprise in this industry that it's not just what you say but also how you say it. This book provides you the information you need to share and how and when to share it.

You know top-producing agents by how they carry themselves. They dress, talk, listen, and act in a certain fashion. This isn't coincidental. Successful agents follow the same steps. This book starts by highlighting the characteristics you want to emulate. I call these top-producer traits.

I start here because it's important that you understand success at the highest levels in this industry isn't only because of what you know. Success is a direct result of *who you are* as a person. To experience top-producer fruits, you need to develop the character and characteristics that make clients want to work with you.

I introduced the concept of the Sales Funnel in *SOLD*. In this book, I go into deep detail about how it works. I developed it as a framework to help my team break down the daunting actions of turning someone from a prospective client into a seller with a closing. While the concept is simple, you can't achieve sustainably high-volume closings without respecting its principles. The Sales Funnel is a map that guides you from one checkpoint to the next through clear, actionable steps. It will help you recognize where you are failing in your business and which skills you need to improve to have better conversion rates, and it will bring you clarity when you're confused.

Without the Sales Funnel to guide you, you'll find that clients will try to lead the transaction by default. For a successful career in real estate, you must have the confidence to remain in the driver's seat of transactions and have your clients follow your lead. Using the stages of the Sales Funnel will help you build your confidence to do just that.

Next, I speak to the four main "tools" that agents need to build up their sales skills, or their ability to build a large volume of work: (1) lead generation, (2) appointments/presentations, (3) psychology, and (4) knowledge. Each tool helps you transition from one stage of the Sales Funnel to the next. When you're ready to move from "good" to "great," use these tools.

SKILL also provides detailed information on using social media to build your business, moving lower-level tasks to assistants, creating a business/vision plan for your company, mastering listings to increase volume, and more. Understanding and applying these concepts will make you a standout among your competition in both quality and confidence.

This book is meant to serve as the mentor that so few of us find in the industry. Use its contents like a trusted guide to help you find your true potential, your unique voice, and your place as a top-producing real estate agent in your market.

If we are honest with ourselves, we'll admit that real estate can be a hard career. What appear to be benefits (freedom of schedule, no boss, unlimited income ceiling, etc.) are often huge challenges (no structure offered, no accountability or leads provided, no income security, etc.). For a happy and rewarding career in real estate, you need a strong income to justify the sacrifices it requires.

There is plenty of competition from big companies looking to replace us with tech. There is plenty of vitriol directed at our commissions. There are plenty of agents who give our industry a bad name from lack of effort and professionalism.

This book is intended to help strengthen your position and allow you to succeed no matter what you face. It offers you the knowledge and guidance great agents provide to grow their clients' wealth, plan their future, or find a safe place to live. And to build your wealth along the way!

CHAPTER ONE

TOP-PRODUCER TRAITS

*"If you want to be a leader who attracts quality people,
the key is to become a person of quality yourself."*

—JIM ROHN

What Is a Top Producer?

Top producers are the agents who stand apart from their peers in their market. They close more deals, make more money, and help more people than the other agents in their office. They have a reputation for selling a large number of homes. Top producers not only generate leads, but they also have more leads come to them. When a top producer speaks about real estate, they speak with the authority and confidence that comes with knowing their craft. They dominate their market.

Their reputation doesn't stop with the local community. Other agents know about them too. When you start working at a brokerage, it doesn't take long before you know who is selling homes, what their specialty is, and how they are leveraging their talents, skills, and resources to outperform the competition. People talk about top producers. They want to be like them, they want their approval, and they want their results.

There's a common maxim in real estate sales: "Eighty percent of the business goes through the top 20 percent of the agents." If you're going to work in this business, you want to be in the top 20 percent. If you're not, you'll find yourself fighting for 20 percent of the business with the other 80 percent of Realtors.

This book is for those who don't want to just call themselves a Realtor—they want to become a top producer and experience everything this profession has to offer. Odds are, you didn't invest all your time and energy into becoming a licensed agent just to be mediocre. Getting to the top 20 percent is the key to the Realtor good life.

Reverse Engineering Success

A common mistake newbies make is to ask, "What do I do first?" and then work forward from there. These newbies learn from their mistakes, just like everybody else. But their path is dictated by trial and error. They take the wrong step, they learn their lesson, and they take the right step next. Rinse and repeat. Progress can be made like this, but it's not ideal. Rather than figure out the path to success by potluck, it makes much more sense to start with the end in mind and work backward. By doing this, you reduce the number of missteps to your desired result. The more direct your path, the faster you'll reach your destination (that is, top-producer status).

Being a top producer in real estate sales is more about who you are than what you do. When you follow top producers, you start to notice many of them have similar character traits. For instance, they have more disciplined work schedules. They use leverage to get ahead. And they insist on high standards in anything they do. If you want to be a top producer, start by valuing what they value. Doing so early in your career will help you develop the habits you'll need to support a big business later on.

Another wrong question new agents often ask is, "How do I get leads?" Although this appears to be a practical place to start, it assumes you'll know what to do with a lead when you get one. The truth is, if the agent knew how to close a lead with a high level of skill, the confidence they would exude would bring leads to them. Instead, I recommend you ask a different question: "Who would I need to be in order to draw a large number of leads?"

Think about how the top producers in an office act, talk, and carry themselves. How do they dress? In which direction do they steer conversations? How do they make you feel after speaking with them? These are the traits you want to emulate. When you come across this same way, clients will find their way to you. If you still want to find leads, you can do so knowing you can close the deal and your efforts weren't in vain.

Understanding who you need to become to get the results you want starts early in the process. This book offers helpful information, but nothing I write could possibly bring the same understanding as watching a top producer in action. The body language, facial expressions, and confidence with which they carry themselves is really what you're after. No text by itself can explain how that works.

The traits used by top producers are not easy to come by. If they were, there would be no top producers—everyone would be getting the same amount of business! Top producers are where they are because they are *better* than their competitors. Building up these characteristics in yourself won't come easily, and it often won't feel natural. If you find that to be the case, *that's okay*. The more difficult the transition is for you, the more valuable it will be when you get it down. It is no different than anything else you have learned in life. As a child, it was challenging to learn how to walk and speak. As an adult, it is hard learning a new exercise like yoga or developing a new skill like cooking. Everything is difficult in the beginning and becomes easier with repetition.

Top-Producer Qualities

In my time working in the real estate sales space, I've found top producers to have certain traits in common. Here's how you can channel and improve on those qualities.

Be More Direct

Those you communicate with perceive directness as a hallmark of confidence and skill. When someone is unsure of the direction they should take or how to communicate an issue, it's usually because of inexperience. Clients understand that the less experience their agent has, the less likely they will do their job well. Avoid looking insecure and inexperienced. Instead, act confident in front of clients. Direct communication is an easy way to accomplish this.

Beating around the bush, failing to answer a question clearly, or fumbling over words all portray a lack of experience that induces hesitation in your clients. Speaking directly to a situation and letting your clients know what comes next before they even ask works wonders in earning their confidence. To establish yourself as a confident leader who's in control, end every conversation by sharing next steps you'll be taking.

Directness in communication also saves you time, which is why top producers develop this trait. It's a requirement when you're operating at a high level with a lot of clients. You need to get things done faster! When you speak clearly and get your point across quickly, your clients tend to mirror this trait and will give you the information you need faster as well. Directness is more efficient and more effective, and portrays more confidence, and those three are important in this job. Start practicing being more direct in both your decision-making and communication style.

Ways to Be More Direct

- Set the boundaries of the conversation from the get-go.
  - *Example:* "Hey, I have five minutes, and I need to ask you something. Here are our options...What information do you need in order to know which direction you'd like to take?"
- When providing options, paint a picture of how those scenarios will likely turn out. This makes it easier—and therefore faster—for your clients to make their decisions.
  - *Example:* "If we ask for a credit of $5,000, the sellers will likely put their house back on the market and find another buyer. That means we'll be out looking at properties again this weekend, and there isn't anything else on the market with a pool. Or we could ask for a credit of $1,500. I think I can get them to give it to us. That should be enough to fix the major problems but not the cosmetic ones."
- Help clients see the value in eliminating options. Many clients make the mistake of trying not to miss out on a great opportunity. This fear of missing out creates a scenario in which the client is overloaded with options and can't decide at all.
  - *Example:* "There are twenty-five houses in town that fit your budget. Ten are in the wrong school district, five need significant work you don't have the money for, and four of them have lots

that are too small for you. That leaves us with six houses I'd like to show you. Let's focus on making sure we don't miss out on the best one of these six!"

Improve Your Skills

It should come as no surprise that top-producing agents are highly skillful in their craft. Top agents are known for something special that makes them better than their competitors, and they often brand themselves this way. Sometimes they sell homes faster, or they earn more money for their clients, or their customer service is superior. Top producers simply do certain things better than agents who perform at a mediocre level.

Luckily for you, there are many skills an agent needs, so there are many ways you can be better than your competition!

Skillful communication is a key skill to develop. Your ability to convey information in a way that keeps your client excited and feeling positive will affect how many houses you sell. Strong communicators highlight the best aspects of the deal for the client, provide possible solutions to problems, are easy to understand, and sound confident in the information they are providing.

Market knowledge is also a skill that requires a high level of mastery. Top agents know how fast houses sell, how much they sell for, and which parts of town are most desirable. This carries over into design as well. You want to help your sellers prepare their homes to be appealing to as many buyers as possible. You also want to know how to help buyers estimate what it will cost to fix up a property to the way they say they would like it. Knowledge of home values, rehab prices, and design styles will set you apart from less experienced agents.

Another beneficial skill is negotiation. Negotiation is an important part of an agent's job, especially with those who are primarily concerned with the financial components of a transaction. Sharing how you handle offers on a client's listing or what you do to eliminate leverage in transactions (when you represent the seller) will showcase your skills as a listing agent. This will work when representing buyers too. Share how you get sellers to cover closing costs or how you get your offers accepted over others in a hot market. Buyer clients will take note of this and be impressed by your negotiation skills when you bring this up in conversation.

Negotiation is not limited primarily to the other agents. More often than not, you will find yourself negotiating with your own clients. Your ability to convince your sellers to give a little in closing costs can make the difference between a house selling in the first two weeks on the market versus six months down the road. Your ability to negotiate your buyers into shortening their inspection period by a week can be the difference in them getting their ideal house or something less than their ideal. Strong negotiators highlight the benefits of the solution they are presenting while helping the other person feel they are getting what they want. If you want to sell a lot of homes, learn how to negotiate with your clients!

Ways to Improve Your Skills
- Improve your communication skills by learning how to get directly to your point.
- Learn how to negotiate so everyone feels like they're getting something of value.
- Start every day with research. See which homes hit the market that morning, look at the listing prices, and note when a listing is posted noticeably lower or higher than a comparable property. Casually mention this information when speaking with clients during lead generation time.
  - *Example:* "Yes, I get a fair commission of 6 percent, but *you* get the best Realtor available in this entire market."

Build Your Charisma
Top-producing agents inspire others. This results in loyal clients returning to you time and time again for their real estate needs as well as referring others your way for the same reason. When you have an army of fans supporting your business, it's hard to fail. You may have this trait naturally. If not, you'll need to cultivate it.

Keep in mind not everyone's charisma is the same. Some people have a gregarious charm that inspires others through fun and goodwill. Others draw people to them through their genuineness or authenticity. Consider someone like Tom Hanks. His popularity in Hollywood is based on his reputation as a "genuine guy" others can relate to. His ability to relate to the working person makes him a movie draw and thus a powerful Hollywood player.

The same can be said of Elon Musk. Most people would describe his personality as downright awkward, and many who work with him claim he is incredibly difficult to get along with. Despite this, Musk has a massive following of devoted fans who believe in him and his ability to be on the cutting edge of progress. Why? Because he is considered smarter than everyone else around him. His intelligence creates a charisma his personality never could.

Charisma comes in all shapes and sizes. Each of us has our own strengths that allow us to inspire this type of devotion. Top-producing agents harness their power to help grow their businesses. What are your charismatic traits? If you don't know, ask the people who know you best. They'll tell you when you are most confident and in which situations you tend to shine. Then, look for ways to spend as much time in those situations as possible.

Ways to Build Your Charisma
- Believe in what you say. It's hard to fake conviction. If you aren't sure, study the material until you are.
- Be aware of how you come across. People notice if you mumble, stare at the floor, or try to blend into the shadows. Work on outwardly expressing the confidence you have inside you.
- Don't try to be someone you're not. If you're introverted, focus the attention of your conversations on the data you've collected that other agents miss. If you know contracts well, mention ways you've kept your clients out of legal problems that other agents can't do. Let people see you through the lens of confidence you project when you are in your element.

Increase Your Leadership

Leaders inspire confidence in others who rely on them for guidance. As a real estate professional, that's the exact situation you'll find yourself in. The better your leadership skills, the more comfortable your clients will be trusting you and following your advice. The less resistance these clients give you, the more deals you can close in a shorter amount of time. Improving your skills as a leader is a nonnegotiable tenet of becoming a top-producing agent.

My best advice for becoming a better leader is to practice the concept Jocko Willink and Leif Babin detail in their book *Extreme Ownership*. They state that every error or mistake ever made is the leader's fault, regardless of who makes the blunder. If a leader takes ownership of everything that happens underneath them, they eventually iron out bumps in the road and become better at preventing mistakes from happening in the first place. When leaders shirk responsibility or place the blame on others, they reduce their ability to influence and impact their business and subordinates. Good leaders own everything.

Good leaders also run toward hard things. As a top-producing agent, you are setting yourself apart from your competitors. This means having higher standards and taking on challenges other agents would shy away from, like hiring and training staff. Some skills—such as leverage in negotiation—are easier in theory than in practice. For this reason, very few are successful at the most difficult aspects of the industry. This is why there is so much room to rise to the top! It is by running toward hard things and not avoiding them that you set yourself apart from the competition. You can have what few have if you are willing to do what few others do. Practicing extreme ownership as a leader means running toward what is hard.

Make it a habit to own the mistakes that occur in your business and let your clients know your plan to fix them. It is true that when a buyer's loan falls through on your listing, it isn't your fault. It is *also* true that you could have checked more thoroughly with the buyer's lender before accepting their offer. When you own the mistake, you empower yourself to make changes in how you move forward, and you reduce the chances of the same mistake happening with the next client.

Similarly, you should see your weaknesses and vulnerabilities as opportunities for growth. Unfamiliar with the lending process? Learn more about how the lending side of our business works. This will make you a better agent and may even open up opportunities to help improve your lending partners' business. These doors only open when we embrace that we can better influence outcomes when we commit to being leaders who do hard things.

The stronger you become as a leader, the more people will be drawn to you as someone who can serve their real estate needs. Your leadership skills therefore directly translate into an increased number of clients. This will also help you build a strong team—or, at a minimum, create a strong staff—working alongside you to scale your business.

Ways to Increase Your Leadership

- Don't just react to problems when they occur; work proactively to stop problems from occurring. This is a key part of creating systems

and improving your clients' overall experience.
- Accept that it is your responsibility to train others to help you. It's not enough to do the work well yourself. If you want to help more clients, you'll also need to hire and train staff well.
- Never blame anyone else when things go wrong. You can explain how the mistake happened, but always accept responsibility for not working to prevent the mistake.
  - *Example*: "I'm sorry, but it looks like the buyer's agent failed to schedule their appraisal and now they are running behind the contracted timelines. I should have been checking in with them to make sure they handled this. I'm going to call them every day to ensure the appraiser arrives as soon as possible."

Be Trustworthy

It's sad this needs to be mentioned, but there is a glaring need for trustworthiness in real estate sales. If you want to be a top producer, you absolutely must excel at being a trustworthy agent known for always putting the interest of your clients before your own. Most importantly, always tell the truth. It's never okay to lie to a client; however, that doesn't mean that all ways of conveying information are the same. Trustworthy agents disclose everything their client should know about a property or a deal, and they practice how they will convey this information.

These agents develop a specific method of delivering vital information, especially if it's a common issue in real estate. This is referred to as a "script." Scripts are, simply put, a means of communicating information to clients in a manner that is easy to understand. Trustworthy agents often put the information in context to help the client weigh its importance and prevent them from overreacting or making a rash decision they'll regret later. Your ability to communicate information effectively will allow you to maintain a high degree of trustworthiness without compromising your sales.

When conveying negative information, always do so by phone call as opposed to email or text. Practice how you will share the information in a way that is completely accurate but that includes a spoonful of sugar to help the medicine go down. Focus on the solution you have in mind and bring the client's attention to that rather than letting it rest on the problem or the potential negative consequences.

Ways to Be Trustworthy

- Focus on the solution.
- Don't "wing" the conversation. When you must convey upsetting news, jot down every important point that needs to be made, then practice until you've established a way of communicating this news that reduces the emotional blow for the client.
- Resist the urge to hide bad news from your clients and hope they don't find out. This will completely erode any trust you've built. Your clients will understand that not everything that goes wrong is your fault, and they often just need to vent. Be direct about conveying bad news and allow them to take their frustration out on you without taking it personally.
  - *Example:* "It appears your home has appraised for $20,000 less than the contracted price. I'm sure this is a shock to you, and I'm very disappointed as well. The buyers have the ability to back out of this deal if we don't reduce our price, and that would mean us putting the house back on the market where this could potentially happen again. I want to avoid that, and I'm going to be speaking with the other agent to see if there is a possibility we could meet somewhere in the middle."

Your Standards Determine Your Success

Many people operate under the assumption that we can have more success simply by working harder. In many ways this is true; it just isn't the whole story. Hard work is not a guarantee of success. During my time in real estate sales, I've noticed there is something more than hard work that makes a top producer.

Top-producing agents are people of character. There is something about who they are as people that separates them from the other agents in their market.

Think about the people you trust the most in life. Are they always the hardest workers? Or are they the people who keep your secret and are always straight with you? When someone shows the strength of character to put your needs above their own on a consistent basis, you trust them and want to be around them. Trustworthiness breeds trust, and trust is the essential ingredient in all good relationships. Real estate is a relationship business. As such, your relationships with others will play a large role in determining your success.

Your sphere of influence won't send you referrals if they don't trust you'll take good care of them.

Your clients won't follow your advice if they don't trust your motives.

Leads won't trust your guidance if they don't trust your honesty.

Other agents won't accept your offer if they don't trust you can bring your buyers to close.

Two of the first things to learn as a top producer are how to make tough decisions and how to have difficult conversations that maintain and even foster others' trust in you. Your character will determine whether you can do this.

Character will also play a large role in your work ethic. Top producers keep their word. When they say they will make a certain number of contacts in a day, they do it. When they agree to read through a contract in its entirety, they do it. Top producers have high standards for themselves, and it shows. The standards you choose for yourself may be the most influential factor that determines your success in business and in life.

As a young agent, I heard Gary Keller (founder of Keller Williams Realty) say, "Your clients are not loyal to you. They are loyal to your standards." This statement set off an avalanche of thoughts in my mind.

The more I grew in the business, the more I found Keller's statement to be true. In fact, as I gained a deeper understanding of this concept, I realized the only thing that set me apart from other agents—and the sole reason clients chose to work with me over others—was the standard I set for how I conducted myself and my reputation with real estate.

Clients are not drawn to me solely because of my knowledge or track record. These things play a role, of course, but more important is that clients are drawn to what I represent. I have built my own portfolio of investment properties through my standards for earning, saving, and investing money. My properties perform well because of my standards for investment criteria.

My knowledge has been acquired through the standard I set for myself for learning, and my ability to articulate concepts and ideas come from the high standards I set for communication. Everything that causes my phone to ring and people to reach out to me can be traced back to the standards I initially created for myself, and these were higher than my competition's standards.

It became clear to me that the path to more success was higher standards. By always raising my standards in business, and in my own character, I have increased my sales and the performance of my company. When my sales grew to the point where I could not keep doing the work alone, I hired people. But I was continually frustrated with their performance, and my company's growth stagnated. Why? Because I hired people who had standards lower than my own.

When I started hiring people with higher standards and enforcing the standards of my company, growth exploded. In 2020, I sold almost four times as much real estate as in 2019 from this one small tweak. I cannot express strongly enough how important this concept is. If you want to be a top producer, the path is remarkably simple—raise the standards at which you do everything.

Top-Producer Standards

Your clients expect you to be the expert when it comes to real estate, so you should expect that of yourself too. Increasing your knowledge is a quick way to set yourself apart from the competition and showcase a higher standard. The following are simple ways to do just that.

Creating and Interpreting CMAs

A CMA (comparative market analysis) is a tool used by agents to determine what a property is worth based on comparable sales of similar properties in similar locations. Every agent should know how to create a CMA. Your clients will judge you based on your accuracy. Choosing the wrong properties as comparable sales—or missing properties that should be included—is a great way to lose credibility with a seller and find yourself out of a job. To start increasing your knowledge in real estate sales, learn how to look at a property through the eyes of an appraiser, and learn how to select the right properties for your CMA.

Creating a CMA is relatively simple but interpreting it for the client is definitely not. Accurate CMA interpretation is a way to stand apart from other agents. Chapter Nine of *SOLD: Every Real Estate Agent's Guide to Building a Profitable Business* (the precursor to this book) provides an in-depth description of how to create a CMA. Your goal is to present this information in such a way as to help your clients see it from your expert perspective and feel good that they are pricing their home according to the market data.

Knowing how to showcase which homes have sat on the market without selling—and explaining why—will guide your clients to understand this information. You do this by showing the homes that have been on the market a long time and explaining how much stress this creates for the sellers. Bringing your clients' attention to the "pending" properties will help them set realistic goals. Pricing your clients' homes in alignment with properties that were successfully put in contract and getting them to improve their homes' condition to meet pending sale prices are the best ways to ensure your clients' homes sell well.

It is not enough to create a CMA, email it to a client, and expect them to interpret it by themselves. I see Realtors do this, and it conveys an extremely low standard of service. It's not uncommon for your clients to think they know more about real estate than they really do. To help them understand what must be done to sell their home, start with interpreting the CMA information you created in a way they can comprehend and feel good that their home is priced appropriately.

Local Market Knowledge

It is safe to assume your clients will expect you to have a high level of local market knowledge. This includes knowing which types of properties sell the fastest and what price points different homes will sell for. It also includes knowing specifics, such as school districts, utility jurisdictions, and which parts of town have the highest property taxes. From a practical standpoint, this type of information will play a small role in your job as an agent. From a marketing standpoint, however, it will be huge. Being able to quickly share this information will separate you from your competitors.

My favorite way to gather this information is by talking with more experienced Realtors in the office. I've often found the best resource is the agent who sells a medium number of homes (twelve to twenty-four a year) and who has been in the business for a long time. These agents usually aren't too busy to help you. Plus, they have done enough deals to have accumulated the knowledge you need. The easiest way to start this conversation is by asking, "What do you think is the best part of town?" When they answer, follow up with, "Why is that?" This opens the door for them to share their thoughts on facts or details you may not have considered on your own.

Contract Knowledge

A significant part of being a top-producing agent is knowing how a contract works and what it says. It's all too common for an agent to know where signatures are needed on the forms but not understand what the client is agreeing to. This can cause major headaches when there is a dispute between buyers and sellers that ends up in mitigation or arbitration. Top-producing agents are expected to help avoid these scenarios.

In addition to avoiding mediation or arbitration disputes, having contract expertise will showcase your professionalism, care for your clients, and dedication to your craft. The best place to do this is in your buyer and listing presentations. I recommend having slides dedicated to the parts of the contract you feel are the most important and using those slides to show how you protect your clients' interests and can outmaneuver the other side.

Wealth-Building Strategies

A run-of-the-mill real estate salesperson can get away with doing the bare minimum of showing and listing houses, writing up contracts, and delivering keys. If you want top-producer status, you'll need to up your game when it comes to knowledge about building wealth through real estate. A study by the Federal Reserve found the average homeowner's net worth is *forty times* that of someone who rents.[1] With results this significant, you can see how Realtors are changing lives by helping clients overcome their fears of buying a house. When your clients see you as a guide and adviser regarding their financing, they are much more likely to trust your advice and share the word with others who should use you.

One wealth-building strategy you can introduce to your clients after you help them buy a home is renting out properties to others. The following is a simple process that breaks down if a property will make or lose money each month for the owner. Understanding and then explaining these steps will set you apart from other agents.

Step One: Calculate Cash Flow
To calculate cash flow, subtract the rent from the property's expenses.

---

1 Keeping Current Matters, "A Homeowner's Net Worth Is 40x Greater Than a Renter's," October 7, 2020, https://www.keepingcurrentmatters.com/2020/10/07/a-homeowners-net-worth-is-40x-greater-than-a-renters/.

Rent information can be found on websites,[2] BiggerPockets' rent estimator tool,[3] or via a property management company's site.

Expenses typically consist of:

- Mortgage (plenty of free apps help calculate this)
- Property taxes (a title company can provide this)
- Homeowners insurance (online quotes are quick and easy to find)
- Property management fees (6 to 10 percent, depending on price point and location)
- Budgeted repairs (5 percent of gross rents is standard)
- Vacancy
- Capital expenditures (think big items like replacing HVAC systems or roofs)

Adding up your expenses and then subtracting that amount from your rent leaves you with your monthly cash flow. Multiply this number by twelve to get your yearly cash flow.

$$\textbf{Cash flow = (Rent - Expenses)} \times \textbf{12}$$
$$\textbf{(Eq. 1)}$$

Step Two: Determine Investment Basis

Most investment properties require 20 to 25 percent down. This can be avoided by helping your client buy a primary residence and renting it out after they have lived there. Many primary residence loans stipulate the buyer must intend to occupy the property as their primary residence but cannot require someone to stay in a property if life circumstances dictate they move.

To determine the investment basis, add the down payment, closing costs, and estimated repairs.

$$\textbf{Investment basis = Down payment + Closing costs + Repairs}$$
$$\textbf{(Eq. 2)}$$

Step Three: Determine ROI

The return on investment (ROI) is used to determine what percentage of

---

2   Check out www.rentometer.com.

3   https://www.biggerpockets.com/insights/property-searches/new.

your client's investment they will receive back in a year's time. To determine this number, take the yearly profit and divide it by the investment basis.

$$\text{ROI} = \text{Yearly profit} / \text{Investment basis}$$
$$(\text{Eq. 3})$$

Step Four: Determine Likely Appreciation

Your last step is to help your client determine if the property's value and ROI will increase over time. To do this, look at market trends over the last five to ten years to get a feel for how much properties increased in value. You can do the same with rents over the last five years. By estimating previous amounts, you can project what rents might be in five years' time, then you take that number and plug it into a new cash flow calculation with the higher rent (Equation 1). Run through the above process and show your clients what their ROI may be five years down the road.

Raising Your Standards with Clients

As discussed earlier, the difference between a top-producing agent and a mediocre agent can be boiled down to their standards. Raising your standards can be challenging, so you'll need to be committed and disciplined about it.

Top producers offer impeccable customer service. Providing an experience that leaves your customers thrilled that they used you and happy to recommend you to others will supercharge your growth in the field. Keep in mind that almost every client you help in your career at one point used a different Realtor, and that Realtor failed to "wow" them enough to keep them as clients.

Look for ways, even small ones, to make your clients feel special. For example, my showing agents bring bottles of water to each showing to give to the clients as well as team-branded folders with printouts of each property and pens so clients can take notes. We also send our clients' children gift certificates to get ice cream on their birthdays and follow up every year on the anniversary of buying their home. We drop off gift baskets after each closing and look for ways to let our clients know they are the lifeblood of our business.

Top producers thus connect with their clients on an emotional level.

They display empathy, understanding, patience, and a sense of calm in the storm. Many clients have practical needs ("answer my calls," "give me good advice," etc.), but what they really want is someone to make them feel that they are doing the right thing and making the right decisions. This reassurance is on the emotional level. If you naturally don't like people or don't enjoy validating emotions, at a minimum you'll have to learn to do so at specific points in the transaction.

Acknowledging your clients' fears, doubts, and other emotions is a part of your job as their guide. Top producers accept and embrace this principle and then work to excel at it.

Raising your standards includes building stronger relationships with your clients. Get to know them not just as transactional components to your business but as friends. Everybody longs for the day of the family doctor, when your physician knew you, your history, and what ailed you. The decrease in bedside manner—and in the overall patient–physician relationship—is lamentable in modern medicine.

What you want to do is make yourself the "family Realtor." You want your clients' friends, family, and coworkers to hear rave reviews about your performance and loyalty to those you serve. Your follow-up game after the close will play a huge role in this. Everyone knows you made a sizable commission on the deal. If the closing day is the last day your clients hear from you, they will absolutely believe that paycheck was the only reason you worked with them. Your relationship will feel transactional to them. Instead, send gifts, set reminders to follow up on their one-year anniversary, and send periodic texts and calls to let your clients know you're thinking of them. This is not only good for relationship-building but also for lead generation.

Raising Your Standards in Negotiating

It's easy for those who work with real estate transactions every day to forget how much money is changing hands. This can lead to a calloused approach to how much things cost. It's commonplace for buyers to spend thousands of dollars on the title, escrow, closing costs, and inspections. It's also commonplace for sellers to pay 5 to 7 percent in commissions. We may be used to these numbers, but our clients sure aren't.

Stand out from the competition by showing you care about how much money your clients are spending and find ways to minimize that amount.

The best way you can do so is by negotiating hard for every dollar and then letting your clients know what you did. They may not always tell you so, but they are watching what you do for them. Not communicating to the client the work you do on their behalf means they won't know, and you won't get the credit. What's worse: the work you don't do. Top producers pride themselves on knowing where they have leverage and how they can use that to benefit their clients in negotiation. This higher standard of saving client money separates top producers from the standard agent.

Raising Your Standards in Communication

Communication is always important, but it becomes even more so when people are stressed, nervous, or excited. Molehills turn into mountains during emotionally intense periods. It's in this spot where we make our living and where you'll need your best communication skills. Unfortunately, top producers also have the least amount of time. The more clients you're working for at the same time, the harder it gets to stay on top of everything. This is why "busy" agents tend to get bad reputations for their communication skills.

The best agents avoid this situation. They quickly respond to phone calls and emails. And they have systems in place for when they can't get to clients' requests. For example, the client doesn't have to talk only to you. Many top producers hire assistants to field calls and forward the requests. To a client, it's often more important that they talk to *someone* rather than speak specifically with you. Anticipating this communication hurdle and preparing a path for clients to get their needs met is critically important.

Once you get to the point where you're closing a good number of deals, it's important to hire someone to help you stay in touch with your clients. Bad reviews and negative word of mouth can hurt you a lot more than the hourly wage you'll pay someone to keep your clients in the loop. This can start with a transaction coordinator calling your clients daily to let them know what is supposed to happen that day and what is left for the rest of the transaction. From there, you can hire an assistant to take over those duties and offer more control over the quality and nature of those interactions. The important thing is that the best agents never let "being busy" become an excuse to not communicate with their clients.

At the end of the day, success is measured by the standards you hold.

Rather than waiting to raise your standards until after you have more leads, more clients, and more closings, consider raising them right now. Dress better, communicate better, be more interested in others than you are in yourself, and know your market more thoroughly than your competitors do, and you will more easily lay the groundwork for your business to thrive.

My advice? Make everything a game. Ask yourself how quickly you can return calls, how detailed you can make your answers to questions, and how good you can make others feel when you speak to them. Once you are good at these things, look for ways to do them faster. Once you're able to do them well and quickly, look for ways to leverage that skill onto another team member, and get that person doing them at the same level as you. Make every day a game in which you perform better than you did the day before. This will step up your standards, and you'll have fun while doing so.

Carl Buehner wrote, "They may forget what you said—but they will never forget how you made them feel." Keep this in mind throughout your day and ultimately throughout your career. It doesn't matter what your intentions are or what's running through your head. People will judge you—and your ability to represent them—based on how you make them feel.

➡ KEY POINTS

- Top producers speak with authority and confidence and use directness, skill, charisma, trustworthiness, leadership, empathy, patience, and a sense of calm.
- Newbies ask, "What do I do first?" and then work forward from there, but that's the wrong order. Reduce the number of missteps by starting with the end in mind. The more direct the path, the faster the destination is reached.
- Focus on who you are, not just what you do.
- Develop the highest standards, keep your word, and display strong ethics.
- Learn how to build trusting relationships with leads; it will determine your success.
- Top producers make tough decisions and have difficult conversations yet still foster and maintain strong levels of trust.

- Help a client by *interpreting* the information you create in the CMA.
- Develop a high level of local market knowledge.
- Being able to help your clients run the numbers on investment properties will help set you apart as an elite in your industry.
- Acknowledge your clients' fears, doubts, and other emotions.
- Top producers know clients just want to be heard, but that just as easily can be handled by a staff member.

CHAPTER TWO

FUNNEL PROGRESSION (TOOL ONE): FINDING PEOPLE

"No leads means no sales."

—GARY KELLER

Top-producing agents have closed enough deals to recognize that while the job can feel unorganized and chaotic at first, it's actually fairly routine and predictable. Each client roughly follows the same pattern of decision-making, and the decisions tend to be similar. As agents close more deals, they start to recognize these patterns and develop the skills to overcome the most common problems they encounter. The most experienced agents develop systems to reduce how frequently these problems arise by preparing their clients for what to expect. For example, no moment arrives that jolts the client out of the escrow.

This chapter will help get you up to speed with the pattern your business will take as you meet more people and start converting deals into closings. Being able to recognize this pattern and then develop the skills you need to keep people moving along the process will allow you to perform at your best when critical transition points occur. Understanding this pattern also means you can focus on improving any necessary skills.

One step in the pattern is the "Sales Funnel," which helps agents do three things.

1. Recognize the consistent pattern/progression of moving a person into a paycheck.
2. Classify where in the process you are at any given interaction with a person or a task.
3. Understand the next step required to move someone from one level of the funnel to the next.

By using the necessary tools to move someone along the funnel, you improve your conversion rates and the number of people you ultimately bring to close. By knowing how to classify a task crossing your desk, you can quickly determine which tool you need to address it. If you find yourself consistently getting stuck at a certain point in the funnel (for instance, getting buyers into contract), you can easily determine the tool you need to improve your numbers. You can use the information in this book or other resources to better your skills in that area.

This chapter will focus on the first part of your funnel—the part where you find your business. The next chapter will focus on teaching you how to close deals. I encourage you to reread these chapters once a year throughout your career. As you grow in your ability to do this job, you'll find more of this information useful than when you were first exposed to it.

Real estate sales can feel chaotic and confusing, but they don't have to. The Sales Funnel functions as a map to help orient you to your surroundings, determine in which direction you need to move in order to make progress, and direct you to which level to focus on next. It is an empowering system designed to provide guidance and clarity.

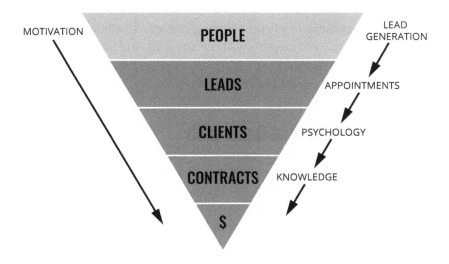

Figure 2.1. Sales Funnel

Sales Funnel

The Sales Funnel is divided into five levels. Each level has a corresponding tool to move the prospective client from their current level to the next one. The levels move from top to bottom and are as follows.

- **People:** This typically refers to people in your database but could refer to anyone in the world.
- **Leads:** A person who (1) wants to buy or sell a house (and has the means to do so), or (2) knows who you are. If either of these conditions is not met, this is not a Lead. (A better understanding would be someone in the "People" category with a higher probability of becoming a Lead.)
- **Clients:** Those who have signed a buyer representation or listing agreement.
- **Contracts:** Offers or purchase agreements that have been fully signed by all involved parties.
- **Closings:** Closed escrows where the title has changed hands from the seller to the buyer and funds have been transferred from the buyer to the seller.

Not everything that catches your attention throughout the day is of equal importance. Problems with Clients related to issues with contracts/

escrows that may delay or prevent closings are more important than People who want to ask you questions about the general state of the market. When you have to decide about which call to spend more time on, the funnel will help you prioritize your tasks.

Keys to Successful Lead Generation

The purposeful, intentional, systematic approach of adding people to your database and staying in touch with them is known as lead generation. It is the first tool in your Sales Funnel.

I like to use the example of an orchard to illustrate the concept of successful lead generation. An orchard takes time and farmer know-how to grow. There is a pattern and rhythm that every farmer must follow to be successful. Once the orchard is mature, it produces fruit year after year. And once an orchard reaches maturity, a big part of the work the farmer does is harvesting—picking the fruit that has been growing on its own.

Each year the farmer sees where things went wrong and adjusts the amount of water used, the water delivery system, or the irrigation techniques. Once these are made, it's time to work on the pests, weeds, and organisms harmful to the orchard. Like a farmer, you as a real estate agent will constantly be contending with others who try to harm your business by stealing clients. Like the farmer, you'll need to ensure that you are planting your lead generation seeds in good soil. And like the farmer's crops, your leads have to bring in enough income year after year.

As a real estate agent, you build a database that is full of potential referrals. However, like the farmer, you've got to cultivate what you grow. Successful lead generation is all about two things: adding people to your database and talking to people who are already in your database. If you can remember this simple fact, your referrals should grow into more business.

If you follow the instructions in this book, you should find yourself with more leads than you can harvest yourself. At that point, you'll need to hire a team. There will be more on how to do this in the next book in this series.

Growing Your Database

"People" is the first level in the funnel. Getting contacts into your database and staying in touch with them is crucial when it comes to generating referrals for your business. If you're not top of mind when someone hears of a potential client, you'll miss out on that lead.

You'll have to first create your database. The simplest way to do so is through a customer relationship manager (CRM), which is a software that stores and organizes your database electronically, making it easier to stay in touch with referrals and clients. Most CRMs use a combination of notifications and reminders to contact people. They have a section to enter notes about your conversations, and they make it easier to send mass emails or texts to simplify communication.

Once you have created a database, the aim is to fill it. Make goals for yourself regarding how many names and contacts you will add each week, then work backward to create a plan to do this. A great target is five names a week. In Chapter Seven ("Strategic Planning"), I provide you with tools my team uses to accomplish goals like this.

Contacting Your Database

As a brand-new agent in your first year of training, you should be making contacts every day. A contact is defined as a face-to-face or voice-to-voice conversation in which you ask for business. If you want to be a top producer, I recommend having at least twenty conversations per day. Having that many will help you in several ways.

- It will keep you top of mind with people in your database so they remember to send you referrals.
- It will force you to build your conversation, rapport-building, and people skills—all of which top agents excel at.
- It will push you to find new ways to bring value to others. If you don't, conversations will quickly become awkward and feel pushy.
- It will drive you to grow your general knowledge of real estate. These conversations will open doors to real estate–related topics, and you will need to shine as the expert.
- It will require you to learn more about the local market and its state, as leads will surely ask questions related to these topics.
- It will help you grow and maintain stronger relationships with the people in your database. As noted earlier in the book, real estate is a relationship business, and these people will be the foundation on which you build your business.
- It will teach you how to naturally control the direction of conversations. You'll have to guide the conversation so that you arrive at a point where you can ask for business without making others feel uncomfortable or making you look inauthentic.

Sending text messages, emails, or other correspondence is good, but for the purposes of this discussion, they don't count. These means of communication are more convenient than face-to-face or voice-to-voice conversations, but they are less effective when your goal is to grow relationships. Talk to someone on the phone or in person. This allows you to catch tonality and facial expressions. It also allows others to catch yours. A text message stating "Good morning! How are you?" is nice, but a phone call where the person can hear the concern and genuine curiosity in your voice goes much further in creating sincerity.

It is important to create a system of accountability for yourself. It can be as simple as a spreadsheet on which you track the twenty people you spoke to that day or as advanced as a CRM that prompts you to contact someone. The important point is not to leave this up to chance or your own willpower. If you do, your subconscious will give you permission to skip it. This is especially critical in the beginning stages of a business. Finding another agent to hold accountable and to hold you accountable is a great way to start building momentum.

Goal of the Contact

There are two components to a successful contact. I like to use the analogy of an irrigation canal.

1. Fill clients with goodwill (like a canal filled with a water).
2. Clients flow goodwill back to you (the canal waters both of you).

If you fill your clients with goodwill in every conversation, the leads will flow back to you.

I provide you with several methods to do this in the rest of this chapter. You know you did your job well when your contact ends the conversation feeling grateful, happy, and appreciative for your relationship. In your calls you are offering the person you are speaking with positive emotions, and it's important that these are genuine. You can always find something positive in another person to highlight and cultivate; if you can't find anything, they shouldn't be a part of your lead generation efforts.

Cultivating positivity also needs to be two-way. You have to direct that goodwill to flow back to you and your business. This is done by asking for referrals. *Most people you contact will send business your way if they know it matters to you and they have a desire to give back to you.* You don't have to feel bad, guilty, or disingenuous. This is especially true when you make your efforts in the relationship genuine and candid. There are many ways to ask for referrals, and it's completely fine to use different methods with different people.

Asking for Business

Many agents find it difficult to ask for business directly, but asking for business is crucial. It is the point of the interaction, and the people in your database need to be aware that you want clients to work with. Don't assume they know. The reason most agents hesitate to ask for business is because they're not sure how to do so naturally. Overcoming this problem can make you a top producer in your first year.

Asking for business without feeling awkward is a two-step process.

1. Build "social capital" by bringing value to your client before asking for anything.
2. Learn how to guide conversations so you can naturally ask for business.

Set yourself up for success by establishing a goal and working backward in the conversation to bring it to that goal.

If you are a competent, capable, hardworking, honest agent, clients should feel lucky to work with you. Before anyone believes this, though, you must believe it yourself. It's natural to have significant self-doubt when you are getting started. This happens for a myriad of reasons. It can come from "impostor syndrome," voices in your head from influential authority figures who doubted you, or even your own awareness that you haven't sold enough houses or don't "know enough" to deserve this person's referrals. Whatever it is, it's your responsibility to isolate why you doubt yourself and create action steps to start removing that doubt. Your business depends on it.

Building Social Capital

Building social capital comes from showing empathy for a client's situation or providing solutions to obstacles. *If you feel uncomfortable asking for business, it may be because you have not yet provided any value to the person you are asking for referrals.* Instead, you may feel like you're asking for charity. That won't be the case if you've built social capital with the person by first contributing to their well-being. This is why I use the canal analogy. You want them to feel so filled with goodwill toward you that they want to give back and relieve that pressure from themselves.

The following is a list of what you can give people before asking for a referral.

- A monthly market report covering their neighborhood
- Information on what property taxes are like in the area where they want to buy
- A recommendation for a handyman who can make home repairs
- Reminders throughout the year to change their HVAC filters
- Comments on their Facebook feed with solutions to whatever problems they mention having
- Gift certificates to their children on their birthdays
- Their favorite coffee delivered to their workplace
- A video on Thanksgiving telling them what you appreciate about them
- Forwarding relevant blog posts or tagging them on social media posts they would enjoy
- Holiday gifts, such as sparklers on the Fourth of July or candy on Halloween
- An invitation to a social gathering you organize, such as to a movie night or a client appreciation party
- Monthly emails with housekeeping tips

Of course, you will feel more comfortable with some approaches than others. The important thing is to find a way to give that works for you—and then give consistently. I promise that if you are giving enough to the right people, they will have no problem giving right back to you when you ask. Focus on building social capital and make it part of your daily lead generation.

Remember, if you are feeling awkward asking for business, you aren't giving enough.

Jab, Jab, Jab, Right Hook

In his book *Jab, Jab, Jab, Right Hook*, Gary Vaynerchuk expounds a sound business philosophy that applies to any sales job. He uses the analogy of a boxer working his opponent with jabs before going for a knockout punch. "Jabs" are the things we provide to others free of charge. They are *gives*. "Hooks" are the times we request something for ourselves. They are *asks*. When you ask your clients for something before having given them anything, it's easy for them to say no. Smart boxers soften their opponents with jabs before taking the risk of throwing a big punch that can easily backfire. You should operate your business in the same way: give, give, give, ask.

Look for the "give, give, give, ask" rhythm in every aspect of your business. Open your conversations by showing people respect and genuine interest in their life before asking them to care about you or your business. Open listing appointments by demonstrating what you can do for a client before asking them to sign a listing agreement. Lay out the benefits of using your preferred lender before asking a client to commit to them. In other words, you should ABJ (always be jabbing)! If you can ABJ, you'll learn to recognize when the time is right to deliver your right hook—and your business will thrive. Top-producing agents are experts at giving to their clients. The best practice is to make a habit of giving continually so that your client begins to feel like they owe you.

The Law of Reciprocity

If you've been giving and giving to someone, the law of reciprocity states that they will feel compelled to give back. If you start paying attention, you'll see this law in action everywhere. Good people subconsciously follow the law of reciprocity. Good agents use this to their advantage to generate leads.

I first saw this law at work when I met Daniel Del Real. Daniel is a real estate agent in Modesto, California. He has a way about him that makes you want to give him the shirt off your back. Daniel is very successful, but you'd never know it. He never talks about himself, never brags, and never leaves you feeling like anything less than an amazing human being. After spending time with Daniel, you simply feel good about yourself. This inevitably makes you want to return the favor. Daniel cleverly lets you know you can pay him back by sending referrals. This single character trait has allowed Daniel to dominate his local market. A quick Instagram search of #bowsondoors will show you just how big his business has grown.

When I first met Daniel, I was so appreciative of the way he made me feel that I found myself wanting to do nice things for him. That feeling grew until the desire to do something for him felt more like a compulsion. In fact, I felt restless and uncomfortable until I could finally give him a very expensive gift. (I didn't send him referrals because I work in his area myself.) I marveled at how well Daniel had mastered this Jedi mind trick. By helping me with my business, setting me at ease when I was nervous, and putting my needs before his own, Daniel created a relationship in which I was actively looking for ways to help him meet his goals.

Daniel was so influential in displaying this concept that I included him in the acknowledgments of the first book in this series, *SOLD: Every Real Estate Agent's Guide to Building a Profitable Business*. The law of reciprocity proves true with him. Get in the habit of thinking of ways you can tap into the law of reciprocity that feel natural and right to you. It's a powerful law of human nature, and mastering it will pay dividends later.

Owning Mindshare

We all know how valuable it is to own real estate, but have you considered how valuable the real estate of the mind may be when it comes to the referral process?

I'm going to run you through a quick exercise in the importance of owning "mindshare." I want you to say out loud the first two brands you think of that make a specific product I'm about to mention.

Ready?

Toothpaste.

You said Crest and Colgate, didn't you? Why? Because they have dominated the toothpaste branding space—they own that real estate in your brain. When you were forced to make a hasty, quick decision, you immediately thought of them.

When someone has a family member, friend, or acquaintance looking to buy or sell a house, they are likely not going to stop everything and do thorough online research to find the real estate agent with the best reviews, list-to-sale ratio, or longest track record. They are going to remember the first one or two real estate agents who pop up in their mind.

What's my point? If you want your lead generation to be effective, you need to be the Crest or Colgate in your sphere of influence. That's why consistency in lead generation is so important. It's too easy to forget about you when you're not top of mind. Consistent phone calls, a strong online presence, social media reminders, yearly events—they all play roles in keeping you top of mind among people in your database. Top producers understand this and make staying on people's radar a priority.

Sample Phone Call Script

Agent: Hey, how's it going? Did I catch you at a bad time?

Contact: Hey, [Agent], not at all. I have a few minutes. What's up?

Agent: Well, I was driving to work today and thinking about how I have so many coworkers that are just kind of a downer. It made me sad that they don't seem to want to have fun at work. That got me thinking about how you and I always had fun together. It didn't really matter what was going on or how bad it got. I always enjoyed the way you carried yourself and what a pleasure you were to work with.

Contact: Wow, I don't really know what to say. I wasn't expecting that. Thank you for noticing. Um, how have you been?

Agent: Great! I'm working in a new career right now, selling houses. I love it. Every day I get to look for a new person to help. I was scrolling through your Facebook feed the other day and noticed how big your kids are getting. How old are they now?

Contact: Yes, they are! Oh my gosh, Hayden is ten years old and Josh is seven. They grow up so fast. Definitely keeping me on my toes.

Agent: I bet! I feel so bad we haven't stayed in touch much over the years. Life gets busy and before you know it so much time has passed! I'd love to see your kids again. It's been so long! Would you be open to meeting for a day at the park? Maybe get lunch and catch up while they play?

Contact: That's a great idea!

Agent: Awesome! I'd love that. I'll email you to schedule it when I'm at the office. Do you mind texting me your email address?

Contact: Absolutely. I'll do that as soon as we get off the phone.

Agent: I'm so excited! I can't wait to hear how your life has been going. It changes so much when we have kids.

Contact: It sure does.

Agent: One of my specialties is helping clients with young children who need a bigger home, bigger yard, better school district, etc. You know how it is when you have kids—priorities change! Would you do me a favor and keep an eye out for anyone who's got kids or may be having them soon? I'd love to talk to them about some loan programs we have and opportunities for young families.

Contact: I can do that, sure. That's no problem at all.

Agent: Great! I'll follow up with you about that later. Thanks so much. It's been great talking to you. Keep an eye out for my email and we'll get that park day on the books!

Contact: Sounds great! Thanks for calling!

As you can see, asking for business doesn't have to be awkward. In this example, the Agent set up the Contact to ask for business by focusing first on the Contact's children (obviously important to them) and then parlaying that into the Agent's desire to help young families. This is much more comfortable and natural than simply calling someone out of the blue and asking for business before taking an interest in their life.

⬛➤ KEY POINTS

- Lead generation is about adding people to your database and talking to people who are in your database.
- Ask for business without feeling awkward through a two-step process: build social capital and learn how to guide conversations.
- Establish a goal in every conversation and work backward to get to that goal.
- Strive for the "give, give, give, ask" rhythm in every aspect of your business. Don't ask for anything before you've given something. If you're uncomfortable asking for referrals, you need to give more.
- "Jabs" (*gives*) are things we provide free of charge and "hooks" (*asks*) are what we request for ourselves. Learn when the time is right to deliver your right hook to make your business thrive.
- Lead generation is the purposeful effort to remain top of mind with those in your database.
  - Mindshare is incredibly important. Strive to become the Crest or Colgate of real estate with people in your database.
  - Consistent phone calls, a strong online presence, social media reminders, and yearly events keep you top of mind among people in your database.

CHAPTER THREE

FUNNEL PROGRESSION (TOOL TWO): CONVERTING CLIENTS

"Ideas are cheap. Ideas are easy. Ideas are common. Everybody has ideas. Ideas are highly, highly overvalued. Execution is all that matters."

—CASEY NEISTAT

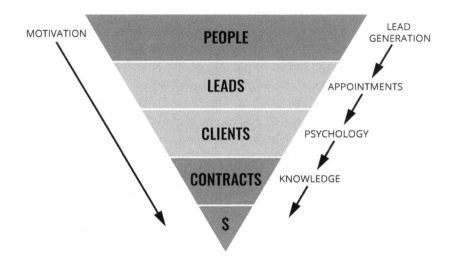

Rapport in a relationship is characterized by mutual trust or emotional affinity. This definition highlights the importance it plays in relationships and includes the element of affinity (goodwill) that you want to build with clients.

Building rapport is absolutely crucial to getting clients to work with you. It is the goal of every relationship, conversation, and piece of marketing you create. Building rapport with those in your database will lead to referrals coming your way. When a referral finds its way to you, you have successfully used the tool of lead generation to move someone from the first level in the Sales Funnel (People) into the second (Leads). Congrats!

Once you've found a lead, focus on building a solid relationship that allows you to showcase your trustworthiness, professionalism, and expertise. We started the book describing top-producer traits. You've been working to emulate them in yourself and your business. This is your opportunity to display them to the lead you've come across. Doing so will be imperative if you want to move this person to the next level of the funnel—from Lead to Client.

The most effective way to do this is through in-person interactions in an environment where you feel comfortable, confident, and in control. While it's possible to accomplish this in a coffee shop or restaurant, these are often noisy places full of distractions and convey a less-than-professional approach. If you want to portray yourself as a top producer, it's better to use your office or another professional work environment.

Your clients will decide which house to buy based on the emotional connection they develop with the property. This usually happens when they see it in person. It is the total package of sight, smell, and touch that creates the immersive, emotional connection. Simple facts or data points (e.g., pictures, information such as it has a pool) are not enough to create this immersive experience. The same applies to developing a connection with you. It doesn't matter how smooth you sound on the phone or how professional your emails read. Humans develop emotional connections in person. Therefore, setting up a face-to-face appointment is your top priority once you've connected with an interested lead. This is the next tool in the Sales Funnel: Appointments/Presentations.

As a new agent, I made the mistake of trying to rush past this step countless times. I did not understand how to build rapport and frankly did not value relationships or emotional connections. Nobody told me how important it was to meet with clients in person, so I didn't. I'd meet a lead at an open house or get a phone call from an interested buyer and immediately try to get them started with the preapproval process before taking the time to get to know them or establish myself as a trustworthy guide. I thought I was saving time. I wasn't. My conversion rate was terrible, and I lost a lot of money in the process.

Luckily, I found a mentor in my office. Sedar (mentioned in *SOLD*) explained that I was losing leads because I was failing to establish initial strong connections. Everything changed with that bit of news. I made it a priority to meet people in my office whenever possible and at their home or a restaurant if they couldn't visit me. I started our interaction by asking questions about what was most important to them, listening, and strategically offering information that showcased my top-producer traits, which made it easy for clients to not only see but also feel that I was the best person to help them in their situation. It became rare for me not to convert Leads to Clients after meeting them in person. With practice and an established system, my conversion rate is now nearly 100 percent.

How did I develop this high success rate? I developed a system to deliver a solid, impressive, professional presentation that functions as a tool, a physical embodiment, and a means to express my traits of being a leader who is direct, skilled, charismatic, and trustworthy. This system was like putting a sword in the hands of a warrior. You want this for yourself.

Strong agents use presentations as tools to help establish a formal agent relationship with a prospect, set appropriate expectations upfront, and move their Leads down the Sales Funnel. Presentations provide a powerful and unique opportunity to prove yourself as the expert and leader, show your client what you can do for them, and relieve their anxieties. They are the best tool I've found for turning Leads into Clients.

When new agents tell me they are having a hard time getting leads to sign buyer representation agreements or listing agreements, it usually turns out that they're not using presentations before asking clients to sign paperwork. Sharing what you know, and more importantly what you can do for your prospect before asking them to commit to you as their agent, is essential. Skipping the step where you provide value first is a violation of the strategies discussed earlier in this book. You should always give before you ask. A formal presentation is the best way I know to do this.

Presentations allow you to showcase what you have to offer, but they do more than that: They allow you to determine if the lead is someone *you* want to take on as a client. Not everybody will be a good fit for you, your team, or your model. Wasting time with the wrong prospects will hurt your productivity and sap the energy you need to stay positive and move Leads along the Sales Funnel. Protecting your own time and energy is just as important as looking for people to spend them on—in our business, we're not looking for just any fit. We're looking for the right fit.

I highlight this point because my philosophy is to give 100 percent to every client. If I'm going to give my all to that person, I want to make sure the person is a good investment of my resources. When you know you're giving your all, it gives you permission to expect the same from others.

Improve Your Close Rate through Preparation

A strong presentation results in an increased close rate in your transactions. This happens because you prepare your clients for what they will experience and come up with a plan for how you will handle any challenges together as a team. Human beings make decisions based on emotion. When a client backs out of a deal, it is almost always because something happened to provoke an emotional reaction stronger than they were prepared to withstand. This can be mitigated by preparing your clients for what's coming.

If you put a plan in place for what you're going to do if/when problems arise, you stand a much better chance of keeping your client when things go wrong. Frequent deal-breaking issues arise with home inspections, low appraisals, and lending complications. These and other frequently encountered problems should be the foundation of the material in your presentation.

When I designed my team's presentations, I compiled a list of the top reasons why our deals fell out of contract, why clients left unhappy, and which transactions required the most communication. I made slides to cover these topics as well as slides covering information most agents neglect to share with their clients. These include helping with loans, which properties we have the best option to get, and how the contract works. This accumulated material became the hinge that swung wide open my team's numbers and volume. We stopped losing so many escrows and started converting almost all our Leads into Clients.

You'll want to cover a list of things with your prospects to prepare them for the emotional journey of buying or selling a home, including:

- How your team works. If you're an individual agent, your "team" will consist of transaction coordinators, lenders, title and escrow workers, home inspectors, handymen, etc.
- What the benefits are of owning real estate versus renting.
- What changes have occurred in home values over the last thirty years.
- What the costs associated with buying a home will be (e.g., monthly payments).
- What the closing costs will be.
- Why preapprovals are necessary.
- How you will send clients homes to view.
- How the process for seeing properties works.
- What emotions they are likely to experience.
- Why to avoid viewing only the best-looking properties.
- What turbulence will commonly occur in the transactions.
- How multiple-offer situations work.
- How the appraisal process works.
- What a home inspection report looks like and how to read one.
- Which lending pitfalls to avoid, such as opening a new line of credit.
- Which property types are options (e.g., single-family versus multifamily).
- What new home construction protocols to expect.
- How they can ask friends to be referrals.

I also include photos of properties other clients have found and loved as well as my résumé.

Get the Agreement Signed

This presentation should impress your leads enough that you can offer them the agency paperwork to sign—after you've softened them up with jabs, of course. Most agents who have a difficult time getting their prospects to sign paperwork are throwing that right hook before the prospect is ready for it. Establish your value first, then look to get paperwork signed. If your presentation has gone well, very few people will have a problem with signing, especially if they believe it is a standard part of the process. My presentation even includes a slide of the buyer representation agreement and why it's in the lead's best interest to sign it.

You need to present the information in such a way that leads can clearly see the benefit to signing the agreement. Later in the book, I provide scripts and additional examples for how to accomplish this. For now, just remember that your leads don't know what is in your head or why you want them to travel the path you do. When the client calls the shots, more often than not the result is a disaster. Our job as agents is to paint a picture that makes the path as clear as possible and highlights why it's in our clients' best interest to walk it.

The technique for doing this is called "frame control."

Frame Control

The key to a strong presentation, and a strong relationship with your clients in general, is establishing frame control. I first learned about this concept from the book *Pitch Anything*, by Oren Klaff, who describes frame control as your ability to get someone to see things from your perspective—referred to as a frame. Think of your perspective in life as the window through which you view the world. Two people looking at the same object will have different perceptions of that object based on their perspectives. This is the basis of much of the conflict and mistrust in the world. We see things differently than other people and only feel safe with people who see things similarly to the way we do.

When two people come together with different perspectives, their frames collide. You might think this would result in a "hybrid frame"—a blending of the two. It doesn't. What happens is the stronger frame takes over the weaker frame. When two people with two different frames collide, the one with the weaker frame ends up seeing things from the perspective of the one with the stronger frame.

Think of times you came across someone who appeared so intelligent, so passionate, and so educated on a specific topic that you immediately adopted their perspective as your own. This frequently happens with religious leaders, business leaders, or others who have achieved very high levels of success in specific areas of their lives. (Would you argue with Steve Jobs about technology innovation or Arnold Schwarzenegger about bodybuilding?)

Frame control isn't a bad thing. When I visit my mechanic and he starts talking about engines, I quickly realize that he knows more than I do about this topic and, as a result, I defer to his opinion. If I see things from his frame or his perspective, I am more likely to go with his recommendation. It would be a disaster if those with less-informed opinions or a weaker perspective on a subject always got their data included in the final algorithm. It's good when the stronger frame triumphs, as long as the stronger frame is also the better frame.

As the real estate expert in the relationship, it's your job to make sure you always know more than your client about what they are trying to accomplish. It's also your job to make sure you carry the stronger frame. Letting your uniformed, uneducated client carry the frame and direct you on what to do can be catastrophic to their ability to achieve a successful outcome, whether landing a house in a hot market or selling their home quickly and for top dollar. Allowing your less-informed client to take the leadership position is not fair to your client.

A strong agent needs their client to understand the situation and make decisions based on the agent's perspective. As real estate professionals, we are experienced in handling the transactions that make up the home-buying or home-selling process. Our clients are not. The more our clients feel we are in control, the more they will defer to our guidance and expertise. The less in control we appear to be, the more likely the client will try to guide and direct us. This is a common problem with new agents who have yet to find their voice or develop their confidence. If a client begins to lead you, even when you know they are wrong, the client has taken control of the frame. A killer presentation is a great way to accomplish frame control.

Establishing a strong frame doesn't just make your job easier; it also helps your clients feel safe and secure under your care. Think of times you were nervous, apprehensive, or scared. Perhaps it was during an emergency. Didn't you instinctively look for the person who seemed most confident and most in control, and didn't you follow their lead? How likely would you be to follow someone who seemed just as scared as you, even if they were wearing the uniform worn by an authority figure?

In this relationship, you are that authority figure. Holding on to that control is how you keep your Leads and Clients moving down the Sales Funnel to eventually close deals. Agents are often people pleasers. Being a people pleaser can make lead generation a lot easier, but it won't help you during the tough parts of the transaction. When a Lead becomes a Client, you need to shift from being a people pleaser to being a strong leader. This is why leads hire you and not someone else.

Establishing a Strong Frame through Your Presentation

There are several things you can do to establish a strong frame. The first is to have your leads come to your office for your presentation. This gives you the opportunity to impress them with your workplace and establishes you as a professional. You look like one, act like one, and work professional hours.

For some leads, coming to your office isn't feasible. If you live in an area with bad traffic or you serve a large territory, you may want to consider an alternative, such as meeting them at their house or in a neutral location. Another option is using an electronic format such as Skype or Zoom. It's not ideal, but it will let you accomplish most of what a presentation is meant to accomplish.

I like to have my leads arrive at the office and wait by the receptionist before I go out to greet them. This lets them know that I work on a schedule and expect them to respect that. It also puts them in an unfamiliar environment where they might feel uncomfortable. At first glance, this may seem cruel. Consider that the process of buying or selling a home will already feel unfamiliar and uncomfortable to anyone who's never done it before. By putting them in an environment that feels the same on the outside as what they are likely feeling on the inside, I actually make it easier for them to get in touch with the full range of emotions they are experiencing with buying or selling a home. Creating an opportunity for my prospects to tap into these emotions is an important step in preparing them for my presentation, during which I can then set them at ease.

Next, I bring them back to my office. I have them sit in chairs across from my desk, which is adjacent to a 70-inch television screen mounted on the wall. I use Apple TV to broadcast my computer's screen onto the television. Before I begin the presentation, I offer my leads something to drink, then I ask them if they have any pressing fears or concerns we should address before we start. Doing this puts me in a position where I am providing for all of their needs and showing them I can be a source of relief from pain, a shelter in the storm they are experiencing on the inside.

After this, I ask them questions about their goals. I always start with questions before jumping into the presentation for three key reasons.

1. If someone has fears or questions at the front of their mind, they won't hear anything I'm saying until their questions are addressed.
2. If I immediately tell a prospect what I want them to do, they will push back. By asking questions, I allow a prospect to take ownership and agree to the process I've set in place in order to get them what they want.
3. If I ask questions first, I can show the prospect that they are the center of the transaction and that their needs are what I care about the most.

When the presentation is over, the lead usually signs an exclusive buyer representation agreement or listing agreement, and they officially become my client.

Local Star Power

In *Pitch Anything*, Klaff describes what he calls "local star power," which is when a person with a traditionally weaker frame takes control in specific situations. Klaff shares an example of a surgeon taking golf lessons from a golf pro. While they are on the course, the golf pro has local star power. Even a highly successful neurosurgeon will follow the directions of the golf pro.

Your experience, knowledge, and confidence as a real estate agent will go a long way toward establishing your own local star power and ensure your frame is stronger than that of your clients. You are the real estate pro!

The following is a list of terms you can use to establish frame control and local star power with your clients.

• **Private Mortgage Insurance (PMI):** If a client doesn't have 20 percent to put down on a home, they will have to pay PMI. This insures the lender against the higher risk of default should the borrower not make their payments. Many clients don't know this, and their lender hasn't told them. By advising them of an additional cost they may have been unaware of, you show expertise (and that you're looking out for their bottom line and not just your commission).

- **Lender-Placed Mortgage Insurance (LPMI):** LPMI is not well known, which is why it's my favorite way to build local star power. LPMI is an option that some lenders offer for borrowers with stronger credit scores. In the case of LPMI, the lender gives the client a slightly higher interest rate but drops the PMI requirements. Ask your lender about the details; in most cases in my market, this leads to an increased mortgage payment of $70 to $80 a month. But the removal of PMI would be a savings of between $300 and $500 a month. Telling your client you will look to get them LPMI is a fantastic way to show that they should follow your guidance.

- **Property Tax Base Rates:** The property tax base rate is the number the county uses to determine how much to charge for property tax. While every municipality is different (and they don't all use the same terms), the concept remains the same. Knowing which parts of town have higher property taxes shows your leads early in the relationship that you can save them money.

- **Homeowners Association (HOA):** An HOA is an association voted into place by a community of homeowners that creates and enforces the rules of the community. HOAs dictate things like what color a house can be painted, where people can park, and who will maintain the common areas. HOAs usually charge a monthly fee, and owners can be fined for rule violations. Explaining this to your leads now can help save them a headache later, and they'll appreciate you for it.

- **Amortization Schedule:** An amortization schedule lists each regular mortgage payment broken down into principal and interest portions for the life of the loan. Use a mortgage calculator app to break this down for your leads and show them how much of their payment will go toward the principal and how much toward interest.

- **Mortgage Interest Deduction:** The mortgage interest deduction is a tax savings that many American homeowners qualify for. Consult with a certified public accountant or a tax attorney for the details, but if you can help your clients understand the tax savings they may receive by buying a home, you will stand out as an expert. I like to give my leads the big picture and then refer them to a specialist for the details of their potential savings.

- **Deposit Protection:** Many buyers know they need to put down a deposit on a house, but they don't understand that in many cases they can get it back. Explain to your leads how contractual contingencies work and, more importantly, how you'll manage their escrow to protect their deposit.
- **New Construction Homes:** Going over new construction options with leads is another way to ensure you are making them aware of all their options. Go over the pros and cons, including how new construction homes may have higher taxes and smaller lots but also will also have fewer maintenance issues and often better floor plans.

A strong presentation can lead your prospects from being uncertain acquaintances to signing on as official clients who trust your judgment, advice, and guidance. Each slide should create a specific emotional impact and speak to your lead's emotions in a way that builds rapport, creates curiosity about your expertise, and increases their confidence in you as their guide. I specifically order my slides to accomplish this.

1. The first slides introduce me and establish my credibility. This is where I list my awards, high-profile past clients, positive reviews, and other noteworthy accomplishments.
2. Next, I detail what makes me different and why. I introduce the members of my team and explain how they work together. I also talk about what makes me excel as a Realtor and where I feel I offer clients the best support and guidance.
3. I move along to address the costs associated with buying a home. I show my prospects that I'm not just after a commission but really want to make sure they can afford the home they want to buy. I explain all the costs involved and what I will do to reduce or eliminate them.
4. I then discuss why owning makes more sense than renting. I show at a macro level how real estate prices have performed over time, and I detail what benefits owners enjoy that renters don't.
5. Next, I share testimonials or videos from past clients saying how they felt at the beginning of the relationship and after they successfully bought or sold their home with me as their agent. Testimonials

go a long way toward easing a lead's unspoken fears.

6. I then give step-by-step directions of what goes into buying a home.
7. I discuss the format for sending listings of available homes and how the showing process will work.
8. At this point, I stop to ask about my prospect's wants and needs. I take notes and make sure they feel heard and understood.
9. After answering their questions, I review the process of writing an offer, show them what a contract looks like, and what they'll be signing with an offer.
10. For leads who are buying, I discuss the importance of being preapproved for a mortgage before looking at homes.
11. For leads who are selling, I review closing costs, including who pays what and what the costs pay for.
12. I also cover the earnest money deposit and how I'll protect it.
13. I discuss contract contingencies and make sure to cover inspections, appraisals, and loans.
14. The next slide is a review of the types of inspections that are available.
15. The following slide goes over home inspections and/or pest inspection reports, and it explains how to read them. I also remind them that all inspections are designed to scare the buyer, so I will be looking only for the bigger, more pertinent items.
16. I review how appraisals work and what to do in the case of a low appraisal.
17. The next topic is turbulence in an escrow account and how everyone feels it. This is when I prepare leads that this is a normal part of a transaction.
18. I discuss multiple-offer situations and how they can have a big impact on a buyer's emotions if they don't get the house.
19. I encourage buyer leads not to chase after the same properties as everyone else but to focus on diamonds in the rough instead.
20. The last thing I do is to ask for referrals. Do they know anyone else who is thinking of buying or selling? If they sign the agreement then and there, I let them know that I'll be asking them several times throughout the transaction for suggestions of others who might benefit from my help.

Presentation Execution

Your presentation alone won't seal the deal. That will depend on you.

The presentation shows off your knowledge, heart, and skill set to the lead, but it can't do all the work for you. If that were the case, you could just have the lead sit there, click through the slides themselves, and walk away loving you! Instead, think of the presentation as Tony Stark's (Iron Man's) armor. Without it, Tony is a brilliant man but cannot fight evil. With his armor, he can execute his ideas.

Presentations are your armor, but even the best armor is pointless if you don't know how to use it. You need to diligently practice delivering your presentations. When new agents join my team, I encourage them to give presentations to everyone they know—friends, family, neighbors. The more they practice, the more comfortable they get with the information, and the better they become at using it to create a connection with each prospect. This connection is what will ultimately move each Lead down the Sales Funnel. The presentation is a tool to get you to the point of personal connection, but it's not a substitute for it.

When I was developing my presentation, I videotaped myself giving it to a team member. I then watched that video to see where I did well, where I struggled, and where I lost connection with the person sitting across from me. I looked at the body language of my prospect, and I noticed their facial expressions as well. I then adjusted my presentation accordingly.

A powerful metric in your new business is to track how many times you give a buyer or seller presentation per week. Of course, your end goal is to give a presentation to a lead. But I encourage new or nonproductive agents to give presentations to everyone—not just leads. Giving presentations to people who are not even prospects will help in the following ways:

1. You'll get more practice, and that will improve your skills as a speaker and presenter.
2. You'll plant seeds in the minds of your listeners, so they'll think of you later when they decide to buy or sell or hear of others who want to buy or sell.
3. You will establish your professionalism, expertise, and trustworthiness.
4. You will have the opportunity to introduce the idea that the listener is "your client," even if they are not yet ready to buy or sell a home.
5. You will improve your psychology skills.
6. You will help cement your relationship with the people in the room.
7. You will discover what information you should add to or delete from your presentation based on questions your listeners ask.

As a general rule, I tell new agents on my team to set a goal of delivering one presentation five days a week. This builds up their confidence and is also an extremely effective method of lead generation for new agents. Who in your sphere of influence wouldn't be impressed with your new career after receiving a professional demonstration of your market knowledge, contract expertise, and negotiating skills? When done correctly, this is an almost guaranteed way to own your audience's mindshare when it comes to real estate.

If you can't do five a week, consider pairing this with your lead generation efforts. If you make twenty contacts a day, use these contacts to offer someone a free consultation/presentation on buying or selling a home. For those who agree, schedule the presentation and deliver it. At the end, when they're impressed with what you've taught them, ask who else they know that you can give this free presentation to. The names they provide will go into your database, be part of the five names a week you add, and provide you with more opportunities to deliver the presentation—which will plant more seeds, create more mindshare, and bring in leads from more people.

In most cases, your successful delivery of a listing or buyer's presentation will be the final piece of your lead generation efforts and will secure you a client. If you've never experienced the feeling of having a lead sign an exclusive buyer representation form, let me tell you—it's an extremely good feeling! You'll breathe a huge sigh of relief once you know that your client is just as committed to working with you as you are with them. When I realized I didn't need to beg, plead, or worry all day about leads using a different agent, my confidence rose. This confidence made it much easier for me to do other parts of my job and increased my rate of success.

Common Objections for Appointments or Presentations

Wise agents acknowledge there will be resistance or objections to the information they provide. This is a natural, healthy way for your leads to work through the issues preventing them from committing to you the way you want them to. When someone shares an objection, that is actually a sign of trust. They are looking to you to help them overcome the part of themselves that is holding back. Never be irritated by an objection. The alternative is they don't share their concerns with you. When that happens, you have no chance to close the lead, as they are not providing you with the information you would need to do so.

The following are common objections you'll encounter during your presentations:

Objection: I don't want to have to sit down and meet with you. I already know what I want.

Response: I completely understand that you already know what you want. I love that! It's very important to me that I get a good understanding of what you want. As the person representing your interests in this transaction, I need to make sure I have a thorough understanding of those interests.

When we meet, I'll walk you through everything that goes into buying a house: the loan process, appraisal, earnest money protection, what a contract looks like, what a home inspection looks like, and a lot more. You'll get a deep understanding of what I need to do behind the scenes for you; but more importantly, I'll have a much better understanding of what's important to you so we can both feel confident that I'm getting you exactly what you want.

Objection: I've already bought a house before. I don't need to see all that.

Response: I'm glad to hear you've bought a property in the past and that you're familiar with the process! In my experience, most Realtors don't do a great job of explaining to their clients what they're doing, what the clients are signing, or what options the clients have. I do things differently.

When I represent my clients, I do everything for them in the same way that I would for myself. I want the opportunity to show you what I'll do for you that you don't see—how I choose which properties to share with you, how I qualify those properties to make sure you have a solid chance of getting them, what due diligence I perform behind the scenes, and how I ensure you get the very best deals. The home-buying process can move quickly, and I want to be certain my clients have every advantage. I can't do that without sitting down with you and showing you what goes into this from my end, so I can make sure I'm serving you the way you want to be served.

Objection: Let's do that after I find the house I want.

Response: That's certainly one way to do it. It may be possible to have these discussions after you locate a potential property. My main concern is that it potentially takes away any competitive advantage we would have over other buyers pursuing the same house. The best houses go fast. I've seen prospective buyers get beaten by a matter of minutes. I'll work hard to find you the right house, research to make sure it checks all your boxes, then fight like crazy to get it for you before anyone else does.

I'm very competitive. I educate my clients first to smooth the pathway to success and make sure they're well prepared to know what's coming. The relatively short time commitment I'm asking for up front is a great investment that will yield huge dividends later in the process.

Objection: I've got a few agents I can ask if I have any questions about anything.

Response: There are certainly a lot of agents out there, and many will be willing to offer their opinions and give away free advice. In my experience, that's not always a good thing. Just like not every coach teaches their players the same way, not every agent counsels their clients the same way. It's more of an art than a science. My job is to protect your financial interests and help you reach your overall goal—and my advice will be centered on that. I'll weigh all of your options, present them to you as clearly as possible, ask you as many relevant questions as necessary, and then give you the advice I think is best for you financially. If you ask ten different agents, you're going to get ten different responses.

I'd like to meet with you so you can see what I do, what I offer, and how well I can help you meet your real estate goals. Just like I want to get to know you better, I want you to get to know me better. It's important to me that you understand where I'm coming from and how I run my business.

Objection: Is real estate really that complicated?

Response: Well, it's the biggest purchase (or sale) of your entire life. And while buying (or selling) real estate can be wonderful, it is also a significant commitment. There are a lot of moving pieces to a transaction, way more than most people realize, and that's why we have real estate agents. Trust me, if the market could get rid of us, it would. The reason we are part of the process is because there are *so* many moving parts and *so* many things that can go wrong.

With thousands upon thousands of dollars on the line, I can make a huge difference in negotiations. When we meet, I'll cover how I negotiate, we'll discuss closing costs, how I avoid problem properties, how I can save you money on your loan, and so much more. I'm confident you'll be surprised at how much goes into a transaction, and you'll relieved to know I can represent you throughout the process. I can't wait to sit down with you and show you what goes on behind the scenes.

Common Presentation and Appointment Mistakes

It will take a certain amount of repetition before you get really good at giving your presentations. This why I recommend practicing as much as possible in front of people who are not yet prospects before presenting to a real lead who equals real money. I've watched several agents on my team learn how to do this, and I had to learn how myself. The following are some of the most common errors I've seen agents make when meeting with leads for the first time. Learn from their experiences so you don't repeat these errors yourself.

Going Too Fast. When people are nervous, they usually speak too fast. That's understandable. It's normal to want to get out of an uncomfortable situation as quickly as possible. If you're nervous about giving a presentation, you may find yourself talking too fast, which makes it hard for the lead to follow the information you're providing. Keep in mind that the point of the presentation isn't to get through it. The presentation is a tool to help you develop a connection with the prospect in order to build trust. It is also an opportunity to showcase your professionalism and expertise.

Speak at a pace consistent with the listener's ability to absorb the information. My favorite way to do this is to mirror a prospect's speech pattern with my own. People often mirror the speech patterns of those they agree with. In my own experience, I've learned that most people talk the way they think—I sure do. Use this information. If the lead speaks faster than you, they probably think quickly and want information delivered quickly. If they speak more slowly than you, that's indicative of the pace at which they process information. You should adjust your presentation speed to match your lead's speaking pace.

Reading Slides Verbatim. Nobody likes to be lectured to. Forcing a client to listen as you read verbatim off slides is boring at best and insulting at worst. If you plan on simply reading directly from your slides, you might as well hand your clicker to the prospect and let them walk themselves through your presentation. This is not an effective way to build rapport or trust.

Instead, use the slides as guides to make your points and use your points to connect with the listener. For example, I like to use analogies to describe unfamiliar concepts to people. When explaining that a contract is not a full commitment to purchase for a buyer, I might compare it to dating versus marriage with one prospect or as a test drive of a vehicle with another. The analogies I use differ based on the personality of each lead. You, too, should adjust the delivery of your presentation to make it as relevant as possible for your specific audience.

Again, as you highlight what you can do for each lead, make the delivery unique to them. This not only keeps you on your toes mentally (and prevents you from delivering your presentation on autopilot), but it also forces you to get to know your prospects better. That effort won't go unnoticed.

Using Filler Words. Put simply, using too many filler words or phrases (like, you know, um, I mean) indicates that you haven't mastered the information you're providing and aren't prepared for the appointment. If you can't be prepared for your own appointment, which you scheduled, how can your prospect expect you to be prepared to represent them in what may be the biggest purchase of their lifetime?

It's okay to be nervous or anxious. Most people don't enjoy public speaking or being in the spotlight. It's not okay to let those fears prevent you from serving your lead to the absolute best of your ability. There are several things you can do to overcome your jitters if you find yourself too nervous when presenting, including:

- Practice more so you can think less.
- Focus less on how you are feeling and more on how they must be feeling.
- Remind yourself that you have complete control over how well you perform. Don't look to your prospect to give you confidence. It has to come from within you. The more dependent you are on others to feel good about yourself, the less control you have over your own success and your business.
- Your prospect will probably have no idea that you're nervous unless you make it known to them.
- If you forget something in your delivery, they will never know.
- They agreed to meet you because they wanted to. You are not imposing on them.

If you want to establish a relationship in which your lead views you as professional and in control, you must be professional and in control. The presentation is where you set the tone for the relationship and move it in the direction you want it to go. Be confident and sound confident. That means avoiding using filler words because they make you sound as if you don't know what's in your own presentation.

Failing to Explain "Why." Your listener may understand only in a general sense why you are providing them with certain information. This means they don't fully understand why the information is significant or what could happen if they don't follow your guidance. Don't expect to get buy-in from a prospect unless they can clearly see the "why" behind what you're asking them to do.

During my presentation, I explain how contingencies work in a transaction and how we set a timeline. This is useful information, but the point is to show that I can protect the lead's deposit and make sure they don't lose money. Providing information serves no purpose if your listeners don't understand how it benefits them.

Make sure you explain everything. For example, when you explain preapprovals, highlight *why* that protects them from disappointment, wasted time, and a last-minute rush in which they may lose out on a home.

Focusing on Yourself, Not the Client. These presentations can often feel like a job interview. Indeed, your goal is to have the lead sign a form appointing you as their agent to represent them when buying or selling real estate. However, at most job interviews, the goal is to talk about yourself and your experience. Be careful you don't adopt that mindset here.

Although I do use the term, I don't like to think of a prospect as "hiring" me. They aren't. If they were, I would work only if I got paid. An agent–client relationship is more of a partnership. If the client doesn't buy (or sell) the house, they lost. I did too because I won't get paid. Either we both win or we both lose together.

Your goal during your presentation isn't to talk about yourself the whole time. Of course you will explain how you work and what you can offer, but your focus needs to remain on the prospect. If the focus is on you, you're doing it wrong!

Not Giving Your Lead the Opportunity to Ask Questions. Some agents are so eager to show off how much they know that they jump right into the presentation without asking any questions first. This is a big mistake. There is an excellent chance the prospect won't listen to anything you say and certainly won't care about it.

Start the appointment by making it about them. Ask a lot of questions and get to know your prospect's needs before you ever talk about yourself. Understand the reasons behind their decision to buy or sell a home. Inquire about their fears, concerns, and worries. If you do this, you can tailor the information in your presentation to that specific prospect. Once you know what they need or are concerned with, then share how your unique skills or abilities will serve them well. Your ease and skill and connection will win over your leads.

Speaking in a Monotone. It's hard for anyone to maintain focus and engagement when a speaker doesn't vary their tone. If you use the same tone for the entire appointment, your client's mind will wander. Your goal is for the presentation to sound more like a conversation and less like a lecture. Stop and ask them questions. If you're meeting with a couple, be sure to include the quieter or less dominant partner. Breaking up your delivery and listening as much as you talk will make the presentation much smoother and keep your prospective clients engaged and excited.

Using Industry Jargon. When I was a police officer, this was something I saw regularly. We'd be working on a time-sensitive police situation and a civilian would inevitably walk up asking for directions or a ticket to be signed off. All too often, my partner would reply with, "Hey, we're 10-7, working a hot 211 right now. Can you 10-23 for now?"

Of course, the civilian had no idea what that meant. Most of the time they just walked away feeling dismissed—and this often led to complaints. Had my partner just used common language to describe our situation, the civilian would never have been upset. (My partner was saying, "Hey, we can't help you right now. A robbery just occurred and we're looking for the suspect. Can you stand by for now and ask us later?")

Not Connecting with the Lead. The information in your slideshow is designed to help you build a relationship with the prospect, but if you're not connecting with the lead, then your presentation has no purpose. The information itself doesn't have magical powers, and it's not going to subliminally convince anyone to work with you. It can, however, bridge the gap between you and the prospect. That's what you're really after.

Keep at the front of your mind that the goal of the meeting is to connect. Use the tools at your disposal to accomplish that and stay focused on your goal.

Failing to Establish Yourself as the Guide. Along with connecting, the other goals are letting the prospect know you are in control, winning their confidence, and getting the agency paperwork signed. If you are hesitant or nervous about taking the lead in the agent–client relationship, then you don't really think you're ready to be someone's fiduciary. That's not okay! You've gone through several courses of instruction, passed a state test, and found a broker to supervise you—you are ready to do this.

If you go through the entire appointment and fail to win the lead's faith that you can guide this relationship, you've lost the prospect. I make sure my leads know I'll be the one "driving the car," but they will be telling me where they want to go. They choose the destination, but I choose the route to get there. Just as there can be only one driver in a car, there can be only one driver in the agent–client relationship. That driver had better be you!

Problems arise in real estate transactions when the agent is unsure or timid about their advice. Although some clients will fight you for control (especially initially), deep down they don't want it. The presentation is designed to show what you know, what you can do for your prospect, and why they should trust you. Make sure they do by the time you're finished.

▶ KEY POINTS

- People develop the strongest emotional connections in person, so meet in person.
- Use presentations to establish a relationship with a prospect, to set expectations, and to move your Lead down the Sales Funnel.
- Important metrics are your weekly number of calls and number of presentations. Use the calls to offer free presentations, and practice on friends, family, and neighbors. Practice more than you think might be necessary.
- Make leads clearly see the benefit of working with you.
- Be the stronger frame to make your job easier and make your clients feel secure in your care.
- Handling a lead's resistance or objections is a natural, healthy way to work through the issues preventing them from committing to you.
  - Mirror a prospect's speech pattern and tempo.
  - Use analogies to describe unfamiliar concepts.
  - Clients who fight you for control don't really want it.

CHAPTER FOUR

FUNNEL PROGRESSION (TOOL THREE): THE PSYCHOLOGY NEEDED TO GET IN CONTRACT

"Approach each customer with the idea of helping him or her to solve a problem or achieve a goal, not of selling a product or service."

—BRIAN TRACY

The first two tools, lead generation and appointments/presentations, are used to find and secure Leads. The next two tools, psychology and knowledge, are used to convert these new Clients into revenue for your business (Contracts and Closings). This chapter will focus on the former of those revenue tools: the psychology needed to push your Clients through the Sales Funnel into Contracts.

Experienced real estate agents recognize that to keep clients satisfied (and properties in escrow), you have to effectively communicate with your clients. It's not about how well you navigate the MLS or fill out contracts. Your ability to understand your clients' psychological state and present information to them in a way that makes them feel confident will be what determines if you put clients in contract or lose them.

The real estate industry is quite stressful, largely because of the tremendous amount of uncertainty involved in each transaction. Whether you're working with buyers or sellers, this environment is rife with worry, fear, and stress. While these emotions are not pleasant, be grateful they exist. Otherwise, buyers and sellers wouldn't need agents to help them.

The first thing to understand is that uncertainty breeds anxiety. Some people handle anxiety better than others (my previous career as a police officer prepared me for my real estate career). Others, like first-time home buyers, are typically not prepared for the amount of anxiety they will experience when purchasing or selling a home. This anxiety can hinder your clients' ability to navigate the labyrinth of emotions during an escrow. We've already established that people use emotions to make decisions. Knowing how to get your clients' emotions into a healthy place will be a huge asset for putting more clients in contract and becoming a top producer.

Consider the many fears and anxieties your clients may experience during a home search, such as:
- Will I find a home I like?
- What price will I have to pay for the home I like?
- How many other buyers will be competing for the home?
- What if I don't get the home? Will I find another one as good?
- What will my monthly payment be?
- Will interest rates increase during my home search?
- What will the home inspection report show?
- What will the home be appraised at?
- What if my loan doesn't go through?
- Will my family and friends approve of this home?
- Is this a safe neighborhood?
- What if I don't like the neighbors?
- What if I pay too much for this home?
- What if I'm buying at the top of the market cycle?
- Will the housing market crash?
- Am I buying a money pit?
- What if buying this home was the wrong decision?

Now consider the fears and anxieties for sellers.
- What will people think of my home?
- Should we remodel before selling?
- How much should we spend on fixing up the house?
- Can I keep my home clean for showings?
- Will I get any offers on my home?
- What if I accept an offer too soon and a better one comes in later?
- Will my buyers back out of the deal?
- Will the home appraise at value?
- How can I trust a home appraisal report?
- Will the buyer ask for unreasonable repairs or credits?
- Will the buyer's loan be approved?
- Are my neighbors going to scare away the buyers?

- Will I regret the decision to sell my home and move?
- Will the market spike after we sell?
- Will the market drop while our house is on the market?
- Will we be able to find a new home to buy?

And these are just some of the possibilities—there are plenty more not included here.

To succeed in real estate, you need to accept that your job involves more than just finding a property, explaining a contract, running the numbers, and negotiating a deal. You must also be a counselor and a confidante, a trusted guide and a persuasive figure. If you want to be a top producer, you'll need to master the psychological aspect of the agent–client relationship.

Top-producing agents master several different aspects of client psychology. I'm going to share with you some of the most powerful concepts I've learned to keep clients feeling comfortable throughout the process of buying or selling a home. Once you understand these concepts, you'll have a much easier time moving clients toward a successful transaction. Remember, the purpose of using psychology is to help turn Clients into Contracts in the Sales Funnel. As you read these techniques, do so with that perspective in mind.

First, I want to stress the importance of the tool of psychology. The tools discussed in the previous two chapters can be learned by anyone. They can be mastered by simple repetition and discipline. Psychology, however, is what separates the talented agents from the mediocre ones. Carl Buehner's quote used in Chapter One rings true: *If you can make your clients feel the way they need to feel to move forward, they will.*

Psychological Concepts to Help Your Business

How the Brain Filters Information

To return to Klaff's *Pitch Anything*, the author points out an important process when it comes to the way the human brain processes information. There is a systematic, repeatable process as information filters through the three main parts of the human brain. Understanding this will help you tailor the way you present information to clients to make sure it's received the way you want.

The three main parts of the brain are:
1. The crocodile (or croc) brain
2. The midbrain
3. The neocortex

According to Klaff's research, humans develop the croc brain first. It is responsible for regulating essential body functions such as breathing and heart rate. Additionally, it filters all incoming stimuli and searches for any potential dangers. It is responsible for our fight-or-flight responses and produces strong, basic emotions like fear, worry, anxiety, and doubt. The croc brain's primary purpose is to keep us alive. Information or stimulus is first received here.

Next is the midbrain, which is responsible for determining the meaning of things within a social context. The midbrain takes a stimulus already screened by the croc brain and analyzes it to determine if it is a threat or not. Consider the sound of your alarm clock loudly going off in the morning. The croc brain hears a loud noise, and it screams, "Threat!" It orders your adrenaline to be released to prepare you for fight or flight. The midbrain receives this information and says, "Wait, it's morning time and I recognize this loud sound. It's the alarm clock. Everything is fine, relax." You experience calm. The midbrain is constantly evaluating stimulus within a social context to determine its threat level and validity.

Finally, the neocortex is the problem-solving part of the brain. It receives the information last. It uses logic and reason to analyze and interpret the input received from the other two parts. This is where we weigh pros and cons, consider multiple alternatives, and justify our decisions. Because this type of analysis is time-consuming, your brain will only engage in it when it believes you are safe and don't face any threats. When we evaluate how information travels through a mind, we can conclude: People do not process information—think things through—until the croc brain and midbrain have informed them that they are safe.

It's common for all three parts of the brain to work together quickly. Consider the following scenario: You're walking through a parking garage late at night. It's dark and empty. Suddenly, you hear a loud sound. The croc brain triggers a release of adrenaline into your body, causing you to jump and preparing you to run away from (or stay and fight against) whatever made that sound. Next, your midbrain looks for more input. What was that sound? Was it a scream? Was it laughter? Is it normal to hear a noise like that at a time and place like this? Is there a second voice also screaming and/or laughing?

You realize the sound was whooping and laughter. You immediately calm down a bit. The neocortex jumps in and provides a rational explanation: "It's Friday night and the bars are closing. That's probably a loud group of college students having a little too much fun."

Klaff points out the information processed by the human brain is initially viewed from the perspective of how it could hurt us; only later does logic kick in. This is a neurological fact real estate agents would do well to consider. Our clients are experiencing stress when buying or selling a home. The brain receives stress very similarly to the way it receives danger. The anxiety involved in buying or selling a home will leave your clients feeling on edge and constantly looking for information that will hurt them. They may even create scenarios in their own minds to justify these fears and anxieties. We have all experienced this with a buyer who completely overreacts to dry rot in a report, or a seller who is unreasonably angry about a buyer's request for an extension of time. Now you understand why.

If you want your clients to listen to you, you first have to calm their fears. When you carefully find comps on a home or look up neighborhood statistics for your client, you use your neocortex. However, when your client receives this information, they process it through their croc brain, which simply scans the information for how it could possibly harm them.

Klaff explains that if you want prospects to see the value in your information, you have to let it work its way through the croc brain and midbrain before they can begin to process it in their neocortex. You can get yourself into hot water with people you don't know by sharing the wrong information too soon. Their croc brain will interpret it as a threat and tell them, "This is a slick salesperson who just wants your money— don't trust them." That's why you should always begin by addressing any fears a client may have, such as concerns about losing money or becoming committed to a mortgage payment they may not want later. Once you've addressed and eased your client's worries, they will be ready to receive information showing them the benefits of any given scenario.

The Communication Formula

Remember, you can share the most brilliant, insightful information on earth, but it will be wasted on people if they are just scanning it from the perspective of how it could hurt them. Always address their fears and concerns first. If you combine this with the art of asking questions instead of making statements, you can create a solid formula of communication that will make your job much easier. The formula looks like this.

1. Address a fear or concern. Let your clients experience their emotions and hear themselves verbalize them.
2. Ask a question to help your clients acknowledge this fear and own it.
3. See whether the client has a solution that will work.
4. Propose your own solution once they realize they are seeking one.

Here are some formula responses for common concerns and fears.

List Price. I know you're worried that pricing your home competitively may result in offers coming in low and that you don't want to leave any money on the table. After you've seen how fast houses like yours are selling, can you think of any reason we won't get multiple offers within a week? Do you have any reason to think getting more buyers could possibly be bad for us? I'd like to list it competitively, get multiple offers, and then use that to drive the price up even higher than what you wanted to list it for.

Buying Before the Market Drops. I can see you're concerned with mistiming the market and buying right before a crash. That's a scary thought! Have you noticed anything specific in the economy that would lead you to believe a market crash is coming? How long are you willing to wait to buy if we are committed to waiting for the next crash? I think our best bet is to buy something with a payment you can comfortably afford. If you are an investor and are worried about the market dropping before you are able to expand your portfolio, I also recommend putting down as little as possible and saving money immediately so you can be prepared to buy more properties if the market crashes.

Not Finding the Perfect House. It seems you're worried that the houses you can afford don't have everything you hoped for and that you feel like you're settling for less than you really want. This is a really strong economy, and there's a lot of competition for the little inventory available. Do you think it makes sense to buy nothing at all if you can't find your dream home on the first shot? What would it look like if we found a property that met your needs and started planning now for the next house that has all the bells and whistles you want? I'd like to get you into the market with something financially responsible and great for your family, then use that as a foothold to start looking for something that really blows your mind next year, when we've had some time to prepare.

Not Wanting to Buy When They Can Rent. It's true that renting is typically cheaper than buying in the short term, and I don't want to see you paying more than you have to. Just out of curiosity, have you ever looked at how high rent prices have become over the last ten years? If rent prices continue to increase the same way over the next ten years, do you know how you're going to be able to save money to buy a house? I'd love to find you something and lock in a fixed-rate payment right away that will seem cheaper and cheaper every year as rents increase.

Not Wanting to Pay a Fair Commission. Look, I understand that commissions feel high on top of all the other costs involved here, and nobody likes to pay them. There's always a Realtor out there who has nothing to offer other than being the cheapest. I'd like to ask you: How much money do you think you'd be leaving on the table if you went with an agent who is less skilled and just cheaper? If you lose $20,000 to save $5,000, does that seem like a win for you? The reason I charge what I charge is because I routinely make my clients much more than anyone other than elite-level Realtors. I'd like to show you what I do to achieve that. Can I give you my presentation?

The Trusted Guide

In his best-selling book *Building a StoryBrand*, Donald Miller lays out a strategy to help small businesses and salespeople connect with consumers. Miller explains that a big mistake salespeople make is trying to show themselves as the hero in the client's story. For the inexperienced salesperson, it's easy to think you are selling yourself and that your clients will only choose you if you can stand apart as the best, smartest, and most capable person in your industry. This causes a lot of agents to make the fatal mistake of turning off their prospects early in the relationship.

Miller contends no client wants to play second fiddle to the salesperson. In fact, the client wants to be the hero themselves; they just feel too insecure, nervous, and scared to take on that role. They don't want to be stuck in the back seat and told to shut up; they want to feel confident in the decisions they make themselves. The best salespeople learn this and adjust how they communicate information accordingly.

Miller gives examples of how almost every movie that portrays a hero's journey follows the same pattern. The story starts with a character who will emerge as the hero. The writer helps the audience get to know the character's personality, feelings, and story. The character is likable, and the audience can relate to them on a personal level.

Next, a problem arises. This problem requires the character to take extreme action.

The character then meets a guide—think Yoda and Obi-Wan Kenobi (any *Star Wars* movie), Rafiki (*The Lion King*), or Dumbledore (any *Harry Potter* movie). The guide's role is to help the character develop a better sense of who they are, what they want, and how to execute the plan to solve their problem. Once the plan is in place, the guide then spurs the character to action—oftentimes pushing them past what they're comfortable doing and forcing them to move forward despite their fear.

Finally, there is a climactic battle in which the hero overcomes a great obstacle and emerges as the victor. This battle ultimately helps our hero find relief from the pain that spurred them to action. It also leaves them in a better place and results in a happily-ever-after moment.

Miller argues if a hero could solve their own problem, the audience would immediately tune out. Why? Because if a hero could solve their own problem, they wouldn't be in trouble in the first place. We all instinctively know and relate to a scenario in which help is needed to accomplish a goal bigger than what we are presently capable of handling. In order to prevail, we need to grow—and we all need a guide to help us do that.

Our job as real estate agents is not to become the hero; it's to be the guide. Our clients are the heroes. They are the ones trying to provide safety and comfort for their family and make financially smart moves for their future.

Our clients feel pain. They want to get away from that pain, just like in the movies. They know they need to do something but aren't exactly sure how to do it. They instinctively realize they need a guide to help them with this process. They don't want someone to steal the show and play the hero. They want help finding their own inner hero. That is why they've come to you—to help them accomplish their goal, not yours. If you recognize this and communicate accordingly, you just might earn the right to become their guide.

As your client's guide, you will be walking them through the hero's journey. You'll be helping them come up with a plan (the initial consultation) and then helping them execute it. They will be looking to you for guidance, reassurance, support, and comfort—the very same things a hero looks to their guide for in the movies. If you do your job well, they will end up escaping the pain they are currently in and accomplishing their goal.

Embrace the role of guide, not hero, and you'll find that clients are eager to work with you. You'll also find that you avoid conflict by sidestepping the power struggle that ensues when two people want to play the hero. I use the techniques taught in *Building a StoryBrand* to communicate with my clients the centrality of their story to our relationship and the process of helping them achieve their goals.

The "Big Why"

Anytime someone takes on an endeavor as difficult as buying or selling a home, there's a strong motivation pushing them to do it. In real estate, we refer to this as the "Big Why." Everybody has a Big Why, but it's not the same one for everybody. During my first meeting with a prospect, I always identify their Big Why. Once you understand your lead's motivation, you can take the following steps to ease their way through the process of buying or selling a home.

Tailor Your Advice to Their Needs

Although a prospect's ultimate goal may be to sell their house, this is not actually their most pressing concern. Instead, their biggest concern is the motivation behind their desire to sell. Do they need to downgrade for retirement? Do they need the capital to pay off high interest debt? Do they need better schools for their children? While we're looking at the process as a straightforward transaction, the client is typically seeing it as a single piece of a larger puzzle.

If you want to be a top producer, you'll need to earn a reputation as someone who gives great advice. And you can't give people great advice until you understand their Big Why. Only by uncovering a prospect's true motivation can you offer them the most appropriate, custom-tailored guidance. When you provide advice that's specifically designed to address a lead's unique motivation, you empower them to make the best decisions possible and ultimately realize their goals. Agents who merely get their clients through a transaction are a dime a dozen.

If a lead believes you understand what matters to them, they'll follow your advice. If they don't, they will stubbornly dig their heels in and resist you. When you feel a lead pushing back over things that seem trivial, recognize they likely don't feel you understand what they want. That's when you must take a step back to find out their Big Why.

Prove You Care About Them, Not the Commission

No matter how well you think you know your client or how well they think they know you, there's always the potential for an undercurrent of mistrust when it comes to your commission. This undercurrent becomes markedly more pronounced when your client is experiencing the inevitable stress that's part of every real estate transaction. Wise agents understand and acknowledge this.

When you present options to your client that they may not love (a normal part of this job), it's easy for the client to feel trapped, forced into a situation, or taken advantage of. For example, let's consider a scenario in which the house they want has three other offers, so you suggest offering $20,000 over list price. You advise them to write this aggressive offer because this is the best house for them. Your client suspects you just want the commission on the extra $20,000.

A 3 percent commission on $20,000 is only $600 and not worth risking losing the goodwill of the client over. But that $600 can feel like a big deal to the person who resents having to pay an extra $20,000. To avoid conflict and mistrust, make sure your advice is always centered on why making the hard decision is best for the client, not best for you, based on your understanding of their motivation.

Consider the following ways of presenting information, which are only possible when you know your client's Big Why.

- "I know it hurts to have to pay $20,000 over list price, and if we could avoid it, we would. But is having to settle for an inferior school district worth the extra $50 to $80 a month you'd save by not spending $20,000 now?"
- "I know it's a bummer that we have multiple other buyers who want this property. We want to avoid a bidding war. That's why I want you to start strong out of the gate with this offer. Do you really want

to wait and find out how high the offers go if the seller counters everyone to submit their highest and best amount?"

- "I know it's not ideal that your house appraised for $20,000 less than we put it in contract for, but there's not much we can do about that. The appraiser is delivering what they believe to be an objective opinion of fair market value. If we don't work with this buyer and instead wait for a new one, what are we going to do if we run into the same problem next time? What happens if we don't sell the house in time for fall registration and your child ends up at the same school again next year?"
- "I know it's a pain having to keep your property ultra-tidy for showings and that it's really intruding on your life—but what will it cost you in terms of the next home we can buy if we get an offer $10,000 to $20,000 less because the house didn't show in its peak condition? Is it worth being unhappy in your next home for thirty years because we didn't want to give our best effort now?"

Your clients are going to be thinking about your commission. They are going to see a big number and question why you think you deserve that much money. Anticipate this, and make sure your advice is always wrapped around the client's Big Why so they don't put you in the uncomfortable position of having to justify your paycheck.

Make Sure They Feel Heard and Understood

One of the biggest shocks in my career as a real estate agent was discovering how important it was for my leads to feel heard and understood—to the extent that they didn't seem to care whether I knew how to fulfill all the practical requirements of my job. This may sound like an overstatement but let me explain.

There are three things that determine how quickly a home sells and for how much. They are:

1. Location
2. Condition
3. Price

While there is an argument to be made for a fourth factor—the agent's ability to negotiate—it plays a small role in comparison to the other three. The best things an agent can do to obtain the highest price for a home are to get it into the best condition possible and then list it at a price that will attract multiple offers. (We'll cover this in Chapter Ten, "Listing Like a Pro.") These multiple offers will then allow the agent to use their negotiating skills to increase the asking price while improving the terms.

The problem is you can very rarely sit down, explain this to your lead, then walk them through how you're going to help accomplish this. Instead, you need to use the limited time you have in your presentation to address any mental blocks they are struggling with. If you don't address these directly, you'll have a tough time getting a signed listing agreement from anybody who isn't already extremely close to you.

Issues that might hold your prospect back (either consciously or subconsciously) can include:

1. What other agents are telling them they do to sell houses.
2. Outdated notions about what makes a house sell.
3. Concern that you won't take their project seriously.
4. Fear that they are overpaying.
5. Advice from family members that contradicts your own.

Addressing the above issues will always make your goal of obtaining a signed listing agreement easier. Not taking the time to understand your lead's Big Why and just jumping into looking at homes or preparing their home for sale might work—as long as you experience zero hiccups, hurdles, or setbacks. But as you know by now, that's not how things usually go. When you do hit those snags, your client will push back if they don't believe you understand what's important to them. This inhibits your ability to move them down the Sales Funnel.

When They Want to Quit, Bring Them Back to Why They Started

This is essential. During the journey (which I'll break down shortly), there will be moments when your client wants to quit or at least take time away from the process. This happens most frequently with buyers who can't find a home in a seller's market, but it can also occur with sellers who fall out of escrow a few times or have a hard time finding a buyer. Unless you can turn your client around, all your hard work to this point will have been for nothing.

Top-producing agents anticipate this problem. The way they combat it is by bringing clients back to their Big Why.

Some of the common Big Whys I've encountered in my time as a real estate agent include:

- I want to build long-term financial wealth for my family.
- I want to get into a better school district for my children.
- I need a bigger home for my growing family.
- I want to house hack (rent out part of the home) and reduce my living expenses.
- I want to sell this house to get rid of my PMI / not have to deal with HOAs / avoid higher property taxes.
- I want to live closer to work.
- I want to live in a more like-minded community.
- I want to take the equity from my primary residence and put it into an investment property.
- I want to sell my home and live somewhere cheaper for retirement.

My advice is to assume many of your clients will have similar Big Whys. You should start preparing now for how you will bring them back to the emotional base that motivated them to start this process in the first place. I've found the best way to determine a client's Big Why is through a method I learned in a Keller Williams class.

Going Three Levels Deep

I first heard of this approach in a Keller Williams training class called "Bold," in which agents are taught methods, systems, and criteria for finding clients and closing deals. (I highly recommend taking this class, even if you aren't with Keller Williams.) A key concept was the idea of going three levels deep with your leads. The goal is to help them access the emotion behind their reason for doing things (their Big Why).

Start by asking a question. Then follow up with three more questions, each one diving deeper into your leads' minds and emotional states. With each successive question, they will experience more of the emotions behind the goal they've stated to you. By the time you reach the last question, they will be open to you emotionally. You may even see tears well up in their eyes. This is the level of depth you need to fully understand what motivates your leads and comprehend what is important to them.

Here's an example of how the method works.

Opening question: "You mentioned you wanted a house with a pool. What about a pool is important to you?"

Lead response: "Well, I've always loved houses with pools. When I was a kid we had a pool, and I had some great memories there."

First level: "That's awesome! What kind of memories?"

Lead response: "We had all my family's birthday parties there! All my cousins, aunts, uncles, neighbor kids, the whole gang. We had such an awesome time. I miss those days."

Second level: "Ah, so it's more than just the pool. What would it mean to you if you could provide those memories to your kids?"

Lead response: "My goodness, I hadn't thought of that before. I suppose it would make me feel like a really good mom. I struggle a lot thinking about how my children don't get a lot of what I got as a kid. I'm so busy working, and when I'm home it's always go, go, go. We never really take much time to make memories."

Third level: "So, if you could provide the experience you had as a child to your own children, how would that make you feel?"

Lead response: "I think I would finally get over this feeling that my career is stealing my kids' childhood. I'd also know I was the one who brought all our families together. I don't think I've seen my nieces and nephews at a birthday party for more than five years now. If I can land a house with a pool and a yard big enough to entertain, it would take a huge monkey off my back. I don't think I realized it was even there!"

Once your lead understands why something is important to them, you'll see their resolve strengthen and their commitment to the process deepen. Emotions have the ability to glue us to a cause, project, or purpose. Without them, we rely solely on willpower, and willpower is unsustainable. In this example, the agent helped the lead realize that for her the pool represented childhood memories and, more important, being a great mother. When that client finds herself wanting to quit later on, this knowledge will help the agent keep her on the path to purchase.

The Pendulum of Fear and Greed

I like to compare real estate sales to a pendulum in which the client's emotional state swings back and forth between fear and greed. Each client, whether a buyer or a seller, tends to follow a similar pattern. As their agent, you'll want to use your psychology skills to help control these emotional swings and use them in a way that allows your clients to stay motivated and moving forward toward their goal.

Consider these two scenarios.

Scenario One: Buyer

After showing homes to your buyer clients for several weeks, you finally find a house they love. It's in their price range and conveniently located in their first-choice school district. The house has been on the market for six days, and the seller is accepting offers as they come. Your clients are visibly excited, and you can tell they are trying to keep that excitement under control.

You ask the clients if they would like to write an offer. They look at each other, slowly nod, and tell you they would. You ask what price they'd like to write it for. They look at each other again, hesitate, then look back at you and say what every single buyer always says at this point: "How low do you think we can go?"

This is the greed end of the emotional pendulum. People will always start here when they feel safe. It's not greed in a bad sense—they just want the best deal possible, and their greed engine is firing on all cylinders. If you ask how low they want to start, they'll see if they can do $10,000 under list price. If you say okay, they'll ask about $20,000. If you agree to that, they'll see if they can go even lower. It will never stop because greed has no natural limit. If it goes unchecked, your client will remain stuck in this mindset, so even if they get the house at asking price, they'll feel they overpaid.

You, being the good buyer's agent that you are, call the listing agent and ask whether there are any other offers on the table and, if so, for how much. The listing agent tells you there are three offers in hand, ten disclosure packets sent out, and every offer they've received is over asking price.

You go back to your clients with this information. Immediately their faces whiten, their jaws clench, and their excitement visibly melts away. In one short conversation, their emotional pendulum has swung all the way from greed to fear. Every neuron in their brain is firing and calling on them to protect what they believe is already theirs. You advise them that someone else is going to get the house if they don't write a strong offer, then you ask them what they'd like to offer. They respond with what every single buyer always says at this point: "How much are we preapproved for? How high can we go?"

This is what fear does to your clients. For all but the most experienced buyers or iron-willed people, there is no middle in the fear and greed pendulum swing. They start off at one extreme and move all the way to the other in no time at all. These emotional swings are what make the home-buying process so stressful for them.

Scenario Two: Seller

Your leads want to sell their home and move to a new state for retirement. They've found a new construction home that's half the price of what they want to get for their current home, so they'll be able to pay cash for it. They put the new home into contract and then reach out to you about selling their current home. You meet with them, give an amazing presentation, and take the listing.

After the presentation, the clients express a deeply rooted fear that their house won't sell. They are on a timeline from the builders, and if they can't sell their home within sixty days, they'll lose the one they're buying. They ask you whether you believe the property will sell, and you assure them it will. They ask you if they should price it even lower, and you tell them you don't believe that's necessary. They tell you that if a lower offer comes in, they will still take it. They have plenty of equity and just want to make sure the house sells so they can get on with their new life.

You put your listing on the MLS, market the house effectively, and it shows very well. Three days later you receive an offer that's 2 percent over asking price. You tell your clients about the offer, and they are initially excited and relieved that someone wants to buy their house. You ask them if they would like to accept the offer or wait for a better one to arrive.

Your clients look at each other, and you watch the initial relief melt away and greed start to enter the equation. Their eyes move rapidly as they start imagining the possibilities. They ask you the same question every seller asks in this situation: "How much more do you think we can get if we wait?"

In the above scenarios, the seller clients started at fear and moved to greed, while the buyer clients started at greed and moved to fear. Remember, information makes people think, but emotions make them act. If you're not careful, your clients will make a decision that has a huge impact on their financial future based on an emotion they just experienced for the first time a few moments ago—and one that was radically different from what they had been feeling up to that point!

As their fiduciary, it's your job to help your clients manage these emotional swings. It is also your job to help them make the best decision possible. To do this, you must make sure you don't succumb to these emotional swings as well. Stay level-headed. If you can maintain your own emotional balance, you will see more clearly and be able to guide your clients in the right direction. When your clients become enslaved to fear, it is very difficult to free them. You can be encouraging, strong, and confident, but sometimes that's not enough. I've found the best way to help my clients forward in these situations is by fighting one fear with another.

FOMO

The fear of missing out (FOMO) is a powerful motivator that can shake your clients free from paralysis. Presenting them with a scenario worse than the one they are afraid of is often more effective than pushing back with positivity or encouragement. This can be effective when your client is afraid to move forward. You combat that by giving them a reason to be afraid to go backward.

Below are some common scenarios in which you can use FOMO to help combat your client's fear of moving forward.

FEAR	FOMO COUNTER
Paying too much for a home.	Someone else buying the home that was meant for them.
Not getting enough for the sale of their house.	Not selling their house at all or selling it for even less to the next buyer.
Having to make the repairs recommended in an inspection report.	Backing out of the deal and having to buy a different house with an even worse inspection report.
Paying over asking price.	Losing the house after a bidding war.
Taking the plunge into owning real estate.	Not buying real estate and losing out on hundreds of thousands of dollars of equity over the next twenty to thirty years.
Paying a higher interest rate with their current lender than they could get with a different lender.	Losing their earnest money deposit because they couldn't close on time due to the cheaper lender's poor customer service.
Paying more for a mortgage than they would in rent.	Paying increasing rents because they didn't take control of their finances through home ownership.
Having their credit run by a lender.	Having interest rates rise while they hesitate.
Buying a house that costs more than they believed homes would ever cost.	Looking back thirty years later, seeing that homes have appreciated significantly, and experiencing massive regret that they didn't buy earlier.
Fear of committing to a thirty-year mortgage.	Not getting a tax incentive on the mortgage interest and missing out on steadily paying down a mortgage over thirty years.
Paying PMI if they don't have 20 percent down.	Paying more for the house than they would today because they waited to save up the rest of their down payment, then paying off that extra amount, plus interest, over thirty years.
Not getting every single thing they want in the home.	Not buying a starter home to use as a steppingstone for their next home (i.e., letting this home buy their next home).
Not wanting to commit to a buyer's agent.	Being represented by an agent who is looking out for someone else's interests, not their own.

I've developed several scripts in my career that I use to trigger my clients' FOMO when I see they are paralyzed and can't take action. These work when my clients are at a crossroads and having a difficult time identifying their best courses of action. Such situations can be very stressful, and they require me as the agent to rise to the occasion.

The following example shows how you can guide your client to move forward and make the best possible decision to reach their goal.

Scenario

Your client makes an offer on a house that receives several offers. The seller sends a multiple counteroffer with these instructions: "Buyer to submit highest and best offer." Your client doesn't want to lose the house but also doesn't want to pay more than they have to. The house is listed at $350,000, and your client offered the asking price. The fear of losing the home is on one side and the greed of not wanting to pay more is on the other. The pendulum is swinging back and forth between the two, and the client is feeling the tension.

Script:

I understand you have a difficult decision to make. On the one hand, you don't want to lose this house. On the other hand, you don't want to feel like a fool who over-paid. The reality is there's no way we can know what the other buyers will be offering. Do you mind if I ask you a few questions to help you determine what you should do?

What if we write a new offer for $360,000, and someone else writes it at $365,000? Imagine that and tell me how you feel. Do you wish you had paid $365,000 yourself, or are you happy for the other buyer because they paid more than the house was worth to you?

Now imagine someone else paid $370,000. Are you happy they got the home at that price because it wasn't worth that much to you? Keep in mind, we did see comparable sales in the neighborhood in the $390,000 to $400,000 range. The sellers listed this house far below market value.

What if we offered $400,000 and then someone else paid $405,000? I really don't want you to have any regrets about how we handled this situation. You shouldn't regret the price you paid, but you also shouldn't regret losing the house. This property meets all your criteria, and the market is clearly showing it's worth way more than the list price because of all the other buyers who are interested in it.

At what price would you say, "I'm happy for those buyers—I would never have paid that price"? I want to find that number and come in strong right there. If we come in weaker, this will turn into an auction, and you'll likely end up paying even more.

▶ KEY POINTS

- Top-producing agents make clients feel confident to move forward and reduce their anxiety by sharing knowledge of what's to come.
- Top-producing agents master several aspects of client psychology. They address fears or concerns; ask questions to help clients acknowledge this fear; see if the client has solutions; propose solutions.
- Real estate agents are the guides, not the heroes.
- Top-producing agents go three levels deep to understand a lead's "Big Why." When clients want to quit, agents bring them back to this.
- There's always the potential for an undercurrent of mistrust when it comes to commissions.
- Clients' emotions swing between fear and greed.
- Use FOMO to help clients afraid of moving forward.
- Study the FOMO script as a basis to come up with your own for common scenarios.

CHAPTER FIVE

FUNNEL PROGRESSION (TOOL FOUR): THE KNOWLEDGE TO CLOSE THE DEAL

"An investment in knowledge pays the best interest."

—BENJAMIN FRANKLIN

The final tool in the Sales Funnel is your knowledge of real estate. While knowledge is important, you may be surprised that it's actually the least important tool for a newer agent because knowledge is the easiest tool to leverage. New or inexperienced agents can leverage knowledge through a transaction coordinator, office broker, team leader, escrow officer, partner, or just a friendly, more experienced agent in the office. You should never let a lack of knowledge keep you from moving prospects along the funnel.

As I just noted, there are multiple ways to gain knowledge. You can also learn indirectly by reading, listening to, and watching published content, including books, articles, social media posts, podcasts, and YouTube videos. BiggerPockets is a great resource for every one of these content channels. And, of course, you can learn from your own personal experience. A good agent will use all methods to keep expanding their knowledge base.

The more knowledge you have, the more escrows you will see all the way through to close. The more deals you close, the more money you'll earn and the more confidence you'll have. This confidence makes it easier to generate leads (Tool No. 1) and completes a full circuit of using your tools. Your next round of deals will come more easily as your increased confidence makes lead generation simpler and more enjoyable.

Think about any area of life in which you have confidence. Don't you feel comfortable making decisions quickly in this area? That's the power of a strong knowledge base. The confidence that stems from this knowledge will give you the feeling of being "in the zone" that every successful Realtor experiences. We know we're going to land every listing, take every buyer, and get every deal. Having the confidence to believe you can do something often creates the reality.

Agents with a strong knowledge base consistently close more deals and experience fewer problems in escrow and before closing. Let's look at some of the common ways top-producing agents use their knowledge to increase their effectiveness and earnings.

Practical Knowledge Application: Anticipating Problems Before They Occur

Certain problems crop up repeatedly in real estate transactions. The most successful agents anticipate these problems and create systems to minimize their negative impact. The following are some of the problems that tend to arise in escrow and the strategies top-producing agents use to solve them.

Inspection Issues

In general, once a seller accepts a buyer's offer, there will be an inspection period during which the buyer may perform due diligence on the property. This inspection period has different names across the country, but the purpose is always the same. During this period, the buyer may hire licensed professionals to perform inspections and issue reports detailing their assessment of the condition of the property. Buyers use these reports to decide whether they want to move forward with the purchase, and their agents use these reports to negotiate credits and purchase-price adjustments. The following are the most common reports.

- Home inspection reports
- Pest inspection reports
- Roof condition reports
- Septic tank reports
- Natural hazard disclosure reports
- Pool inspection reports
- Title reports
- HOA documentation

The first thing you can do to minimize inspection issues is to familiarize yourself with these reports. As a buyer's agent, learn how to read and, more importantly, how to interpret these reports. This will put you in a position to convey the information in a way that prevents your clients from overreacting. You will also be able to solve any problems revealed in the reports and keep your clients optimistic about the home's condition.

As a buyer's agent, understand the items often found in these reports. Feel free to return to this chapter when advising your clients on their options related to inspection reports or other issues that arise during the inspection period.

Pest Infestation

The purpose of a pest inspection is to uncover any signs of infestation or damage and the potential for either in the future. Inspectors commonly check for rodents, scorpions, snakes, spiders, termites, area-specific insects, and fungus (dry rot). When there is clear evidence of the presence of a pest, the report refers to this as Section 1 damage. When there is evidence pointing to the possibility of a future infestation, the report will refer to this as Section 2 damage. The following table breaks down examples of Section 1 and Section 2 damage.

ITEM	SECTION 1 EXAMPLES	SECTION 2 EXAMPLES
Rodents	Droppings, dead rodents, chewed wiring.	Holes in the exterior where a rodent could easily enter, trees hanging over the roofline where rodents could drop down.
Spiders	Spider webs, eggs, dangerous spider specimens are present.	Climate conditions or temperature conditions where spiders prefer to nest.
Termites	Tubes, tunnels, or chewed wood; termite carcasses or an active hive.	Wood touching ground likely to attract termites, paper debris left under the home that will draw them.
Dry rot/fungus	Soft wood, wood with holes, peeling wood fibers.	Worn paint leaving wood exposed to fungus, areas where water is incorrectly draining from roof or ground and coming in direct contact with wood.

In a pest inspection report, inspectors will often label an area of the home where they noted Section 1 or Section 2 damage, then provide a price for what they would charge to repair the damage. These labels are usually in alphabetical order and then in numerical order. For example, a list may look like this: 1A, 1B, 1C, 2A, 2B, etc.

The price quoted by the inspector to make each repair is usually found at the bottom of the report and corresponds to the label assigned to that problem. You'll find the grand total at the bottom of the report. It's important to make sure you explain to buyers that not everything listed on the report has to be done and the prices are not set in stone. These are often negotiable, and it's not uncommon to find another contractor, handyman, or inspector who will do the repairs for less money.

Dry Rot or Fungus Damage

In areas with even moderate amounts of rain, dry rot frequently shows up in pest inspection reports. Because it is labeled as a "fungus," the name itself can easily scare clients. Be sure to explain to them that this term commonly refers to dry rot, and it's one of the most frequently encountered issues in pest inspection reports.

It's worth telling them that dry rot repairs are not as difficult to fix as other pest inspection problems, like termites. Skilled handymen and contractors can solve the majority of dry rot issues for much less than the report will quote. It can be as easy as cutting out bad wood, replacing it with new wood, and painting it. Sometimes simply using wood filler can fix the problem if the dry rot isn't too bad.

Don't let the high quoted cost of dry rot repair scare your clients into backing out of the deal. Always get a second opinion; your clients will feel much more comfortable once they've reviewed more than one quote.

Easements

An easement is a specific right to use another person's land for a particular purpose. Easements are usually recorded with the county and reveal themselves on title reports that are run during the escrow period. Easements are very rare in certain parts of the country, such as those with tract home communities. In other parts of the country, such as in rural areas, they are much more common. An easement itself isn't inherently concerning, but the moment your client hears, "Someone else can use my land and I can't stop them," it's likely to trigger scary thoughts in their croc brain. Get out in front of this by explaining exactly what this easement means and how it will affect their use of the property.

Some easements transfer with the title; others do not. There might be nothing to worry about if the easement won't transfer when your client buys the home. However, if it does, talk to the title or escrow officer about how the easement will affect your client's use of the property, who is allowed to use it, and under what circumstances. This will leave you better prepared to act with certainty and calmness when your client cannot.

HOA Assessments

A homeowners association (HOA) is an entity formed to help manage and maintain the value of a specific group of properties or housing developments. HOAs create standards that homeowners must adhere to, enforce code violations, and often provide amenities to the members. These amenities frequently include a controlled entrance protected by security at a guard shack; neighborhood security patrols; common-area landscaping and maintenance; pools and clubhouses; water, sewer, and trash collection services; and exterior maintenance.

Members pay monthly fees to belong to the HOA, and the association keeps a certain amount of this money in reserve. Sometimes an issue will arise in an area that the HOA is responsible for maintaining, and there will be an insufficient amount of money in reserve to make the repairs. When this happens, the HOA will issue an assessment, whereby all association members are required to pay a certain amount of money to make up for the shortfall. These assessments obviously have a negative impact on the owners' finances.

When buying a property that is a part of an HOA, help your client understand the financial position of the HOA before they commit to buying there. It's your responsibility to check if the HOA is in litigation (if it's being sued, the reserves could be drained and assessments imposed to rebuild the reserve), whether there are currently any assessments that need to be collected, and if there is currently a healthy amount of money in the community's reserves.

Foundation Problems

Foundations are the F-word of real estate. The minute most would-be homeowners hear about a problem in this area, they decide they want nothing to do with the property. I advise my clients when they experience a strong negative emotion like this to take the issue causing them fear and turn it into a number. That number is how much it will cost to repair the problem. This is particularly helpful with foundation problems. These are much less scary when we consider them as a dollar amount.

To be a top-producing agent, familiarize yourself with the different types of foundations in your area and the problems that can arise with them. Foundations are a part of the structure, and just like any other structural component, they wear down and eventually need to be repaired or replaced. Many of your clients will assume that a foundation problem means the house is ready to collapse. This is not usually the case, as not many of us have seen houses just collapse while we're driving down the street! Being able to articulate how a foundation works and how it's repaired will highlight your professionalism in the eyes of your clients.

For example, there are three main types of foundations in California, where I live. While different states have different soil types and foundation options, these are the main three I've seen.

Raised foundations are those where the house sits on a system of beams resting on concrete piers. These foundations are ideal, as there is a crawl space underneath the home that gives access for repairs. It's also better when it comes to running plumbing and electrical infrastructure, as the contractor has a much easier time running their lines underneath the home and doesn't have to drill into concrete to do so. These foundations also prevent moisture from building underneath the property and rotting away its base because the house sits above ground and not where water can pool.

Concrete slab foundations are those where the home is built on a large slab of concrete reinforced with steel bars and wired mesh. These are the cheapest foundations to build, but they're less ideal for running plumbing and electrical lines because there is no access underneath the structure. These foundations are more likely to be found in warmer climates; cold weather can cause them to crack.

Basement foundations are built with a high foundation wall and a concrete slab at the base. These can be room height or can be partial basement foundations that are much shorter. Basement foundations can be built to be tall enough to create an entirely separate living quarter or function as storage. Many homeowners will dig out the area under the basement foundation to increase the height of the area underneath, then run plumbing, electrical, and gas lines to the area to create that storage or living quarter.

With concrete slab and basement foundations, you may see large cracks running through the concrete. If left untreated, this can lead to pest infestations and eventual compromises in structural integrity. A foundation repair company can come in, cut out the cracked portion of slab, pour new concrete in its place, and use an epoxy gel and rebar for reinforcement. Make sure you get a quote for this work during your inspection period and see if you can negotiate for the seller to pay for it.

Issues with raised foundations are different. A foundation repair company can come in, jack the house up (similar to jacking up a car to change a tire), and repair or replace the damaged foundational components. If there is easy access to the area and the house can be lifted without much difficulty, I've found these repairs to cost much less than originally feared, often in the $5,000 to $10,000 price range or less.

Remember, when your client hears the words "problem with the foundation," their croc brain will go to a worst-case scenario. Focus on converting emotions into numbers to bring your client back to a place of confidence. Then you can speak to their neocortex and provide a sensible solution to keep the deal in escrow.

Plumbing Leaks

Plumbing leaks are another potentially expensive problem you'll encounter in a home inspection report. Some are minor and relatively inexpensive to repair, as when the plumber has easy access to the plumbing line, knows exactly where to find the leak, and no significant water damage has occurred.

Repairs become expensive when the water or sewage line is difficult to find and/or access. If the line has been leaking for a long time and there is rot or fungus forming on wood in the home—especially if that wood is an important part of the home's structural components (foundation, framing, subfloor, etc.)—repairs can involve serious expense.

Whenever an inspection report shows a plumbing leak, look for a plumber, contractor, or experienced handyman to give you an estimate on what it will cost to make the repairs. Don't assume the leak will be minor or major until an expert has provided you and your client with their professional opinion.

Unsafe Electrical Conditions

Electrical problems can be a major hurdle to overcome for several reasons. First, they can be major safety hazards. When this is the case, the buyer cannot delay getting the work done; it needs to be tackled soon after closing. This is particularly problematic when your client is putting a big down payment on a property and paying closing costs in addition to that. Not every buyer will have enough money to make electrical repairs. That leads to the second problem, which is: Electrical problems are not cheap to fix.

This means that the responsibility for these repairs will often fall to the seller. Sellers do not like having to make repairs before escrow closes, because there is no guarantee the escrow is going to close and they may have spent that money for nothing (safety concerns notwithstanding).

Unless the problem is something as simple as including a ground fault circuit interrupter (GFCI), you're probably going to have to hire a professional. This means high labor wages. On top of that, you can't replace a single aspect of an electrical system like you can with one line of plumbing or one board of wood. If one part of the system is unsafe, there's a very good chance you'll have to replace the entire system.

When you spot an unsafe electrical condition, talk to the inspector who pointed it out and get a bid from a licensed electrician very early. If you have to back out of the deal, you want to do it before putting your client through the ringer.

Roof Life

The condition of the roof—or the remaining life in one—will play a big factor in the overall condition of a property. In dryer areas, such as parts of California, Arizona, and New Mexico, buyers will be much less concerned with the condition of the roof than buyers in areas where it rains frequently. When your client gets a roof inspection, the inspector will often call out areas where the roof could use repair and provide an estimate of what they believe the remaining life of the roof to be.

When a roof is nearing the end of its life, you should expect that it will need to be replaced. This is usually something the seller is going to need to credit the buyer for in all but the hottest of seller's markets. Roof repairs are not cheap. They can range from $8,500 to $12,000 across the country. A bad roof can kill a deal. If you're representing the buyer, you'll likely need to ask for sizable credits from the seller so your client can replace the roof as soon as the deal closes.

Cosmetic Repairs

The final thing to understand when reading inspection reports is the cosmetic fixes. Most items that show up on the report will be cosmetic fixes, and they range from linoleum scuffs to chipped paint to missing cabinet fixtures. It's important to recognize these issues because you'll need to explain to your client why it's not something that should concern them, and that the seller isn't likely to repair any of it.

Inspection reports are inherently scary. They are designed to protect the inspector from being sued if they miss anything. This means the inspector will include as many things as possible. That can feel overwhelming to the home buyer when they are reviewing the report, and most buyers will believe they or the sellers are supposed to fix everything. This is not the case! An incredibly powerful skill to keep your clients in escrow is the ability to explain which items are concerning and which are not. The more you grow your knowledge base in this area, the more properties you will move all the way to close.

Buyer's Remorse

When a buyer is looking at homes, their subconscious is working overtime. Because our subconscious desperately wants to do for us what it thinks we want it to, it begins looking for ways to present us with information it knows will please us. When buyers first start looking at homes, they are excited, optimistic, and positive. Their subconscious is painting a picture for them viewed through rose-colored glasses. Everything is an opportunity, their creative juices are flowing, and nothing feels like it's too hard to overcome.

You'll see this manifest itself in the comments buyers make during the home search. When a buyer loves one particular element of a property (say, the kitchen, the park across the street, or the sparkling pool), they will frequently make justifications for other parts of the home that do not meet their criteria. I've heard them talk about turning one-story homes into two-story homes, extending the home into the backyard, or taking the property down to the studs to rebuild it from the ground up. This is all incredibly unrealistic, but it doesn't feel that way when the subconscious is constantly whispering, "Do it, do it, do it!"

This is the honeymoon phase. Having worked with a large number of buyers, I've noticed the same pattern every time.

The buyers will start the process eager, excited, and optimistic. They will look at homes and think of creative ways to justify making them work. They will write offers and hold their breath waiting to hear if they get the house. When they don't, they will feel rejected and disappointed, but eventually they pick themselves back up. When an offer is finally accepted, they will scream, hug each other, call their loved ones to tell them they got the house, hang up the phone, then look at each other and say the same exact thing as the reality of the situation hits them: "What did we just do?"

There is something about going into contract and the weight of that commitment that typically triggers fear in the buyer. In that singular moment, their excitement can turn to ashes as fear of the unknown sets in. They start wondering:

- What if we can't afford the payment?
- What if there were better houses out there?
- What if we decide we don't want to be tied down to a mortgage?
- What if the economy collapses?

You can be sure their subconscious hears these questions being asked, and like the good servant it is, it completely changes course. Rather than pointing out all the amazing opportunities this house represents, it will immediately begin feeding all the things that could go wrong or problems that could arise. In the blink of an eye, the entire trajectory of a buyer's emotional condition changes. The honeymoon phase has abruptly ended. The buyer is now staring at their "marriage" to this house and asking if they are really ready for the commitment it requires.

It is in this emotional state when molehills become mountains. The subconscious is doing everything it can to give them reasons to back out of the deal. It happens to every buyer—all of them—and you should assume it will happen to yours. Be prepared when it does. Top buyer agents prepare for this. They begin that preparation during the first appointment and cover it during the presentation. They continually reiterate these realities throughout the home search period and warn the clients about what they'll experience when they go into contract. I train all the agents on my team to be top buyer agents.

Strategies for Listing Agents

As the listing agent, you have no control over the agent who is representing the buyers. You won't be able to influence the buyer's emotions or present information in a way that keeps them encouraged. If, as the listing agent, you want to keep your deals in contract so they close more frequently, you need a plan in place for when buyers inevitably hit the "buyer's remorse phase." In the next section, I'll go over techniques you can use and systems you can build to protect your seller clients' interests after your listing has gone into contract and you can't control or influence the other side.

Inspection Report Problems for Listing Agents

As a listing agent, you can save yourself a lot of trouble by having your clients pay for and order these inspections before listing the property. Inspection reports are the No. 1 thing buyers use as leverage to get credits from sellers. As you can see from the section above, the more skilled a buyer's agent is at understanding these reports, the more leverage they have when asking sellers for credits.

By providing these reports to buyers upfront, even before they write their offer, you can save your clients a considerable sum later in the process when buyers may have you in a compromising situation. I encourage all my sellers to get their reports. This one strategy saves my clients thousands of dollars. Here's why it works.

When buyers go into contract and enter the buyer's remorse phase, the last thing you want is inspection reports with bad news about the property. Unfortunately, reports are full of bad news; even more unfortunately, this is the exact phase when buyers tend to see them. Since you can't control how the buyer's agent presents this information, you should assume the buyer won't handle it well and thus must proactively prepare for this response.

Remember the honeymoon phase when the subconscious is working overtime to dismiss every concern and make light of every issue? Wouldn't that be a better time to present buyers with any inspection report issues? Wouldn't it behoove your sellers to show the buyers the scariest part of the whole transaction when they are in the very best frame of mind to view it? Presenting potential buyers with reports before remorse hits them will prevent the majority of them from backing out of escrow later. It will also reduce the likelihood of them asking for any repairs or credits. It will definitely provide you with more leverage in representing the seller if they do ask.

This one trick will save your clients thousands of dollars. However, many sellers don't want to pay for these reports upfront. That's why I make it a part of my presentation. I tell them why they should do it, how it saves them money in the long run, and why it could be too expensive to do it later in the process. Before providing potential buyers with the report, I ask the seller if there is anything on the report they can repair that won't be a pain or an inconvenience to them. It's always a positive touch when you present the report along with a list of items that have already been repaired or replaced.

Low Appraisals

Low appraisals are another killer of escrows, and you'll want to prepare for them. This preparation can mitigate the negative impact they'll have on your seller. An appraisal is an expert's opinion on the value of a property. It is based on comparable sales in the neighborhood, with adjustments made to the value based on things like amenities, conditions, and upgrades. Appraisals are typically required by banks when giving loans on properties and are paid for by the buyer. Since the majority of deals use loans, appraisals are a staple in the homebuying process.

If an appraisal comes in above or equal to the contract price, there's no problem. When an appraisal comes in below the contract price, there's a problem. Lenders don't want to lend on a property if it's being purchased for more than it's worth. A lender always considers what might happen if they have to foreclose and sell the asset to recoup their investment. There's less chance of them being able to do that if the home is worth less than the amount the buyer borrowed to buy it. In the case of a low appraisal, there are four possible outcomes.

1. The buyer pays the difference out of pocket.
2. The buyer backs out of the deal, if they have an appraisal contingency.
3. The seller drops the contract price to match the appraised value.
4. Both sides negotiate and meet somewhere in the middle.

If a buyer is putting down 10 percent of the home's value to purchase, the bank is putting down the other 90 percent. If a house is contracted to be purchased at $200,000, the bank will be contributing $180,000 of that (200,000 x 0.90 = 180,000). If the property appraises for $190,000, the bank is willing to give 90 percent of $190,000, not 90 percent of the original $200,000 price.

In Option 1, the buyer can pay that extra $10,000 and buy the property at the price they put in the contract.

In Option 2, the buyer can back out of the deal based on the low appraisal value if the seller is unwilling to compromise and the buyer has an appraisal contingency.

In Option 3, the seller drops the price to $190,000 and the bank contributes 90 percent of that amount.

In Option 4, the seller may agree to reduce the price to $195,000 instead of $200,000 and the buyer would then contribute the other $5,000 (not the original $10,000 when the purchase price was $200,000).

As you may notice, appraisals do not help sellers. An appraisal contingency gives the buyer leverage to ask for a reduction in price. If you want to protect your seller's interests, you want to limit the buyer's ability to do this before putting the property in contract. The best way to do this is to not allow the buyers to have an appraisal contingency.

Without a contingency, the buyers would lose their earnest money deposit if they don't close. It is very difficult to get buyers to agree to this, and it only works when there are multiple offers on the house, buyers are frustrated trying to get into contract, or buyers have enough money in the bank to cover the difference should they want to.

The next best way to protect your seller clients is to negotiate upfront how a low appraisal will be handled. If you can't get the buyers to waive their appraisal contingency, ask them to agree to pay a specified amount over a lower appraisal price. This amount will vary depending on your market, but it can vary from $1,000 to $100,000 depending on the price of homes in the area. Negotiating this upfront puts power in the hands of the sellers, as they can't be held hostage by a low appraisal and buyers threatening to back out.

You can also shorten the time period buyers have to back out based on a low appraisal. If buyers are forced to decide to stay in the deal or back out quickly, it gives your seller clients more time to get their house back on the market.

If you cannot limit the effects of a low appraisal before going into contract, you still have two options before agreeing to reduce the contract price. The first is to challenge the appraisal. Some banks will allow this and are willing to send a second appraiser to the property to see if the new appraiser comes up with a different appraised value. Your second option is to have the buyers change lenders and have that lender send an independent appraiser to the property to do their assessment. Neither of these options is guaranteed to change the original situation, but they're better than nothing when you need to do something to help your clients.

Loan Problems

Though not nearly as common as appraisal issues, loans falling through can stop deals from closing in escrow. In today's real estate environment, most buyers are preapproved for a loan, and the major hurdles that prevent a loan from being approved are handled upfront and ahead of time. This cuts down on a significant number of loan problems, but it won't eliminate everything. When loans do fall apart, it's often for one of these reasons as follows:

- The borrower opens a new line of credit; this throws off their debt-to-income ratio.
- The borrower failed to disclose debt they are carrying.
- The borrower is in an unstable position in their job (such as in a probation period).
- The borrower has not worked at their job for a long enough period of time.
- The borrower is using funds for the down payment that were not sourced properly.
- Interest rates rise to the point where the price the borrower is pre-approved for drops because their debt-to-income ratio is affected.
- The borrower thinks they can include commission, bonuses, or other non-salaried compensation, and the underwriter says they cannot.

While it's not your responsibility to ensure your client's funding comes through, it is in your best interest to make sure it does. You don't get paid until that house closes. This applies when you're the seller's agent too. In my system, when I'm the seller's agent, I have my transaction coordinator call the buyer's lender to confirm that the appraisal was ordered on time and that the buyer has provided all the necessary documentation to ensure the loan will close.

Before accepting an offer, you should call the buyer's lender to make sure they have all the appropriate paperwork to preapprove a loan. This will often include:

- The two most recent pay stubs.
- The last two years' tax returns.
- The last two years' W-2 forms.
- Proof of funds.
- A completed mortgage application.

Many lenders will issue preapprovals without first gathering the necessary information. They do this because buyers don't want to take the time to provide them before looking for a property. Once the buyer finds a property they love (your listing), there is now an urgency to put it in contract. This often results in the lender saying that they've collected documents that they actually haven't. The less verification the lender has done ahead of time, the more likely something could have changed in the buyer's loan profile and the loan won't be approved.

You can limit how often this happens by verifying with the buyer's lender before accepting an offer. This is the smartest best way to proceed.

Offers Contingent on Selling or Buying Another Property

Another factor that kills escrows is when the listing purchase is contingent on the buyer selling their current home first. These contingencies allow the buyer to back out of the deal with your client if they can't sell their house within a specific amount of time. For the buyer, this is great. For the seller, this is less than ideal.

As a general rule, I advise my seller clients against accepting offers that are contingent on selling a property first. While every market is different (and sometimes you feel you have no choice), there are ways to handle this scenario without pushing the buyers away and leaving your seller without any options.

When you receive an offer contingent on selling a property, don't assume that property is already on the MLS. Some buyers don't even start the process of listing their home until they've found a home they want to buy first! You don't want to let your seller clients get excited about having a buyer if they aren't a real buyer. A buyer who does not have the funds or ability to purchase their listing should not be considered a real buyer.

My preferred way to deal with this scenario is to politely and enthusiastically tell the buyer that I would love to go into contract with them, but they need to put their current home under contract first. I then ask the buyer if it's okay for my team to check in with them weekly to see how they are progressing. This takes the sting out of my rejection of their offer and lets them know I am willing to work with them. After that, I ask if I can post their listing on my social media to see if I can generate interest to help them sell it. Taking this approach helps me avoid going into a bad contract for my clients without offending what might be the only buyer interested in the house.

Outside Influences

Outside influence is a major disruption of escrows. What's worse, you usually don't see it coming. A big area of concern is who is influencing your client's decisions. Things can start off great but turn ugly if the wrong voices are in their head. This leads to doubt, mistrust, and often-times a breakdown in your relationship. When you first meet leads, it's wise to ask them who else is influencing their decisions.

When your lead is the seller, ask questions to determine what pre-conceived notions they have about the process, then follow up with more questions to determine where they came from.

- "How much do you believe your house is worth? Really, that's inter-esting. Where'd you get that number from?"
- "What are your biggest concerns with selling your home? Okay, got it. What makes you believe that will be a challenge?"
- "You'd like an open house every weekend? I understand. What's important about open houses to you? Who told you that?"

Most of your leads will reveal who is influencing their ideas about real estate if you ask them the right way. Once they let you know it's their parents, their neighbors, their in-laws, or some other authority figure, you'll be able to prepare for those problems. Many people have had terrible experiences with real estate. They've lost big money, had an agent take advantage of them, or worse. For others, they've never gotten over a bad real estate decision they made or forgotten who suggested they make it. There are boundless motivations behind nonexpert advice. If you want to keep your deals in escrow, make sure your voice is the loudest in your client's head.

When you are representing the sellers, make the effort to ask the buyer's agent questions that reveal who is in their client's head. I've seen many deals fall apart because of an outside influence causing the buyer to back out of the deal. Although the sellers did nothing wrong, they were negatively impacted by the buyer's decision to listen to someone other than their agent.

Before you advise your clients to accept an offer delivered from a buyer, always ask the buyer's agent where the funds are coming from. If the buyer is receiving down payment money from their parents, they will often be susceptible to their parents' opinion. This can catch you off guard because the parents are usually not a part of the process until the property is in contract and they go see it for the first time.

This is a recipe for disaster. If the parents see something in the home they don't like or hear advice they don't agree with, they can easily pull the plug on the deal before you're even aware they are involved. Knowing where your buyer's funding is coming from will help you get out in front of problems like this. See if you can meet the other people who are financially involved in the transaction and win their approval before they go into contract, thereby protecting your escrows.

What Top-Producing Agents Do

Top-producing agents design a pattern for themselves that allows their business to grow, and this pattern allows them to consistently close large numbers of deals. As I stated earlier in the book, newbies can avoid trial and error by finding a mentor. Because this book is intended to function as the role of mentor in your journey, I've compiled the following list of items you need to learn.

Set Expectations Correctly

Top-producing agents set expectations with their clients. Preventing issues will keep your clients engaged and optimistic, which is why you must make setting client expectations a priority.

Earlier in the book I talked about the importance of setting appointments and delivering presentations. The presentation is your opportunity to build rapport and seal the relationship as a fiduciary to your clients. It is also the time when you correctly set expectations and take the nasty surprises and unforeseen hard turns out of the equation. The better your client is prepared for the emotional spikes that are coming, the better they will handle them. This will keep more of your deals in escrow.

The following are examples of scripts for commonly encountered problems with both buyer and seller clients.

Buyer Scripts

AREA OF CONCERN FOR BUYER CLIENTS	SCRIPT TO SET EXPECTATIONS
It's a seller's market and hard to find a home for buyers.	This is a red-hot market, and that's great because it means the economy is thriving and it's the right time to buy a home. Something to be aware of is there are almost always several buyers for every property you're going to like. Be prepared that we'll likely have to write offers over asking price, and it may take a few tries before we can put something in contract.
They don't want to move quickly to put a home under contract because of too many questions looming in their mind.	You're going to have a million questions about the conditions of the homes we look at before you feel comfortable. That's totally normal and something we expect. Once we put a property into contract, we will have a period of time to conduct inspections, look up data, and peer deeper into our concerns. A contract is not a commitment to buy.
They'll be scared after reading an inspection report.	When we order inspections, the inspector is going to provide an incredibly detailed report that describes every fault they can possibly find in a house. These reports will scare you with all the information they contain! Try not to worry about that. Every house has a lot wrong with it, even the one you live in now. We aren't going to worry about small, trivial, or cosmetic items. We are looking for big problems like a bad roof, faulty electrical system, leaky plumbing, or major foundation problems. Here's an example of what an inspection report looks like. Let's go through it together.
They realize property taxes are higher than they expected.	Different parts of town may have different rates of property taxes. The city may charge differently depending on the amenities in one area over another. I know you love the homes in this area, but the taxes will be higher. It may cost an additional $100 a month. Does that sound worthwhile to you?

They worry about interest rates rising.	I know it's important we keep your monthly payment as low as possible. I'd like to ensure that, but we don't get any say over what rates are going to do while we are looking at homes. Oftentimes lenders will let you lock your rate for a fee. Would you like to do that now, or are you okay gambling and just seeing where rates go while we look?
They want to view a lot of houses before making up their mind.	I know it can feel overwhelming with all the choices you have to make when looking at homes, and you want to make sure you choose the right one. My job is to help you do that by prescreening properties and only showing you houses that not only match your criteria but that we also have a realistic chance of getting. I don't want you to try to do my job for me. Is there anything more I should know about your needs before you'll feel comfortable writing an offer on the house that matches your criteria?

Seller Scripts

AREA OF CONCERN FOR SELLER CLIENTS	SCRIPT TO SET EXPECTATIONS
The buyer is asking for credits after going into contract.	One thing to be aware of is that the price we go into contract at isn't guaranteed to be the price we close at. The buyer will conduct various inspections to show the condition of the house as well as an appraisal to help determine its value. After receiving these reports, the buyer will have the ability to back out of the deal and find a different property. Oftentimes, they will ask you to make repairs or give them credits to cover the cost of making these repairs themselves. I will do my best to negotiate these down for you, but it will ultimately be your decision to provide what they ask for or put the house back on the market and sell to a different buyer.
They want to wait until winter to list their home because it's more convenient, but there are fewer buyers looking at that time.	I understand you'd prefer to take a few more months to get ready to sell, and I'd love to be able to help you do that. Unfortunately, if we wait until then, there will be fewer buyers looking at homes. Your home will still sell, but it will likely take longer and possibly not sell for as much. Does that still sound like the better scenario for you?

They don't want to go through the inconvenience of multiple showings.	I can totally understand that. Nobody likes strangers traipsing through their home and the pain of having to keep it clean and ready all the time. However, you hired me to get top dollar for your home. My strategy is to get as many offers as I can, then negotiate them as high as possible. I need showings to get offers. While this may be a pain now, do you think it will be worth it later if it means tens of thousands of dollars more in your bank account?
They want to sell for as much as the house down the street.	I would like that as well! My goal is to get you as much as we possibly can. When we put your house under contract, the buyer's lender will require an appraisal to be done. That appraisal will provide a value based on comparable sales. If your neighbor's home is a comparable sale, it will be included. In this case, though, that house is significantly larger than yours, and there's nothing you can do about that. We'll get you as much as we can for the size your house is, not the size of that other house.

Your ability to set expectations correctly will have a massive impact on the number of clients you put into escrow and, ultimately, on the profitability of your business. You will experience smoother escrows, more enjoyable transactions, and an overall better relationship with your clients. If you want raving fans sending you referrals, start focusing on preparing clients for what to expect when they start looking at homes and what they'll experience once they put one in contract.

Meet Transaction Timelines

Top-producing agents do a good job of meeting the timelines agreed upon in the purchase contract and keeping everyone happy during the transaction. When a timeline is missed, it tends to trigger anxiety and sometimes even panic on the other side. Rarely are good decisions made when anxiety and panic enter the real estate equation. The sign of a top-notch agent is having a system in place to keep your escrows moving along smoothly and hitting your timelines.

There are several ways to make sure you hit your timelines. The first is hiring a transaction coordinator (TC) to monitor timelines and remind you when they are approaching. Most TCs or transaction managers charge a flat fee per file to organize the paperwork and keep things moving. Another way is to use CRM software to remind you of approaching timelines and tasks that need to be completed. There are several CRMs on the market.

On my team, we use a combination of a CRM and a TC to make sure timelines are met. By staying ahead of when tasks are due and knowing which contingencies need to be removed, we rarely get caught off guard or get behind schedule. This system allows me to have several properties in contract (I have thirty at the time of this writing) and manage them all with a TC being supported by a CRM.

One important step to ensure you hit timelines effectively is to order what you need immediately after going into escrow. The day after I put a property under contract, I schedule all my inspections for as soon as possible and remind the lender to order the appraisal. If an inspector is too busy to go as soon as I'd like, I find another who isn't and use them instead. It's important to leave your client time to review the report and possibly get quotes on repairs. If you wait until the last minute to review inspection reports, you may not have enough time to decide which next steps are the best ones to take.

When you know your client will need more time to reach a decision, let the other agent know that earlier rather than later. If you can provide an explanation (there was more dry rot than we thought, we're getting a second opinion on the roof, etc.), they are much more likely to go to bat for you with their client than if you surprise them with a last-minute request for more time. Letting them know as soon as possible shows you are organized, on top of your file, and doing your job. This avoids the skepticism and mistrust that occurs when you unexpectedly reach out with a request for an extension.

Stay in Touch with Transaction Vendors

It's easy as a real estate agent to assume you are the only person involved in the transaction, especially when you are the only one talking with your client—and you usually are. Top-producing agents remember that there are more people participating in the transaction than just themselves and their client, and they keep all relevant parties included in the communication. This decreases the likelihood of an escrow being extended because someone didn't realize they were supposed to be doing something that everyone else expected. These additional players include lenders and title/escrow companies.

Lenders need a copy of the contract and need to be told when the house is in escrow. They then order the appraisal and submit the loan to underwriting for review. Many times underwriters will kick the loans back and request more information. If you're late getting the contract to the lender and something is wrong in the file, there's a good chance they won't be on the necessary timeline to have loan approval before the loan contingency is due.

Title/escrow companies are often a huge and overlooked piece of the puzzle. They need to be made aware of changes in the contract (i.e., calculating new commission amounts if the purchase price changes), changes to dates in the close of escrow (i.e., calculating prorated property taxes), and changes in the lender (i.e., changing who they are receiving funds from). If you forget to notify the title company of changes in the trajectory of the deal, you may find yourself with a delayed closing. Top-producing agents avoid that by making sure all transaction vendors are kept up to speed with the details of the transaction.

Completing the Closing Circuit

When you master funnel progression, you eventually end up mastering closing. Closing is a good thing to master, as it's the only way you make money. And there are several pretty nice perks that accompany multiple closings, beside making more money. These perks include that it's easier for you to close new clients, it speeds up how quickly you move them through your funnel, and it puts new leads in the top of your funnel more easily. This self-serving cycle helps speed up the rate at which you are closing new deals and grows your business exponentially over time.

When you create a working cycle, the loop between the bottom and the top of your Sales Funnel closes. This creates a circuit that allows energy, opportunity, and benefits to flow from the closing back to the top of the funnel, putting in more prospects that work downward. There are several ways this benefits you.

One major perk to being a top producer is that you start gaining recognition in your office as someone who does a lot of business. This can lead to more referrals coming from outside agents who call your office and ask for the top producers there. It can also lead to other agents in your office sending you some of their clients to work with when they're too busy or don't feel qualified to help that particular client.

Another perk is that top-producing agents are often given awards by the office that recognize their superior production levels. These awards are important marketing tools that can bring you more business. Being able to share on social media, flyers, and signage that you were awarded recognition or given a title as a top producer will increase your credibility and enhance your perceived level of professionalism. This helps with mindshare: You're the Realtor they think of when they want to sell their house or buy a home. This fills up your funnel, giving you even more clients to work with.

More closings will also result in more online reviews, which are sources of lead generation for your business. With every closing you have, ask your clients to leave you an online review on Zillow, Google, Yelp, or anywhere else you believe people are likely to be looking for Realtor information. Many top-producing agents generate 5 percent to 10 percent of their business specifically from people who found their information online as a top agent in the area.

More closings equal more money. More money equals a bigger marketing budget. A bigger marketing budget should equal more leads making their way into your funnel. This is another reason closing more deals will make you even more money. By spending money to get your name out in front of more people, you fill your funnel up with more potential prospects to work down the funnel, and the result is more closings.

In addition to all these benefits, quite possibly the biggest perk to closing more deals is the confidence you'll build in yourself. Confidence is a huge component to being a top-producing agent. I address it multiple times throughout this book, because it is that important! The more confidence you have, the more you talk about real estate, and the more convincing you sound because you actually know what you're talking about. You are your own best marketing tool. The way you dress, speak, act, and sound will do more to convince people to list or buy with you than any gimmick, technique, or lead source in the world. Closing more deals increases your confidence because your knowledge grows. This leads to more people making their way into your Sales Funnel and thus more profits into your business.

The reality in the real estate industry is that the bar is set very low for agents. The testing process is not too difficult, the education requirements are minimal, and the qualifications to hold a license are not hard to achieve. There is not much supervision, not much training, and not much accountability. This has created an environment in which many clients are left disappointed and jaded after their experience with their Realtor. The good news is that this is good news.

With the bar set so low for agents, it's not difficult to make it to the top of the heap. Many top-producing agents in my area make more money in a year than a doctor does. This is physician money, without physician hours, risk, stress, insurance, or eight years of student debt. For those who commit themselves to mastering real estate, there is virtually no ceiling. The low bar for agents can be your friend. You just have to rise to the occasion. That means focusing on your business and running it like a business, not as a hobby.

When you close multiple deals and start making money, you'll need to monitor it. You'll need bookkeepers and accountants to keep good track of your income, expenses, and profit—and that you're paying your taxes. The biggest tool in your toolbox to help with this will be a profit and loss statement (commonly known as a P&L). P&Ls are a business owner's best friend. They tell the story of how much you sold and made, but more importantly how much you kept.

It is so easy to focus only on the amount of your commission check and miss how much money you have to spend to stay in the business. MLS fees, brokerage fees, lockboxes, access to lockboxes, insurance, gas, signs, clothes, marketing—it all adds up. Make sure you track these things on your P&L and review it at least monthly. Before I started tracking my income and expenses, I had many months where I assumed I had made money but I had actually lost it. Running a successful business isn't just about making a lot of money. That is a metric your ego uses. It's about keeping a lot of money. That's the metric that matters to your business.

As you run an increasingly profitable business, you'll find yourself able to reinvest money back into your own success. One of the biggest investments I made into my own business was to buy an expensive CRM (it costs nearly $1,000 a month). But this CRM allows me to systematically communicate with those in my database, maintain all their contact and personal information, manage my transactions, assign projects to team members—and helps the agents on my team all do the same. Once I applied this CRM to my business, it became the backbone of our operations and allowed me to scale faster than I ever could have without it.

Another way profit will help you grow is by providing the opportunity to attend additional training. I attend approximately four to six events a year where I learn from other real estate agents, investors, and businesspeople who share ways they've been successful in their business, in their market, and in increasing their profit margin. This information isn't always readily accessible in other places, and it is incredibly valuable. If you're reading this book and wondering why nobody told you this information earlier, it's because you weren't attending the training where it was shared. Reinvesting in your own education can have a massive impact on your future success.

The last thing to consider about increasing closings in order to increase new opportunities is that more profit allows you to start hiring more help. Without a doubt, the No. 1 move I made on the David Greene Team was to hire my first TC, Krista. Krista has helped me in so many ways. She got me organized, helped me secure new leads, and helped me follow up with old leads. She also has conversations with clients that typically take up a lot of time. Her help has allowed me to focus on what the rest of the team needs most: lead generation and setting appointments. When you close deals and build a profit, hire your own Krista. This will lead to more clients making their way down your funnel and thus more money in your bottom line.

➡ KEY POINTS

- Familiarize yourself with common inspection issues to best prepare your clients.
- Your ability to interpret an inspection report is crucial in helping your clients make good decisions.
- As a listing agent, provide inspections upfront to the buyers; this will prevent homes from falling out of escrow and reduce the amount of credits the buyer may ask for later.
- As a buyer agent, prevent properties from falling out of escrow by reviewing an inspection report early and preparing clients for what to expect.
- During the buyer's remorse phase, the buyer will subconsciously look for reasons to back out of a deal; prepare your buyer clients to keep your deals in escrow.
- To avoid loan contingency problems, as a buyer's agent, ensure your client is completely preapproved and doesn't open new lines of credit. As a listing agent, contact the lender to verify the buyers have turned in all paperwork.

- Set client expectations clearly, meet transaction timelines, stay in touch with transaction vendors.
- More closings equal more money, which equals a bigger marketing budget, which equals more leads in your Sales Funnel.
- Reinvest money back into your own success.
- Attend trainings and seminars.

CHAPTER SIX

COMMON PROBLEMS WITH EACH TOOL

"All problems become smaller if you don't dodge them but confront them."

—WILLIAM F. HALSEY

Now that we've covered the four tools that will help you to become a top-producing real estate agent, I want to walk you through common problems that come up with each one. But first, a general word about proficiency.

As with any other kinds of tools, it will take time to learn to use these effectively. Nobody picks up a tool for the first time and uses it perfectly. Proficiency comes with focused, repeated effort. It will take time to master funnel progression, but the good news is that you control how quickly that happens.

It is better to practice in advance than wait for on-the-job experience. You can practice your presentation on live leads, but is it wise to make your mistakes in scenarios that will likely make you lose potential clients in the process? It's much better to practice using your tools before it really matters. The point here is obvious: Sharpen your tools as often as you can (give your seller and buyer presentations to your friends and team members and family members, read real estate books, etc.) so that when you actually need your tools, they are at your ready.

Your proficiency level will be based on repetition, not time. For example, I sold more homes in my first two years than most agents in my office had in ten because I made sure that my growth trajectory was steep. My proficiency was greater simply because I closed more deals, worked with more clients, handled more problems, and grew my confidence faster than those agents who spent more time in the field than me but didn't have as much experience as me. Repetition plus effort equals proficiency.

Now let's get into the potential pitfalls with each tool so that you can avoid them.

Common Problems with Lead Generation

Every business that generates revenue has two components: creating business and servicing that business. I analogize these two components to "catching fish" and "cleaning fish." Catching fish is creating revenue or generating business, otherwise known as "sales." Signing new clients and securing contracts are ways of catching fish. Cleaning fish is the act of servicing business that's already been developed. Processing files, collecting payments, and providing service are ways of cleaning fish. A business needs both components to thrive.

As a solo real estate agent, you'll do both components yourself. You will be responsible for finding clients (lead generation), securing clients (presentations), servicing clients (psychology/putting houses in contract), and closing clients (knowledge/closing escrows). Although you're responsible for all of it, that doesn't mean it's all equally important. Without a doubt, catching fish is far more important to your revenue stream.

This is why the first thing you'll hire out is someone to do the fish cleaning. Top-producing agents don't often excel at administration; they are usually terrible at this. If you want to be a top producer, then lead generation is the tool you'll use.

Several things can ruin good lead generation, including:
- Being self-consciousness
- Being inconsistent
- Being disorganized
- Being lazy
- Being unconfident

Every agent must fight their way to overcome these problems. You'll notice the majority of areas to improve to become a top-producing Realtor are emotional and therefore within your control. Most people don't overcome these issues because they aren't self-aware enough, they aren't willing to release their self-limiting beliefs, or they've decided the pain of change is not worth the reward. Let's now look at these one by one.

Being Self-Conscious

Self-consciousness erodes confidence and assertiveness. Good lead generation is all about adding value to others by staying in touch with them and reminding them that you'd like them to send you referrals. If you want to add value to others, you need to focus on them. Great lead generation involves being aware of the desires, problems, and concerns of another person and then showing that you care about those things too. Self-consciousness prevents that from happening because it drives your focus onto you instead of the other person.

Everyone feels self-conscious at times, especially when starting out in a new career. It's really difficult to want to make phone calls when you don't know what to say or are afraid of what someone might ask you. Many new agents struggle with the need to start posting on social media, putting out their picture, or sharing information about themselves online. These are completely normal concerns. The key to defeating self-consciousness is to take your focus off yourself—your feelings, your worries, your insecurities—and put it on the person you want to bring value to.

Ultimately, you will overcome self-consciousness when you genuinely want to help people and care about their lives. You'll find that you no longer worry about what people think of you.

Another factor in overcoming self-consciousness is acknowledging that the other party has no idea what you are "supposed" to know when it comes to real estate. To them, you are the expert simply because you have a license. If you haven't closed a lot of deals or don't currently have any listings, it won't matter to them. All they will see is what you choose to show them.

If you feel timid, nervous, or uncomfortable, they will feel that too. If you feel confident, engaging, and decisive, they will feel that as well. Many of the people in your database have a desire to buy or sell a home. Most won't know how to do it. Confidence is contagious. Remember, you set the tone of the conversation, so be brave.

Being Inconsistent

Consistency is a hallmark of success, and inconsistency all but destroys it. Consider workouts—most of us think the intensity of a workout will determine our results. Intensity does play a role, but consistency is much more important. When you brought massive intensity to your first workout in six months, you likely ended up incredibly sore the next day and weren't able to work out for weeks after. What's worse, by the time you could work out again, you'd experienced a huge opportunity cost. How many workouts did you miss while you were sore?

Intensity needs consistency. You can't work out at your peak level until you've consistently built a baseline that allows your body to push to new levels of intensity. Lead generating works this way as well. Doing it regularly builds up your skill set, conditions you to rejection, and strengthens you for any challenges. You get better at lead generation and enjoy it more when you routinely work at it. It gives you the opportunity to increase the number of requests for referrals and business. Consistency and intensity work best when they work together.

Consistency in lead generation is important because the goal is to stay top of mind. After you have a great conversation with a friend over the phone, you are likely to jump to the top of their mind when it comes to real estate. This means that any lead that crosses their path in the near future is likely to come toward you. The problem occurs when too much time passes and you slowly sink from the top of their mind to somewhere in the middle. To stay top of mind, you have to consistently work to stay there.

Good lead generation is about staying in front of your clients and remaining their Realtor of choice. Without this consistency, prospects, appointments, escrows, and closings go way down. Because lead generation is the first step in the funnel and the basis for everything else, being consistent matters.

Being Disorganized

When you are disorganized, your lead generation will suffer. You must have a system in place to remind you who to talk to, what to say, and what you said last. My CRM allows me to take notes of every conversation I have with clients and prospects. I take these notes as we speak, and I pull them up before every subsequent conversation. This allows me to remember what we last spoke about so I can jump-start the conversation right where we left off. It helps the client know how important their relationship is to me and makes it easier for them to open up to me.

I often note what issues clients are having with their children, how their relationships are going, what their work situation is like, how they're doing with their fitness plans, and what their goals are for the year. This allows my lead generation conversations to be structured and purposeful, and it allows me to be confident and decisive on what topics to bring up with each client. Staying organized is the backbone of this structure.

I also set aside time in my calendar to dedicate to generating leads. By organizing my schedule around lead generation, I am prioritizing the most important part of my business and working everything else around that. Lead generation time makes sure I have conversations with my clients and leads to stay top of mind.

Lead generation can happen via social media, video creations, meetups, seminars, lunch and learns, or phone calls. But if you're not organized, none of this can happen consistently. Remain faithful to staying organized and your lead generation will reflect positive results.

Being Lazy

Laziness is the enemy of success in everything, and real estate sales is no exception. Laziness can take many forms, but it's always based on the same thing: lack of drive.

Many people believe laziness is equivalent to slothfulness. That is, lazy people don't want to work hard because they don't like to expend energy. I believe this is the case for some people, but I don't assume the aversion toward exerting energy is the only form of laziness. I believe laziness is the outward expression of other psychological issues, like lack of confidence, fear of success, fear of the unknown, fear of rejection, and so on. These issues can cause you to not take action, which appears the same as laziness.

If you find yourself uninspired to do the work necessary to be successful, start by considering these two potential culprits.

On the surface level, it's possible that your Big Why isn't big enough. If you were more motivated, the excuses you make for not taking action would disappear like mist in the sun. Motivated people have an inner source of fuel that removes whatever pull is working against them. They always push through and hit new heights. Why did you choose to become a real estate agent in the first place? And how would success help you achieve your goals?

There could also be deeper psychological issues going on. For instance, what's causing your deep-seated fear of rejection? Why do you feel you don't deserve bigger success? Why does hard work scare you so much? Working in real estate exposes our weaknesses and self-limiting beliefs. Those who embrace this work grow personally and professionally. When you feel laziness creeping into your work ethic, it's usually a sign that you need to dig deeper into your own psyche. You need to have an honest conversation with yourself or a trusted counselor about where it's coming from and how you can change it.

Being Unconfident

Nobody likes to feel insecure or have self-doubts, but when you aren't confident, it shows. The art of appearing self-assured when you're not feeling it takes time to develop. The best way to get there is by focusing on consistency in your work. Consistency brings experience, and experience develops confidence. If you wait to act until you're confident, you'll never move. That's like waiting to be strong before you go lift weights.

The process for developing confidence involves a combination of experience and knowledge. The more you know, the calmer and more collected you'll feel. Strong lead generation is possible when you feel confident, are having fun, and are enjoyable to talk to. You want your leads and clients to want to hear from you or watch the next video you post. Your confidence and self-assuredness will draw them to you. By focusing on building your confidence, you're also focusing on building your lead generation.

Common Problems with Appointments/Presentations

When it comes to appointments/presentations, there are several major mistakes new or inexperienced agents make. I've compiled a list so you can prevent making them yourself.

Setting Expectations

Because I work as a team with several support members helping me to service clients, it's important I make sure the leads understand this during their presentation, so I set those expectations immediately.

I put them at ease by sharing what I know, the fastest way for them to get from Point A to Point B, and that I understand how to handle emergencies that may arise. I also warn them that there will most likely be turbulence during the process, but that they shouldn't let it deter them.

I describe my top-notch team and explain that they will also work with clients to make sure the process is as smooth as possible and that they can answer any questions or concerns throughout the process. After all, we work as a team.

This prepares the prospects that it won't always be me making the phone call to tell them about the inspection schedule or that their loan has been approved. When the lead knows what to expect, then as a client they normally go along with whatever you advise. Preparing your prospect for what's coming is crucial to landing them as a client, buying/selling a house, and keeping them in escrow. Skipping this step will cause major problems down the road. Even if you don't have any assistants (yet), letting leads know exactly what they can expect from you as their agent will go a long way toward a successful and pleasant process.

Skipping the Appointment

The biggest mistake I see most agents make is not doing presentations at all. Many agents don't want to make the time to meet with a lead to go over a presentation, but that time investment can pay huge dividends. Choosing to conduct a presentation with a potential client will help you (1) determine whether you and the lead want to work together; (2) show the value you can add and get a buyer representation agreement signed right away; (3) prepare the lead for headaches and fears they will likely experience during the escrow or home buying/selling process, which can increase your closing rate; (4) set expectations appropriately so you have an easier job of keeping the client happy; and (5) avoid having to explain a form, option, or decision later when there's no time.

Skipping presentations to save time now will end up costing you much more time in the future. My favorite aspect of scheduling that appointment is that it means I have the time—according to my own schedule—to focus on the lead when I don't feel rushed, pulled in several directions, or unable to give them my full attention. By scheduling the presentation for a time that is convenient for me, I can make sure the lead has a good experience.

Setting an Appointment but Not Giving a Presentation

Setting and keeping an office appointment is definitely better than not setting an appointment at all, but you're selling yourself short if you don't use a prepared and practiced presentation. In-person meetings help solidify relationships, but you have to work much harder to sell yourself without a strong presentation. And you run the risk of selling yourself too hard in a meeting, which can absolutely backfire.

Consider how you feel when you first meet someone who tells you how amazing *they* are. Chances are you're skeptical, irritated, and looking for ways to prove them wrong. Now consider how you feel when a third party tells you how amazing *someone else* is. Odds are you're curious, optimistic, and eager to see for yourself. It's always better for someone else to brag about you, and a good presentation will do that for you.

Being the Hero—Not the Guide

When I referred to Miller's "storybranding" concept earlier in the book, I explained the importance of focusing on how you can help your client be the hero of their story as opposed to being one yourself. This makes it easier for your client to feel good about taking your advice and trusting that you have their best interests at heart.

An easy way to ruin a new relationship is to talk about yourself too much. It may feel natural to do so, especially when meeting someone for the first time. We all want to be liked. But trying too hard to get your lead's approval will feel off-putting instead of friendly to that prospect. The desire to be liked is amplified in high-stress situations, such as when trying to land a new client. Additionally, you may feel nervous and feel the need to prove your skills and value. One big way that your nerves can hijack your meeting with a potential client is by making you talk too much about yourself.

Having a presentation and a clear process can take your nerves out of the game. When you have a structured presentation, you think less about yourself and more about making the lead feel good. You want to make them feel confident that they are making the right decision by hiring you. You want to congratulate them on how well they've done to save up money, how impressive their decision to buy/sell is, how they've put themselves in a situation to be successful, and how excited you'd be to work with them. This meeting is about them.

Ask them about their needs, fears, and concerns. Ask them what is most important in an agent and what is most important to them in this buy/sell transaction. Ask them to tell you what a perfect transaction looks like, and what they'd like to be able to say when the process is finished. This will give you a blueprint of how to structure your interactions with them as clients to make sure you give them the service they expect. If you do that, you won't have to say much about yourself at all.

Not Allowing the Lead to Feel Heard

When you talk too much about yourself it not only makes you look grandiose and narcissistic, but it also makes your lead feel like they aren't important. As stated in the Bible, the "mouth speaks from the overflow of the heart (Matthew 12:34)". This means the things you choose to speak about reveal what really matters to you. If you don't ask enough questions about your lead's feelings and experiences, they'll know that those things don't matter much to you. This will prevent any trust that is needed to make the relationship work.

Make sure your lead feels heard. This is true even when the information they are presenting isn't something you believe matters in the transaction. If the lead doesn't feel heard now, they are much less likely as a client to listen to you later. In this relationship, you are the expert, and you know what they need to do to sell their home or find their next house. How can you help them do that if they don't heed your advice? Here are some areas you can focus on to make sure your leads feel heard.

- Listen about the improvements they made to their house, even if they don't affect the sale price, because they reflect an emotional investment in the property. Ask questions about molding, flooring, and backyard landscaping. The leads likely had a hand in all those decisions.
- Ask buyers about their fears in buying a house. This will tell you exactly what you need to address to make them feel confident.
- Ask sellers what is most important to them in the process. It may not be price. Maybe they need to find something quickly or move to a certain area. Some clients want the highest price, while others want a fast sale and don't care as much about the money.
- Ask how their children feel about the transaction. Many kids feel scared of where they'll end up or sad about leaving their friends. If you can help the kids feel better, you'll score major points with the parents.
- Be sure to ask both sides of a couple what is important to them, and don't interrupt them. It's too easy to leave the less dominant partner feeling left out and unheard.

- Take notes. This goes a long way in showing you value their input.
- And, of course, ask them what they'll be most excited about when the transaction is complete.

Not Showing Your Value

Another big mistake I've seen many agents make is not highlighting their value when meeting with leads. While this may seem like a silly mistake to make, there are valid reasons for why it happens. A high percentage of agents tend to be a high "I" (Influence) on the DISC personality assessment (if you haven't yet taken this behavioral test, I encourage you to look into it). High "I" individuals value being liked and being personable. For those with this disposition, it's easy to forget that the goal is to show their value as an agent. Instead, they get caught up in gaining the approval of the lead and being more concerned with being liked than being valuable.

For agents higher on the "D" (Dominance) scale, they tend to be more concerned with efficiency and speed than showing their value. For these agents, they may focus more on how quickly they can get the presentation finished than on how powerful the presentation is. This is a major mistake. You're conducting the presentation for a reason. It's not a mindless box to check so you can move to the next step. If you complete the presentation in record time but don't win over the prospect, you've actually wasted everyone's time in your haste to save it.

Always remember that the point of the presentation is to show your value. You should be doing that the whole time.

Not Instilling a Sense of Confidence and Security

When you're trying to win over a buyer or a seller, the odds of this prospect experiencing fear, uncertainty, and anxiety are quite high. When you meet with them, you're sharing the technical elements of the transaction, but more importantly you're also easing those fears and sharing with them your confidence in getting the job done. If you finish your presentation but the prospect doesn't feel secure and relieved, you did something wrong.

The presentation is designed to showcase your knowledge, skills, and confidence so that the lead signs as a client and gives you control of the process. This won't happen unless you show them that they'll be in great hands. Hide your fears and nervousness. Speak confidently and boldly. Be excited! Your leads will pick up on that energy and feel the same way.

That's how you want to start off your relationship with them.

Common Problems with Psychology

In my first year in full-time sales, I had an office directly across from the desk of another agent—I'll call him Tom. Tom enjoyed working with investors who just wanted a transaction and didn't need to have their emotional needs met. Tom wanted to turn real estate sales into a 9-to-5 job. He liked his weekends off, didn't want to work nights, and didn't want to form a relationship with his clients. Tom would lead-generate to probate lawyers and others he believed would provide him motivated buyers and sellers. He was always looking for an "easy" client.

Tom would be visibly frustrated when clients had questions he didn't want to answer. He often said in the office, "I just want a transaction-based process. I'm tired of these clients wanting a relationship with me. I'm a professional, not a friend." Tom didn't sell a lot of homes. In fact, he rarely sold any. A few months into my full-time career, Tom could no longer pay his desk fees at the office. Shortly after that, Tom was out of the industry.

I tried several times to talk with Tom about how I found clients. I explained I spent a lot of time talking to those in my sphere of influence, bringing value to others, and asking for referrals. When I held open houses, I would frequently take those I met there out to dinner for our first appointment and pay for it myself. My business was based on forming a relationship first, using that connection to showcase my knowledge and skills with real estate, then asking for referrals after that.

Tom never tried to build his business that way, and it showed. Now I'm not saying everybody is a naturally friendly person—truth be told, it wasn't natural for me in the beginning. If your leads are coming from lawyers, lenders, or even other agents, then those are the people you need to form relationships with. How you make people feel and the energy they get from you will play a huge role in the success of your business.

A career in real estate sales is, at its core, a sales career. As such, relationships will always matter.

Not being aware of how you make your clients feel will cost you a lot of money in real estate. So will a host of other mistakes when it comes to the psychology of dealing with clients. The following are some of the big mistakes I've seen agents make when it comes to missing the psychology of clients and the effect this has on closing deals.

Being Aware of Only Your Own Feelings

Every human being is mostly aware of how they feel. If you want the law of reciprocity to work on your behalf, you need to be aware of your clients' feelings as much as your own.

When you worry too much about your own interests in the transaction, it shows. If your primary concern is getting paid or the amount of your commission, your clients can tell. This is not a way to create a raving fan. Conversely, if you show concern about what your client is experiencing and relate to their emotions, they are more likely to care about your interests in the transaction. This includes your commission, your time, and even your own emotional state.

This is why I always meet with leads in person to discuss their concerns before we ever talk real estate. It's important that I show early on that I care about their feelings and worries. You will absolutely be tempted to vent to your clients at times, but I regret every occasion when I shared my negative emotions about the process with my clients. They are looking to me to be their trusted guide, not someone they have to be strong for. When you need to vent, go to other agents, family members, coaches, or friends—never go to your clients.

Learning to be in tune with your clients is an important skill to develop, but for many agents it won't come easily at first. However, after you're experienced in this practice, it will make the job of representing them so much easier.

You'll notice when your client's tone changes, their response time changes, or they seem less enthused. When you notice these changes, it's very important that you reach out directly to find out what the problem is and nip it in the bud. If an unhappy client stays unhappy for too long, it can get to a point where you can't bring them back.

You want to stoke the fires of their excitement while decreasing the fires of their fears; if you know how to connect with their feelings, you can respond faster and more effectively to their emotional changes.

Focusing Too Much on the Transaction and Not Enough on the Relationship

The law of reciprocity is key to growing a solid, long-term real estate business. However, when you're not working with many clients, you're also not making much money. This can lead to a fear of deals falling apart, which makes it difficult to function as a fiduciary to the client and put their interests first.

On the other hand, selling too many homes can cause the same problem.

As top producers start closing a lot of deals, it becomes difficult to focus on the relationship instead of the transaction. When you're too busy, then maintaining contact with the client suffers and so does staying attuned to their emotional state. When business is good, a lot of things are calling for the time, attention, and focus of top-producing agents. This can easily put you at risk of neglecting your relationships with your clients.

No matter where you are in your business, there will always be tasks that get in the way of making the relationship with your clients your first and foremost responsibility. The problem is that clients will refer business to you based on your relationship with them, not just on how well you performed. In my experience, clients will remember what you did for them in the moment, but over time they may forget. What they do remember is your relationship and how you made them feel.

The primary focus of your business, always, is your relationships. You can hire someone to manage transactions, show houses, prepare listings, and whatever else needs to be done—but you can't hire someone to manage your relationships. If you did, they would end up being the one the clients remembered and referred business to. Whether you're struggling or overflowing with opportunity, always put your relationships with clients first.

Common Problems with Knowledge

Knowledge of how real estate works will help close you more deals, but it's important to note it rarely comes into play until you have a deal in escrow. Since this is the fourth tool in a five-tool process, it's a mistake to wait until you feel you have enough knowledge before you begin lead generation, the first tool. If you wait to lead-generate until you have knowledge, you may never get the experience you need. Learn from others by listening to podcasts, reading books, and consulting other Realtors, but keep working while you're learning. Knowledge will come with time, but you can practice the other tools right away.

Not Using Other People's Experiences to Build Your Own

While knowledge will come with experience, it doesn't have to be your own experience. There are many people who have experience you can leverage in your transactions. Your broker, team lead, or mentor agent can help you when you come across something you don't know.

There are many people involved in a transaction who have an interest in it closing. This can include the lender, title company, escrow coordinator, transaction coordinator, and even the other agent. These people can become your resources and sources of knowledge. Don't make the mistake of thinking you have to learn everything the hard way. Plenty of people will want the deal to close just as much as you do and will be happy to help you resolve any specific problems, if just you ask for help.

Not Learning the Jobs of Others in the Transaction Process

In a W-2 job, we typically focus solely on our own responsibilities. In real estate, we won't get paid unless everyone does their own job, and neither will they. The transaction truly "takes a village" in every sense, and you can help by learning what others do in the village of the transaction process. In this industry, teamwork makes the dream work.

When a lender overcomes an obstacle, ask them how they resolved the problem and why the problem happened in the first place. It might help you if a future client of yours has a similar problem with their loan. It will also help you learn how to avoid these mistakes. You don't want to rely on other people (like lenders) to advise your clients on what to do or not to do. You can't control the quality of their work. You can only control your own.

The same is true for title problems, construction problems, inspection problems, and more. Make it a habit to learn as much as possible and ask, "How?" when they tell you something went wrong but they fixed it. How did they fix it? If you make this a consistent habit, your knowledge base will grow fast and so will your results.

Assuming All Deals Will Be More or Less the Same

In some jobs, every day is more or less the same. Not so with real estate. Every transaction—every single one—will be different. Each escrow poses its own challenges, hurdles, issues, and personalities to be navigated. This forces you to stay sharp whether you've been an agent for two months or twenty years.

It's a big mistake to assume what you did last time will work this time. As difficult as it may seem, you must resist the urge to fall into a routine and try to do the same things or use the same strategies on every deal. What worked on one client will not work on another, and what made sense in one situation will not in another. Your best bet is to make a practice of putting yourself in the other person's shoes and asking yourself how you would feel if you were them. You'll do this with clients, agents, vendors, and sometimes your own broker. No two deals will be the same and accepting that will reduce the mistakes you make with the knowledge tool.

If you are aware of the common problems you'll encounter with each tool, you'll most likely increase your proficiency with a shorter learning curve. Many Realtors don't even understand these are tools they should be using. Your use of them will give you a clear advantage over others, so practice them consistently and ask others for help to quickly improve your proficiency and conversion rates.

◼️➤ KEY POINTS

- Finding new business and servicing existing business are both needed to thrive, but finding new business has a bigger impact on your revenue.
- To overcome self-consciousness, focus more on the other person and less on yourself.
- To overcome inconsistency, focus on lead generating, the first step in the Sales Funnel.
- To overcome disorganization, create a system for yourself.
- To overcome laziness, recheck your Big Why or consider talking with a trusted person.
- To overcome feeling unconfident, increase your experience and knowledge base.
- Don't skip presentations.
- Real estate is about relationships, not just about transactions.
- Ask for advice.
- No two transactions are the same.
- Practice before you need to use your tools to increase your proficiency and your overall conversion ratio.

CHAPTER SEVEN

STRATEGIC PLANNING

"I can't change the direction of the wind, but I can adjust my sails to always reach my destination."

—JIMMY DEAN

Empowerment through Planning

Your subconscious mind will lead you wherever you program it to go. If your subconscious is unclear on what you want, it will often default to leading you away from where you *don't* want to go. In the absence of clear direction, we resort to the avoidance of pain. This pain can come in the form of wasted time, rejection, or uncertainty. Telling our subconscious where we want to go, instead of where we don't want to go, is the first step in taking control of our results. The direction we give to our subconscious can be defined as "vision."

Top-producing agents don't stumble into their success. It is not a surprise when it happens, and it is not a mystery why they continue to produce. Top producers understand they take specific actions that lead to the specific results they desire. While not every top agent takes the exact same actions, they do take *some* form of action. Understanding what specific actions you must take is a key component to building the business of your dreams.

You'll know you've achieved your correct mindset when you are no longer surprised by your success. When results are an expected return on actions you've strategically implemented, you'll be operating with the mindset of a top producer. This chapter will share some of the tools I've learned to build a plan, work the plan, and stay on course with the plan. These tools will help you build your business via purpose and strategy.

The Importance of Vision

John Graham, author of *Stick Your Neck Out: A Street-Smart Guide to Creating Change in Your Community and Beyond*, states on his website concerning vision: "[Vision is] a clear, strong mental picture of a desired result that doesn't yet exist. It can't be an idle wish or hope, but a picture of the real fruits of real efforts." (What he has to say is inspiring, so you should read the whole thing.)[4]

As the owner-operator of your business (and a potential team leader someday), you are responsible for providing your vision. Without it, it's incredibly easy to become confused, lost, or uninspired regarding the direction of your company and the necessary actions to get you where you want to go. In fact, without vision, you may not understand what success means to you. Vision in our industry can be described as both your end goal and the path it takes to get there.

Of every industry I've been a part of, real estate affords the most variety in ways to achieve success. In both investing in real estate and selling it, there are *so* many paths to arrive at the same result. No two agents find success the same way, and that is a part of what makes this industry so beautiful. It also highlights why vision is so important in *your* business. Since there is no clear path for every agent to follow, a prerequisite for knowing which path to follow is having the vision to see what it looks like first.

Reverse Engineering

The concept of reverse engineering has always been fascinating to me. It involves starting with a finished project, taking it apart, and learning

---

4   John Graham, "#5 – The Importance of Vision," *Life on the Edge*, https://www.johngraham.org/coach/5the-importance-of-vision.

how the pieces fit together. Once you see the "vision" of what the thing became (and how it got there), you can replicate its production. Many times you'll find you had 80 percent of the understanding already—studying it just revealed the 20 percent you were missing.

Isn't that fascinating in life? We can have 80 percent of the solution, or even 99 percent of it, but without 100 percent, we may as well have nothing. Our business works that way too. Getting 99 percent of the way to landing a client or a closed escrow is worth the exact same as if we never even got 1 percent of the way there. This is why commitment to the end goal is so important. You don't get paid for what you start—only what you finish.

Top agents use the concept of reverse engineering to help plan their business. This can also be described as starting with the end in mind. The easiest way to do this is to decide how much money you want to make in a year. Once you've done so, determine how many houses you'd have to sell to accomplish that. Once you have that number, determine which actions you'd have to take to sell that number of houses. While this may seem oversimplified, it is this process of "taking apart" the end result that will expose what you don't yet know how to do.

For instance, if you determine you need to sell fifty homes to meet your goal, and you ask yourself what actions are needed, you may quickly realize you're unsure of which actions you're currently taking that lead to closing homes now. This gives you an important missing piece from your puzzle. Working backward, you'll have to tally the homes you closed last year, ask yourself how you found those clients, and recall the actions you took that led to meeting and securing them. This process of reverse engineering reveals what your subconscious does not yet know. It provides the missing steps you need to reach the success, or goal, you want.

GPS 1:3:5

GPS stand for Goals, Priorities, and Strategies. This is a reverse engineering tool that helps clarify the specific actions you need to take, as detailed as possible, to achieve your yearly goal. The 1:3:5 is a ratio that means 1 Goal, 3 Priorities to achieve the goal, and 5 Strategies to hit those priorities. The five strategies are the detailed steps you must focus on throughout your day.

As an example, let's assume your goal is to make $500,000 in gross commission income (GCI). Your average price point is $400,000 and your average commission is 2.5 percent. This means your average commission is $10,000. You'd have to sell fifty homes to meet that goal.

1 Goal
1. Fifty homes sold (to reach $500,000 in GCI).

3 Priorities
1. Sphere of influence (SOI) (thirty homes).
2. Open houses/sign calls on listings (ten homes).
3. Past client referrals (ten homes).

5 Strategies for SOI
1. Grow database weekly by five people.
2. Make twenty daily phone calls to SOI.
3. Hold quarterly client appreciation events.
4. Have monthly "meetups" to teach real estate tips.
5. Write three weekly posts to social media regarding real estate, and that invite responses and comments.

5 Strategies for Open Houses/Sign Calls on Listings
1. Hold three open houses a week.
2. Reach out to Realtors in your office once a week to find listings they are not holding open.
3. Follow up with every open house lead three times after meeting them.
4. Average two listings a month with a call to action on the yard "for sale" sign to call you.
5. Knock on fifty doors in the neighborhood of your open house to introduce yourself to the neighbors and invite them to the open house.

5 Strategies for Past Client Referrals
1. Check in with every past client once quarterly.
2. Send out monthly newsletter to past clients with real estate market info.
3. Send out quarterly updated home value estimates to past clients.
4. Send handwritten cards to each past client every six months.
5. Ask every past client what their goals are for the year. When they ask about yours, share the fifty homes sold goal and request they notify you of anyone they hear of who wants to buy or sell a home.

The five strategies for each of the three priorities will give you the daily activities that ensure your day is aligned with your ultimate goal of fifty homes sold for the year. Without this clear direction, it's easy to spend your day on unproductive activities. The sneaky enemy to your success will be the time you spend doing things that *are* productive—but not productive toward your goal. Your subconscious wants to help you. It will let you know when you're being productive or unproductive. The key is to program it to only direct you toward the type of productivity your conscious mind has determined is best.

4-1-1

This tool stands for 4 weeks–1 month–1 year. This tool works similarly to the GPS 1:3:5 in that it breaks down your goals (your big one and other goals feeding your big one) into smaller, more manageable, easier-to-accomplish pieces.

Example:
One Year (yearly goals)
- Sell fifty homes.
- Hold 140 open houses.
- Represent twenty sellers.
- Continue education on real estate.
- Increase database by 240 people.

One Month (monthly goals)
- Every month make 430 voice-to-voice or face-to-face contacts where you request business.
- Every month hold twelve open homes.
- Every month take on two listings.
- Every month take one training course/class online or in person.
- Every month add twenty people to your database.

Four Weeks (weekly goals)
- Every week make 108 contacts with your database.
- Every week hold three open homes.
- Every week set one listing appointment.

- Every week listen to two podcasts about real estate.
- Every week add five people to your database

By breaking your goals down into weekly chunks and looking at them every day, you can continually remind yourself what your goals are and keep them top of mind. Another way to state this is to consciously observe what you're trying to accomplish, then push it down into your subconscious to remember. When you remind yourself that you want to add five people to your database every week, you can make it a habit to find one new person every day, get their contact information, and add it to your database. This reminder comes in handy when you make a connection at the oil change shop or when you meet someone standing in line at the grocery store.

33 Touches

The 33-touch system was developed by Gary Keller and shared in his best-selling book *The Millionaire Real Estate Agent*. Keller contends you can expect to receive two referrals a year for every twelve people in your database if you "touch" that person thirty-three times. A touch is defined as a contact. The idea is to stay top of mind to people in your database by finding new, unique, and genuine ways to stay in touch with them. While this information is possibly outdated (social media has changed how frequently people stay at the front of anyone's mind given our decreasing attention spans), the David Greene Team uses the following system to stay in touch with our clients. We call it the High Touch Sphere campaign.

- Monthly market report (email with their home's estimated value) (twelve/year)
- Monthly social media comment (twelve/year)
- Monthly newsletter (twelve/year)
- Monthly text message (twelve/year)
- Quarterly phone call (four/year)
- Quarterly handwritten note to follow up phone call (four/year)
- Quarterly invitation to meetup, event, or client appreciation party (four/year)
- Yearly anniversary card/congratulations (one/year)
- Ice cream gift card for each child in their family on their birthdays
- Happy Birthday card (one/year)

This is a total of more than sixty-four touches and does not include the videos, posts, or messages our clients see on social media. The key to a successful touch campaign is to not spam your database with useless information. Finding ways to stay relevant and interesting during this process is what will separate top producers from those who find themselves blocked. Always think of new ways to be interesting and entertaining to those in your database.

Daily Plan

Your daily plan is calendar control. Most people respond best to a structured workday, so it's important to create this structure for yourself (most jobs create a structure for their employees, but now you are your own boss). Without structure, it's easy to spend your day doing the wrong things, unimportant things, or sometimes nothing. The best practice for scheduling your day is to put in the most important things first.

When it comes to your business, lead generation will always be the most important thing you do. Block off your mornings for pure lead generation time. While phone calls are usually the most efficient way to connect with your database, you can also use this time for writing handwritten notes or commenting on people's social media. Making videos to post on your own social media, creating newsletters, or attending group activities where you talk about real estate are all good uses of lead generation time.

You'll also want to send out requests for information that may take a significant amount of time to receive a response. Many requests require several people to be involved and thus cannot be completed with one action. If you know a problem you're trying to solve will require significant time, start the ball rolling on that process early in the day. You can then block off a chunk of time after lunch to follow up with the morning requests you sent out. This can help move things along that were ignored or slipped through the cracks.

Once lead generation and requests for information are completed, decide what's next. Some tasks are daily, like checking emails or following up on offers that were sent. Others can be done two days a week, such as lead follow-up with cold leads or attending office trainings. In my business, we use the motto: "If it's not on the calendar, it doesn't exist." This is how important it is that things be added to the calendar.

Appointments with clients and tasks with due dates must absolutely be added immediately.

Lead versus Lag Measures

In *The 4 Disciplines of Execution*, authors Chris McChesney, Sean Covey, and Jim Huling lay out the difference between what they refer to as "lead measures" and "lag measures" when tracking progress toward a measurable goal. Lead measures are the activities that have a direct impact on hitting your goal, and lag measures are the numbers that speak to how well your lead measures worked.

Suppose your goal is to lose weight. If you track your weight every morning, you're tracking a lag measure. Tracking lag measures is what most of us naturally do when trying to accomplish a goal. Unfortunately, this approach has some drawbacks—the biggest being that by the time you've tracked a lag measure, there's nothing you can do to improve it.

A much wiser method is to track lead measures. For a weight-loss goal, this could be the number of days you ate less than the maximum number of calories allowed or the amount of time you spent exercising. Top producers in any field focus on improving the performance and consistency of the lead measures that will give them the results they want. When it comes to setting daily goals for yourself as a real estate agent, you should do the same.

It's wise to track the actions you'll take to find new leads. On my team, we track both lead and lag measures. I look at lag measures once a month when I review the numbers with my chief financial officer. These lag measures let me see whether we are on the right track, and if we're not, what adjustments I need to make. Some of the lag measures I track are:
- Company profit
- Company profit compared to last month
- Deals closed
- GCI
- Profit margin
- Expenses
- Names added to my database
- Seller-to-buyer ratio
- Closing percentage of properties put in escrow

Lead measures, on the other hand, should be tracked weekly and focused on daily because they will have a direct impact on the success of your business. Even more important is to focus on improving your skills related to the lead measures you are tracking. Improving your ability to execute on lead measures can be a fast way to become a top-producing agent. Agents who make more headway on this aspect of their business surpass their competition and gain market share. Examples of lead measures to track are:

- Number of contacts made daily
- Number of buyer presentations given
- Number of listing presentations given
- Number of comparative market analyses (CMAs) run and delivered to home sellers not looking to sell yet
- Number of names added to database
- Number of open houses held

As you can see, your consistency with your lead measures is reflected in your lag measures. Get into the habit of focusing on lead measures daily, then reviewing lag measures weekly or monthly. It is crucial to excelling with the Sales Funnel and a helpful way to keep yourself on track in the ocean of freedom you're given as a real estate agent.

Having a funnel is important but only if you're skilled at using it. Most new agents are never trained in the tools used to move prospects down the funnel. This shows up very clearly in their lack of production. There are two factors that determine how many deals you will close: the number of people you put in your Sales Funnel, and your skill at progressing them through it.

Remember, you have chosen a high-risk, high-reward profession. To be successful, you must achieve elite-level status. This is accomplished by combining a high level of proficiency with your tools with a strong lead generation method. Hitting the elite level is important. You're either in the top 20 percent of agents making great money or down in the bottom 80 percent fighting for the scraps.

By focusing on the training and tools provided in this chapter, you can avoid discouragement and temptation to quit when things become difficult. Grab ahold of these tools. Practice them when you're alone and with other people. They are the key to becoming a top-producing agent earning a six-figure salary.

PLAN

PLAN (Prospect, Lead Follow-Up, Appointments, and Negotiate) is an acronym that describes the four steps agents take to create the revenue for their business. Focusing on these four will be the foundation of becoming a top producer. When you eventually scale your business with leverage, these will be the last four things you turn over to your staff.

Prospect

Prospecting is reaching out to people and asking for business.

Lead Follow-Up

When combined with Prospect, you have "lead generation" (the first tool in the Sales Funnel). Following up with leads is incredibly important and often overlooked at the expense of prospecting. Many leads require more than one touch to convert to a client. When we fail to schedule time for lead follow-up, we experience what is called "lead bleed." Lead bleed used to single-handedly cost my business more than every other step combined. When I created systems to reduce this cost, my gross volume quadrupled in one year.

Appointments

Setting appointments and converting on them is the second most important activity, outside of lead generation, to build your business. Since the purpose of lead generation is to set appointments, tracking appointments is an important metric. Appointments create clients.

Negotiate

Agents negotiate in several ways. The most important occurs when putting buyers or sellers into contract. Without contracts, you can't make money. After a property is in contract, there are times when you must negotiate just to save the deal. It's important to note that while this is a pertinent component of your job, it is still not making you money. Rather, it's saving you money you already earned. Top-producing agents limit the amount of time they spend negotiating on escrows they have already put in contract and focus on putting new clients in contract instead.

There are several ways you can save time negotiating escrows to keep them in contract.

1. Do what you can to limit the ways houses can fall out of contract.
   a. Negotiate repairs upfront with the seller.
   b. Negotiate with the seller's agent how a potential low value appraisal will be handled when you make your original offer.
   c. Ensure your clients have turned in all documentation to the lender before submitting your offer.
2. Prepare your clients for what will occur during the escrow process so it doesn't catch them off guard.
   a. Conduct a buyer's presentation with your clients that explains what they are about to experience.
   b. Let your clients know they will experience turbulence but that it is a natural part of the home-buying process.
   c. Explain how the contract and deposits work early in the process.
3. Know your clients' wants and needs at a deep level before committing to working with them.

Every day as an agent you will be bombarded with threats to your business. These almost always come via non-PLAN tasks. Agents spend hours creating marketing flyers that few will ever see, and they don't realize they are losing money with every minute spent on it. "Is this PLAN?" is a question you should ask yourself throughout the day. It can help reduce the amount of wasted time, wasted money, and wasted opportunity in your business.

Hourglass Theory

I developed the hourglass theory in response to how to take control of the chaos in communication I was experiencing when I started working with a high volume of clients. The real estate process is stressful. When people feel stressed or anxious, they tend to communicate with urgency yet more sporadically. Ironically, they want a fast response because time seems to speed up during stressful situations. This is why clients often complain about Realtors never answering their phone; this is how it feels to them.

This situation is compounded as a top producer because you have a high number of clients. Lots of requests for communication multiplied by lots of people equals many opportunities for poor communication and disappointed expectations. Leaving people feeling like they cannot depend on you does not create raving fans. If you want to create repeat business, you *have* to give high customer service at high volume levels.

The enemy to keeping up with communication is lack of organization. Clients reaching out via several mediums several times a day without any direction as to how you work best with communication is a recipe for chaos. To avoid this, let your clients know your preferred form of communication and what they can expect in terms of response time.

In the movie 300, a small group of Spartan warriors hold off a much larger army by forcing the enemy soldiers into one small, easily defendable choke point. This is the essence of hourglass theory. Your agenda is to take all the random pieces of communication that come through various mediums and direct it into one central location. That's how you eliminate important information from being missed. You can then delegate that information be handled by team members (or yourself) in a controlled manner.

The flow of information should look like an hourglass:

WORKFLOW

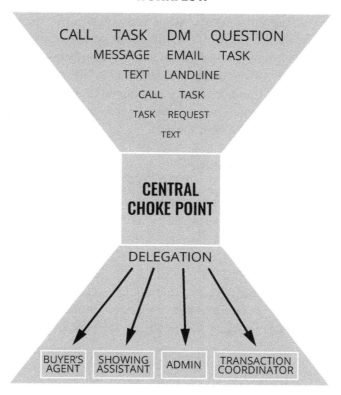

The top of the model reflects all the different ways information makes its way to you: text messages, voicemails, phone calls, emails, social media messages, and people stopping by to speak with you while you're working. Add a smart phone that won't stop going off (especially when you're with a client) and you have lots of unnecessary stress in your life.

The bottom of the model reflects the different team members who could be assigned tasks after the information is collected. As the people are given assignments, you find yourself with the peace of mind that comes with knowing things are getting done. You've conquered the chaos created by the high volume of communication.

The key is to take all this information from the top of the model and push it to one location. If you work alone, this can be your email or your CRM (we create a task in our CRM every time something needs to be done). In our CRM, tasks can be assigned to any team member. This is how we ensure things don't get lost. Email can work in a similar way. By asking clients to email you instead of call or text, you ensure an unread message is waiting for your attention and you don't forget to respond. Ever get a text, need a minute to think about your response, then get a phone call before you reply? And then you don't reply because you forgot about the text? We've all been there. Your client is left with the impression you don't care about them because you ignored them.

The following are ways you can gently push clients to your preferred communication; in this case, it's email.

When Talking on the Phone

"Hey [Client name]. That's a good question. I'm driving right now and don't want to miss this. Would you mind emailing me so I can check it when I get back to the office?"

"Hey [Client Name], that sounds great. I have to jump into my next meeting, but can you send me an email so I can address this as soon as I'm out? It's a valid concern."

"Hey [Client Name], I've been meaning to talk to you about this. I've got some information I compiled about it that I'd like to send you. Can you email me this question and I'll respond back with the information?"

When Texting

"Hey! Thanks for bringing this up. I want to make sure I don't forget this. Can you email me this question, and I'll get back to you about it when I'm in the office?"

"Hey! I was meaning to call you about this. I'm in a crowded room right now and can't talk. Can you email me at [email address] and then I'll call you about it when it's quieter?"

When It's the Beginning of the Relationship

"It's very important to me that I give you my full attention when I'm with you. One way we can avoid missed communication is if you always email me your questions or requests. If it's urgent, please text or call me to let me know an email was sent; that way I can look into it right away. If you text me without an email, there's a chance I'll miss your text and then miss the opportunity to get you what you needed. Can we commit to communicating this way with each other?"

"As a professional, it's important to me that we set clear expectations on what you can expect from here on out. There may be times I want to get information from you to help me do my job. When that occurs after business hours (say, 8:00 p.m.), I commit to emailing you rather than calling. Should it be urgent, I'll text to let you know an email was sent."

While email and a CRM are handy tools for individual agents, many agents will choose to hire an administrative aide to keep up with client demand. It's important to let your clients know upfront how this person benefits them. When you hire someone to buffer communication between you and clients and conduct the administrative tasks that many of your clients will request, the following script can be useful.

"My main job as a Realtor is to get you the perfect house/ sell your house for as much as I can. To do that, I will spend copious amounts of time on the phone with the other agent or their lender trying to negotiate top dollar. Many times I find myself conflicted with time between working with the other agent and speaking to my own client about what's going on. To avoid that, I've hired [team member name] to act as a concierge for my clients. Please let them know *anything* you'd like, and they'll let me know what you need and how we can help you get it. I want to make you money, and I also want to provide a great experience."

As information is funneled to the choke point, you have the opportunity to disperse it out among the people on your team to ensure nothing is overlooked. This should become a staple of your day. The information comes in, it's funneled to one central location, it's decided who should be responsible for it, then it is given to that person. Rinse and repeat.

This can feel awkward at first when you've always been the only one doing everything. Part of becoming a successful entrepreneur is leveraging yourself out of the things in your business that don't feed your business. It may feel like you can't trust anyone else to run a CMA, but as long as you train someone to do it the same way you specify, they could become better at it than you. What's important is every task gets funneled to the correct person and that it gets completed. It's not important if it's not completed by you.

⮞ KEY POINTS

- Tell your subconscious where you want to go instead of where you don't want to go. This will give your subconscious its "vision," which is both the end goal and the path to get there.
- Reverse engineering is the concept of beginning with the end and deconstructing it to determine the necessary steps to arrive there.
- GPS 1:3:5 is used to reverse engineer success.
- 4:1:1 breaks your goal down into trackable metrics.
- Plan your day with a calendar to not waste your time, and make lead generation the first thing you do.
- Lead measures are activities you track that lead to results and lag measures are the results you track. Focus on lead measures to become a top producer.
- PLAN: the only actions to take in a day for generating revenue.
- Hourglass theory takes the chaos of random communication by forcing it into a central location, organizing it, and then delegating it to the appropriate parties. This will eliminate lead bleed and improve your customer service.

CHAPTER ➤ EIGHT

SOCIAL MEDIA

"Don't use social media to impress people; use it to impact people."

—DAVE WILLIS

As a top-producing agent looking to fill your Sales Funnel with lead opportunities, social media is really a nonnegotiable weapon to have in your arsenal. For some people, it can feel awkward to put more of your life on social media (I was, and to a degree still am, one of them). However, there is simply no more powerful way to connect with a large group of people with a small amount of time and effort. Do whatever you must to get comfortable in this arena.

For those who don't like social media at all . . . I still advise you to get over it. I never had any form of social media before becoming an agent. I didn't like sharing much about myself, and in the profession of law enforcement we were advised not to make it easy to find us. After I got my real estate license in 2015, I intended to keep it that way. It was only after several mentors advised me it really wasn't an option that I went online. If my goal was to become a top-producing agent, I simply needed to find a way to stay in front of people's eyeballs. The mindshare you can have with a social media platform is second to none.

For those who already enjoy social media, you may have to make some changes too. It's not simply putting content out—what you put out matters. Unprofessional or offensive content is a quick way to tell the world you don't take yourself seriously and they shouldn't take you seriously either. The same can be true of self-absorbed/ego-feeding content and monotonous, boring content. People in your sphere will pay attention to what you post and will judge you on it. For many leads, it is the only thing they have to judge you by.

What you post is not just a reflection of who you are but also of how you want to be seen. Real estate sales is a lifestyle choice. If you want to be taken seriously by others and win their trust and confidence to represent them, this needs to make its way into your social media content. Finding the right mix of industry-related and personally engaging posts can be a tough formula to nail down. When done right, however, it's very powerful.

Stats on Social Media Usage

For those who question if social media is really a nonnegotiable factor in your business, consider the following stats as reported in 2018.[5]

- 77 percent of Realtors use social media
  - 97 percent use Facebook
  - 59 percent use LinkedIn
  - 39 percent use Instagram
- Social media is the top tech tool used by agents, representing 47 percent of leads
- The three most valuable technology tools used by agents (by approval ratings):
  - MLS (64 percent)
  - Smart lockboxes/key devices (39 percent)
  - Social media platforms (28 percent)
- 77 percent of Realtors actively use some form of social media for real estate
- 47 percent of real estate businesses find social media results in the highest-quality leads versus other sources
- 99 percent of millennials (and 90 percent of baby boomers) begin their home search online (as opposed to in-person referrals)

---

5 National Association of REALTORS® Research Group, "Real Estate in a Digital Age: 2018 Report," December 12, 2018, https://www.nar.realtor/sites/default/files/documents/2018-real-estate-in-a-digital-world-12-12-2018.pdf.

Social media is where the eyeballs are. If you want to stay top of mind, this is how you do it. In addition to posting things about your everyday life, there are numerous ways you can show your SOI how your business is doing and why they should be calling you when they or someone they know needs a real estate agent. You want to avoid being a one-trick pony. Nobody likes to see the same post over and over (and over) again. Consider the following ten ways to switch up your real estate content to keep it fresh and avoiding becoming predictable.

Social Media Content

Sponsored Ads

Sponsored ads get your content in front of your spheres in higher numbers than organic posts. Social media companies cannot show all of your posts to all of your audience. If they did, everyone's feeds/walls would become so saturated with content the users would stop going to the site because the information wouldn't be interesting to them. To avoid this, social media platforms use complex mathematical algorithms to determine what users like and don't like.

These algorithms tend to be weighted by a combination of likes, views, comments, and other forms of engagement the users participate in with the content that crosses their feed. The more engagement you have with a particular type of post or user, the more likely you are to see more of those posts in the future. Agents who understand this do better on social media. If you can create more engagement with your audience by posting content people respond to, your posts are more likely to be seen by more people.

Even the best content that is organically made won't reach the total audience you want. If you want to reach people in a specific demographic, you'll need to pay for a sponsored ad. Platforms like Facebook and Instagram allow users to craft a particular ad or piece of content and pay to have it show up on other people's feeds who match the specific demographics they pay for. Sponsored ads are one way to get your content in front of more people—and more specifically, the right people.

Testimonial Videos

Videos that express your clients' admiration and appreciation for the job you did for them go a long way in bringing in leads. This is because social proof is a powerful influence over how others make decisions. Social proof is the concept that people will make decisions that are heavily influenced by the decisions of others. The concept was first made popular in the Solomon Asch conformity experiment of 1951. During this study, researchers found an unknowing participant would choose an obviously wrong answer to a test if the others in the room (who were in on the experiment) chose the same wrong answer first. The study showed the psychological effects of peer pressure on decision-making

This same concept works when it comes to choosing a Realtor. For those who don't know you, or those who may be on the fence about hiring you, a solid endorsement from a source that is perceived to be credible can make a huge difference in swaying their decision. Having your happy clients make videos about how wonderful you are to work with is an easy way to capitalize on this concept. Posting these videos to social media (and your website) is a handy way to make sure the rest of your sphere sees them and is reminded of how good you are at what you do.

Online Reviews

Posting online reviews functions the same way as testimonial videos: They are a form of social proof and increase the likelihood of new leads choosing you when they are ready to buy or sell. It's best practice to get these online reviews on Zillow, Yelp, and other platforms. If clients have already made them, post them on your social media too. Showing prospects how happy your clients are with their decision to pick you is never a bad thing for business.

To make these most effective, encourage your clients to come up with specific details about the transaction or the role you played in it. Commenting on your patience, resources, knowledge, or negotiating ability will go further to create credibility and intrigue than generic comments about your professionalism or thoroughness. This is a good example of how simple the review can be:

He never made us feel
pressured and pointed out
maintenance upkeeps to
consider when looking at
houses, as well as what'll hold
value and most expensive to
replace/remodel.

Sold, Pending, and Coming Soon Ads

Social media also makes it easy to "market" your past sales for others to see. My team posts on social media for each listing we take. We use a variety of pictures for the same properties to showcase different aspects of the listings and prevent looking like we posted the same content several times. During times when your business is not doing so well, you can post the same listing five different times to make it appear to your sphere you have more business than you do and to create more engagement on your page. This can easily be done in the following way:

1. **Coming Soon!** Picture of front of house with second picture of home's best feature
2. **Just Listed!** Front of house
3. **Pending!** Best pictures of the interior or backyard
4. **Just Sold!** Same picture as Just Listed, or something similar
5. **Congrats to our clients!** Picture of clients standing in front of home, smiling and holding some of your marketing (you can tag your clients in these)

Posts like this not only remind your followers you are selling homes and keep you top of mind, but they also make it easier for them to engage with you. Everyone loves commenting on good-looking houses or congratulating your clients on their accomplishments. This also makes it easier for your sphere to reach out to you when they are thinking about selling their own homes or wanting to buy a new one.

When you get to a point that you are selling enough homes to stay in front of people, you can slow down on the "five posts per listings" strategy and just post each "Coming Soon!" or "Pending!" listing individually.

Company/Personal Milestones

People enjoy seeing awards or accolades that are given to those who deserve them, and the world of real estate is no exception. Social media is a great place to show people the awards you've received from your broker or other sources. You can also show where you rank in lists of other top-producing Realtors or within your own office. On my team, we look for ways to post wins we had over specific periods of time. This can be getting a property under contract when there were several other buyers, selling a property for significantly over market value, or putting a large number of clients under contract. These posts can be simple and fun, as shown below.

Attractive Property Photos/Videos

Frankly, there's no reason you shouldn't be doing this every chance you get. People like to see attractive homes, and they will definitely be tempted to reach out to you when a post arouses their curiosity. Whenever you're showing homes and see a stunning kitchen, incredible backyard, sparkling pool, or great view, take a picture. You can post these photos on your social media while the clients view the home when you'd normally be doing nothing but waiting anyway.

The same is true for videos. People love seeing what homes look like, and it's extra appealing to do so from the comfort of their own home. As you make the videos, talk about what you like and tell viewers to comment on the post or to ask their questions or to get more information. This solicits engagement and is a strong form of lead generation. A simple picture can put the idea in someone's head how important an outdoor space is for entertaining and start the juices flowing that it may be time to leave that apartment complex and start the house hunt.

Industry and Market News

Posting information about local market news is a powerful way to establish yourself as an expert in that area. It can be posts about your favorite restaurant, car mechanic, or hiking trail and sharing some information about why you like it. Posts like this brand you as a "local market expert"—a pretty important title to some buyers. They also give you an opportunity to blend your personal life with your professional one. Making clips of your favorite dish in a popular local restaurant or a sparkling cocktail will show your fun side while also setting yourself apart as the one buyers need to contact for the inside scoop.

This same principle also works for macroeconomic real estate information. Articles, posts, or studies relating to interest rate trends, inventory, or buyer trends show you as a bright business mind and a trustworthy source of information. This can be as simple as taking a real estate article from any website you enjoy and making a brief comment about how you see the trends it mentions affecting your business or local market. If you throw in how you've adjusted your strategy to take the information into account, it will make you look cutting edge and more intelligent than your competition.

Renovation Ideas

This is another opportunity to look like an expert and show the value you bring above and beyond access to the MLS. Posts that highlight new design trends are likely to catch people's attention and pique their interest. To increase your appeal as an in-the-loop listing agent, you can also include what buyers *don't* like. Taking before and after pictures (such as a bathroom with brass fixtures before and then with brushed nickel after) can start a conversation on your page and elicit engagement from the viewers. Who doesn't like to share their design ideas about what they do and don't like? These kinds of posts will boost your status with social media algorithms and get them seen by more people.

Event Invitations

Holding seminars, meetups, and parties is a dynamic way to generate leads. Posting about them on social media is even better. Putting out an invitation for people to attend a social or educational event shows that you are making things happen and are an active participant in the community bringing value to those in your world. It can be as easy as posting a link to an Eventbrite page and having people sign up from there.

Make this strategy even more effective by taking pictures at the event and posting them afterward on your social media and website. You can combine this with the video testimonial strategy. Post videos of people saying how much fun they had and how happy they are to have attended. It will make everyone else wish they'd been there. Showing your personable side will make it easier for leads to reach out to you when they have questions or are ready to buy/sell. Making yourself approachable is a big piece to being successful, and so is using social media to grow your business.

Blog Posts

Not everyone writes blog posts, but if you do, this is a key place to share your knowledge. Some people write about the overall world of real estate while others focus on investing, particular strategies in that niche, or educational pieces home buyers and sellers might be interested in. Writing and posting helps set you apart as an industry expert and shows people you have a lot going on between your ears. Readers feel like they can get to know you, without you having to make the time to speak with them individually.

If you don't write blog posts, that's okay. Look for posts on design styles, information on the city you work in, or overall economic trends to post on your page to give people something to engage with. People will look at what you choose to post and assume it is information that matters to you. The type of post you share will indicate your personality and your value system to your audience. Since people want to work with those they know, like, and trust, letting people get to know you is an important piece of that formula.

Using Social Media as a CRM

In addition to keeping you top of mind within your sphere, social media can be used to stay in touch with those in your sphere. Posting content is a good way to let them see what you're up to, but personally reaching out to message them about a post will strengthen your connections and make it easier for them to reach out when they need something. Some agents buy a CRM (e.g., HubSpot, Top Producer, or Salesforce) to manage their database while others use their social media for the same purpose.

Social media platforms have direct messaging systems where you can send private messages to others on the site. This is a quick way to start conversations with those you have lost touch or contact with. For some reason, a text message out of the blue can feel awkward or forced, but a direct message (DM) doesn't have that same effect. When it comes to reconnecting with those you haven't seen or spoken to in a while, it's easier to start with a DM. From there, you can ask for their phone number to text them or email to write to them.

This is my preferred method for obtaining contact information for my main database. Social media makes the progression smoother. If you don't have a CRM or database manager, social media can substitute as one. Because you are likely to see posts from those you engage with the most (or who engage with you), it stands to reason those are the people you should be staying in touch with to stay top of mind. These are your raving fans. These people are likely to give you referrals and want to support your business. You want to treat them well.

Keep these connections strong by leaving encouraging, positive, and humorous comments. If they respond, that tells the platform to show them more of your content. I also like to send DMs to those who post something inspiring or brave rather than always leaving a public comment. Take the time to let someone know how they positively impacted your life. Make them feel good about themselves, and they will reciprocate with positive emotions toward you.

Social media is often blamed for creating shallowness in the culture, but it doesn't have to be that way. Just like anything else, it's a tool that can be used for any purpose you choose.

Marketing Listings

The bigger your social media following, the more it will help your business. On listing appointments, I share with my seller leads that I will put their property on my social media channels to draw interest even before going live on the MLS. This is a powerful tool I use to show them how I provide better service than other Realtors.

What the leads don't realize is this is also a way for me to find buyers for the property. Not all states allow dual agency, but for those that do, finding your own buyer, providing them with inspection reports and disclosures, then having them waive the inspection contingency can be a big plus for your sellers.

If you combine this with getting the buyers fully approved for the loan with a reputable lender and negotiating ahead of time how a low appraisal will be handled, you can bring your client a highly qualified buyer with a strong chance of the escrow closing. This increases the desirability of having your seller accept an offer from a buyer you are also representing.

This is a win for you, the seller, *and* the buyer, especially when it's a hot market and buyers are having a hard time getting into contract. Advertising your listings on social media allows you to create these types of scenarios and sets your seller up for success based on your social media prowess.

Marketing your listings on social media is a free way to let your SOI know you're doing business and you're a capable Realtor. Choosing the best-looking pictures and then marketing the best highlights of the listing makes you look professional with your sellers and lets future clients know you're qualified to help them. If you aren't putting listings on social media, you're wasting free advertising and future leads.

The formula for posting a listing is simple and includes:

1. Post a good-looking picture of the home.
2. Include relevant data and a brief description.
3. Say what you love about the home or what makes it unique or a deal.
4. Ask for responses.

Here is an example of a description.

Charming 3 bed, 2 bath starter home in the highly desirable neighborhood of Lovely Oaks! Even the pickiest buyers will love the updated kitchen, open floor plan, and generously sized bedrooms that accompany this hard-to-find home. Backyard has fruit trees and plenty of space for a future pool, and the cul-de-sac location makes this a great place to start/raise a family! We'll be hitting the market soon so DM/email me with any questions and let's talk about what's going on in the market and how I can help you land a gem like this!

David Greene
Jun 26 · 🌐

Coming soon to Brentwood, CA. 3,785 square feet, 4 bedrooms, 4 bathrooms, and a backyard that will make you never want to come inside. Huge kitchen, grand family room, several fireplaces, walk in closets, and more. This home has too much to mention and is going to make some family very, very happy. DM or comment if you'd like to know more. Just in time for summer! Info@davidgreene24.com

👍❤️😮 77   25 Comments 10 Shares

👍 Like   💬 Comment   ↪ Share

Attractive posts boost your business in the following ways:
1. They give your followers a reason to continue to follow you; you have access to early inventory.
2. They make you relevant and exciting; they get a sneak peek at "off-market" deals that aren't yet on Zillow, Redfin, etc.
3. They show people what's new in your business.
4. They establish you as an industry expert for your local market.
5. They allow you to find buyers for the property to potentially "double end" (if allowed by your state).

6. They allow you to find buyers for *different* properties by starting a conversation with those looking to buy a home who reach out to you.
7. They are free marketing for your company, and you never know who is taking notice.

Triggering Interest

The ultimate goal of using social media to grow your business is to trigger interest from those who follow you and to convert them into clients. Because "People" make up the first stage in your funnel, posting on social media is a form of lead generation. A "Lead" in the Sales Funnel is defined as someone who knows who you are *and* has a home to buy or sell. That means you need people to feel comfortable reaching out to you when they have a home to buy or sell.

I call this triggering interest. In fishing, when an angler moves the bait correctly, it triggers the fish's instinctual urge to chase and bite the prey. The better a fisherman is at doing this, the less hungry a fish needs to be to take the bait. The same is true in your real estate business. An extremely motivated (hungry) buyer or seller will contact you on any kind of post (good or bad), but when your post is good you can get someone to reach out about buying or selling a property (and hopefully both at the same time; but again, only if your state allows Realtors to represent both the buyer and the seller). They'll do this even when they didn't realize they wanted to buy or sell until they saw your post. This happens when you trigger interest.

Creating Posts

Think about the times you've been scrolling through your feed and see a post that catches your attention. Sometimes you stop to read the post. This is good for the poster. Other times, you know you want to comment on the post or engage with the writer. This is even better. It's often because the poster has an intriguing personality and has written a post that elicits your emotional response.

I've found the posts that elicit the most engagement have a strong dash of humility and a specific call to action from the viewer. For example, "Let me know what you think of this," "Here's an old picture of me. Can you believe I used to look like that?," or "Here's a peek at a vulnerable part of my life. Has this happened to you?"—each has a strong emotional pull likely to create a response. If you want to keep your audience engaged with you, open up. Show them what's going on behind the scenes. Humans like to reward the courage it takes to do this and will offer emotional support in the form of a comment.

Here is an example of a good-natured post that elicited a large number of responses. It was written by Ben Kinney, a Keller Williams mega agent.

Ben Kinney
19h · 🌐   ...

A friend of mine said during COVID lockdown - "Ben a lot of things have changed for you over the last 10-15 years" and I replied what do you think hasn't changed for me? (Me expecting something like your 💜) She replied with a simple and true answer "Your professional photo."

Sad but true I guess 😅. Well here are a few ph... See More

⭕😮😆 Sheila Chand and 354 others   221 Comments

Ben's willingness to poke fun at himself for using old Realtor photos (a common source of jest in the industry) and then share the actual photos made it easier for readers to post comments, tease him, or offer encouragement for how good he still looks. Posts like this boost how often those who comment on his posts will see more of them and make it easier for them to contact him when they have a buyer, seller, or even a recruit for his team.

Poll Ideas

Instagram, Facebook, and Twitter allow you to create polls that are designed to initiate engagement with your audience. If you're looking to trigger interest, this is about as easy as it gets. Realtors can choose all sorts of subjects to run a poll. The following are some ideas you can use to start your own polls to trigger interest.

- Landscaping options
- Floral options
- Room conversions
- Backsplash options
- Island counter/standard counter
- Garage conversion/no garage conversion
- What size garage is ideal?
- Tile roof/shingle roof
- Flooring options
- Front door color
- Stone/brick walkway
- One-section/two-section sink
- Cabinets or hanging shelves
- granite/quartz counters
- One-story/two-story
- 30-year/15-year mortgages
- Take a guess. Is this home over/under 2,000 square feet?
- Condo/townhome preference
- Duplex style/split-level home
- House hack/traditional purchase
- Conventional/drought-resistant lawn
- Fruit trees/shade trees
- Stucco/siding
- Textured drywall/smooth
- Crown molding/no crown molding

Going Live

Facebook and Instagram also have "live" features that allow you to start a live question-and-answer session with the followers of your page. When you do this, your followers get a notification that you have gone live and are given the option to click on a banner and join the session. When they do, they see you and hear you speaking, but you don't see them. At this point, they can ask you questions, and you can answer them right there in the session.

This is a fun and creative way to engage with your audience and connect with several of them at the same time. Be sure to say the names of those asking questions and making comments: Everyone loves to hear their own name and feel especially connected to you after hearing it.

I've found these live sessions are a useful way to share what you're learning or observing in the market. It's an easy way to tell people how hot/cold the market is, where the deals are, what's happening with interest rates, and other relevant market data that will make you stand out from other agents. Those who are less educated about the real estate space can learn about it from behind the privacy, safety, and security of their screen, while you build your confidence and make it easier for them to reach out when they're ready.

The live feature is especially good for people with strong oratory skills who can articulate their thoughts clearly and on the spot. It can be a fun, exciting, and powerful way to stay connected. However, if you're not comfortable speaking to groups or aren't yet confident, this probably isn't the best method for you. It's difficult to hide those weaknesses when you're live. If you can't improvise quickly, since you don't know what you'll be asked, there is nothing wrong with using the other methods of social media to trigger interest and engagement.

Using Videos

When it comes to using video to help you sell houses, consider the following stats.[6]

- According to Google, six out of ten people would rather watch online videos than television.
- According to Insivia, mobile video consumption rises by 100 percent every year, and viewers retain 95 percent of a message when they watch it in a video compared with 10 percent when reading it in text.
- According to Cisco, by 2022, online videos will make up more than

---

6   Biteable, "Video marketing statistics: The state of video marketing in 2021," accessed September 13, 2021, https://biteable.com/blog/video-marketing-statistics.

82 percent of all consumer internet traffic, which is fifteen times higher than in 2017.

- According to Alexa, YouTube is the second most popular website after Google, and YouTube claims its users view more than one billion hours of video each day.

These are some impressive statistics! You should be using video to connect with your SOI on social media and to communicate information, market data, and how your followers can support you. If you're not entirely comfortable with video yet, that's okay. There is nothing wrong with starting slowly and working your way up. When a client closes on a home, I send them a video to congratulate them and remind them of the best parts of the deal. If we helped save them money, beat out other buyers, or negotiated a higher price from the buyers, I casually mention that to remind them I worked hard for their finances. I then remind them to keep an eye out in the mail because we'll be sending them a gift soon.

We also use video to highlight the best-looking parts of houses our showing agents see during tours. These videos get posted on our social media and encourage buyers to reach out and ask us about the market or the specific home. These videos tell those considering selling their home that we work with a large number of buyers, and it would be a good idea to call us to see if any of them would be interested in touring their property. Videos demand to be watched, and watching videos creates a response.

I take videos of my own listings and post those to social media or send them out to my database of buyers. Unlike being live on Facebook, here I'm careful not to say anyone's name specifically. This way I can point out the best features of the home and the person watching thinks it was recorded just for them. Video gives a much more accurate depiction of a home than pictures, which are easier to doctor. Sending video shows a more authentic presentation.

I also use promotional "explainer-style" videos to connect with clients.[7] These videos explain who I am, what my pedigree is, and why people should work with me—all while detailing my past history and the fun side of me. I send these videos to new leads I've just met and to anyone I don't believe is familiar with my story or brand. This type of video can be made for under $250 and is a creative way to let new leads

---

7   You can find them at www.youtube.com/davidgreenerealestate.

and clients learn more about you and your company.

If you follow me on YouTube or Instagram (@DavidGreene24), you are also likely familiar with my in-car video segments. In these posts, I use a hands-free device to record myself while driving to talk about various topics I feel will bring value to my audience. These talks range from success-based principles to psychological tricks to get ahead in life. I often relate them to real estate sales generally or my business specifically to show people the kind of information I'm learning and how I apply these principles to getting my clients a better interest rate or selling their house for more money.

Recently, I hired an editor to create a short introduction to these videos showing me in various aspects of my business (on TV, speaking from my desk, driving in my car, etc.). It's a quick and subtle reminder that I'm very active in real estate and a trustworthy source to lean on when looking to buy or sell a house. Video makes it easy to communicate these small, subtle details. This is one reason video is expected to be even more popular in the future.

Finding Balance

It can be tricky to know what type of content to post. Hitting the right mix of personal and business isn't easy to do. Some people simply aren't comfortable sharing much of their personal life. These folks will often err on the side of business posts. And some people randomly post whatever crosses their mind, whether personal or business, or stick to the same type of post time and time again. These accounts are predictable, stale, and unexciting.

I can't tell you exactly what to post. Before 2020, most social media experts recommended businesses post 80 percent personal or educational content and 20 percent direct business posts.[8] Now, a lot of those rules are up in the air. The reality is there is no formula to follow for what to post or when to post it. Every business and every person is different. Trying to follow someone else's formula for success is no guarantee it will work for you.

I recommend a paradigm shift from this unilateral business versus personal thinking. I prefer my concept of "always working, never

---

8   Tanya Hall, "The New 80/20 Rule of Social Media Marketing: Creating Your Own Ratio for Social Media that Accelerates Your Brand Stategy," Inc., November 16, 2018, https://www.inc.com/tanya-hall/the-new-80/20-rule-of-social-media.html.

working." A Realtor's day is never just personal or just business. Since our work and personal lives are so closely blended, it makes sense to incorporate both into our social media life. Our posts should be both business and personal *because* our lives are both business and personal.

Make a post about your favorite restaurant and include a picture of your delicious meal. Something like this is sure to get a response from your followers. In the text of the post, include things like: "At my favorite Vietnamese restaurant. This is why I love living in Oakville! If you live anywhere near here you have to try it. If you don't, you're missing out!"

By mentioning the city in which the restaurant is located, you remind your audience where you work, why they should want to live there, and that you're a local market expert—without appearing pushy or demanding. You can do the same for so many other relevant life events.

- A post about the Little League game where your child got a hit; it's a reminder that small-town memories like this are worth their weight in gold.
- A post about a new stop sign in town and how it makes the streets safer for the kids.
- A video of you running on a nearby trail, or views from the top of the trail, with a comment about how much you love living in an area with outdoor activities.
- A post with pictures or video of a parade or social setting where people are having fun. This makes others want to be a part of that community.

If you approach it correctly, you can post about anything and make it both personal and business. This forces you to dive deeper into the "always working, never working" mindset so crucial to conducting a large number of transactions without burning out and losing business.

One piece of advice is to follow those you love on social media and try to emulate them. What kind of content are they posting? What is it about their delivery that you like so much? By reverse engineering their style, you can find small ways to improve your own content. Over time, you too will become confident with social media and reap the rewards it provides.

If you plan on being in real estate for more than two or three years, look for ways to grow your sales. With each year, more people are using social media to research products and companies. Consider just ten years ago—when you wanted to learn more about a company or product, you went onto the internet and looked up their website. Can you remember the last time you looked someone up online and went to their website to learn more about them? This rarely happens anymore.

People trust social media as it's usually a more accurate window into the life of a personality or branded company. If you think people aren't looking you up after they meet you, you're wrong. Assume leads are going to look you up, so put content out there for them to find that gives them a reason to trust you. If you put the pieces where they belong, the clients will fall into place.

KEY POINTS

- Social media is a nonnegotiable tool in your arsenal.
- Unprofessional or offensive content will show the world you don't take yourself seriously, and they shouldn't either.
- Find the mix of business and personal engagement that's right for you.
- The more engagement someone makes with a particular post or user, the more likely they are to see more of those posts in the future.
- To make testimonials or reviews most effective, encourage your clients to come up with specific details about the transaction or the role you played in it.
- Posting information about local market news is a great way to establish yourself as an expert in that area.
- Leave calls to action in posts to create responses.
- Posts should be both business and personal because a Realtor's life is both.

CHAPTER NINE

FINDING HELP

"If you want to go fast, go alone. If you want to go far, go together."

—AFRICAN PROVERB

Do-It-Herself Donna was a terrific Realtor, and everyone knew it. Donna was her office's top producer and won several prestigious awards. She was also a lovely person. Everyone spoke well of Donna. The agents who worked with her loved her, and so did the clients she represented. Donna was so good, in fact, that even her clients' family members would send her referrals. If anyone was ever meant to be a Realtor, it was Donna. She excelled at the role.

Everyone could see the closings, the rewards, and the great reviews. What they couldn't see was the toll it took on Donna because she never let it show. She was always smiling, always giving, and always cheerful. Whether someone wanted to write an offer on a house or simply talk about the state of the market, Donna treated them all the same. This gave her a stellar reputation, but it certainly wasn't without a price. Donna was suffering from depression and burnout. Some days, it was all she could do to pick up her phone. She was afraid to tell others what she was going through because she feared it might affect their desire to send her leads. Suffering in silence, Donna soldiered on.

Financially, she was doing great. Donna sold seventy to eighty homes a year and consistently led her MLS in production. She invested the money wisely, buying several investment properties that paid her passive income and set her up nicely for retirement. Donna knew real estate, and she used that knowledge wisely by helping more clients buy houses, then recycling that money back into her investment deals. She was a smart cookie.

Ten years into her career, at a time when she should have been enjoying the fruits of her labors, traveling, and working minimal hours, Donna was in full-blown crisis mode. Her marriage was on the rocks, her kids were getting in trouble at school, and she was about as unhappy as she had ever been. In another few years, Donna knew she would have to quit. But she had become *so* good at her job that her phone never stopped ringing. The constant pressure was breaking her. Clients called her, her office broker called her, new agents asked to be mentored by her, and the list went on. Everyone wanted something from Donna, but nobody was really giving back.

Donna was facing a tough decision. She couldn't go on like this. She needed either to quit, take a sabbatical, or find an assistant. Donna fell prey to one of the worst agent traps—she loved her job so much and did it so well that she began to look to her career to meet all of her personal needs—emotional needs, personal needs, financial needs, relationship needs.

If you're not careful, you too could end up like Do-It-Herself Donna. The irony of being a top-producing agent is when you get good enough, it can become hard to quit. Who wants to throw away everything they've built? But who can go on like this? It's the great Catch-22 of real estate.

If you want to survive in this industry, you must accept there will come a time when you need help. You have to accept this, submit to this, and welcome this. It's not easy to find the right support, but then again, it's not easy to become a top-producing agent. Easy is not how we succeed in this world.

No matter how efficient you are or how much you like work, it's not a matter of *if* you'll need help. It's a matter of *when*. Even if you somehow were able to get everything done yourself while selling one hundred homes a year (I've never seen this done, by the way), the fact remains you could have sold *three hundred* homes with the appropriate help. Too many agents make the mistake of saying, "I don't need help; I can do it myself." They miss the point. It's not about if you can do it yourself. It's about if it makes sense to do it that way.

Consider the things a real estate agent has to do. I won't list them here because it would take an entire other book to do that. It's marketing for leads to meeting leads to finding houses and everything before, after, and during. Real estate can easily consume your days without even selling a home. With everything that needs to be done in a transaction, there are only four things that will actually make you money, and I've covered this in Chapter Seven. Remember that PLAN is:

1. Prospect
2. Follow up leads
3. Attend appointments
4. Negotiate

Even the best agents who fail to stay in the PLAN zone will see their productivity drop, and so will their revenue. It is a constant fight to stay within PLAN, but if you don't, you'll be leaving a lot of money on the table.

To avoid doing the things that don't make you money, find others to do them. This is where finding help comes in. In this chapter we will cover how to know when it's time to find help, what options you have, how to create win-win propositions, and which positions you should hire for first. This is not about hiring a comprehensive full-team model (that will be in *SCALE*, the next book in this series). This is about getting some of the most time-consuming tasks off your plate so you can focus on finding leads, putting them in contract, and keeping them there all the way to close.

Ways to Scale

As we discuss the people that will help you grow your business, it's important to note there are a few different ways to scale. At different stages in your career you'll likely employ different methods, so it's important to understand the pros and cons of each. This way you'll recognize which method will work best for where you are now and when it may be time to switch to a different method.

Scaling operates on a spectrum. On one end of the spectrum, you will spend less money, but you'll also use more of your own time or receive less benefit. This is a lower financial risk. At the other end of the spectrum, you'll pay more, but you won't have to put in as much effort or you'll receive more of a direct benefit. Most agents should start off with the former and build toward the latter as their business becomes more profitable. If your business is already highly profitable, consider starting off with increased scaling.

The Partner

The partnership is the easiest way for you to split up the tasks that need to be done in your business without having to directly pay someone for their time. This works best if you are unsure how much revenue your business will generate month to month or if you don't have a steady stream of income to pay someone a salary. This also works best when saving money is your primary concern.

To create a partnership, find another agent in your office to help you with the tasks that take up most of your time. Rather than paying them by the hour, you will compensate them by some other means. This typically comes in the form of giving them a split of the commission on deals they help with, on-the-job training, or both.

New agents in the office can help you with several of the tasks that take up a lot of your time, but they don't know how to do these things themselves yet. In exchange for your training and the opportunity for them to learn a new skill, they perform these tasks and allow you to PLAN more. Some of the easiest, most productive tasks to get help with are:

- Entering listings into the MLS
- Scheduling showings for buyers
- Showing homes to buyers
- Holding open houses
- Creating marketing materials
- Attending home inspections
- Attending appraisals
- Conducting walk-throughs
- Calling lenders to follow up on preapproval status for your buyers
- Reviewing and organizing offers received on your listings
- Scheduling/taking photos of your listings
- Entering new buyer/seller leads into your lead intake system (e.g., spreadsheet, whiteboard, CRM)
- Calling the agent on the other side of the transaction for the status of different escrow points
- Doing your TC work so they can learn it

- Looking up comparable sales for houses your buyers want to write offers on
- Running CMAs for your listings
- Setting up for listing appointments
- Advertising and putting out your open house signs

When looking for partners, look for hungry, inexperienced agents who want to learn the business in exchange for helping you with the work. You can then offer to split commissions when they reach the point when their contributions are helping you close deals. Splitting commissions is more expensive for you than paying an hourly wage, but it is less risky when you don't close the deals.

The Paid Hire

The paid hire is someone who does parts of the job in exchange for an hourly salary. This type of partnership is riskier for you. If you don't close deals, you still have to pay the hire. The time for this type of hire is when you are closing a significant number of deals. It is much cheaper to pay someone hourly than to give them a larger chunk of the overall commission. This scaling works best for top producers and those who can expect a consistent revenue stream. This is often those with more mature businesses or experience in the industry.

When you are paying someone for work, you have to keep a close eye on your company's profitability to make sure you can both continue to pay your employee and see that their presence is making your business more money, not less. If you are not already reviewing monthly profit and loss statements, you'll need to add that to your calendar. Paid hires make the most sense when a company has a healthy revenue stream and needs to divide the workflow into several parts.

This is the traditional way of running a business. Most companies don't start hiring until they have reached a significant level of profitability. When you have a decent number of salaried employees, you will have to hire or promote managers to oversee them. When you need these types of leaders, you are nearing the time when the next scaling will make sense.

The Equity Hire

Equity hires are positions in which someone is brought on to take over some leadership aspects of the business. This can include management (e.g., operations oversight, salespeople oversight) who is responsible for ensuring results, such as deals closing or reaching sales numbers. It can also include growth management, such as hiring new agents, training new agents, or expanding your operation into more markets or different industries (e.g., title, loans, construction).

An equity hire is similar to bringing on a partner, but rather than just giving them a split of a commission, you are giving them a share of the company's profit. This can be purely monetary (e.g., they receive 20 percent of company profit as their salary) or more incentive based (they receive a percentage of the profitability of those they manage or oversee). This compensation model makes more sense at this level because you want your leaders to be incentivized by the performance of those they oversee. This is important because that is the same way *you* are compensated. You only do well when those in your company perform well.

By giving your leaders a share of the profits, you are tying their success or failure to your own. This maintains incentive for you to keep developing your leaders and incentive for them to continue leading in the way you want them to. This is the most expensive form of compensation—giving away company profits after all risk is accounted for—but it also has the highest upside. Developing leaders to help run your company instead of only piecemeal transactions can have monumental results for your business.

You'll need help growing your business to achieve its full potential, whether that's a partner getting a share of a deal, a paid hire getting an hourly wage, or an equity hire getting a share of company profitability. If you expand too early, you can end up losing revenue by hiring others before you have anything for them to do. If you hire too late, it can be catastrophic because you lose out on thousands and thousands of dollars in potential revenue. Learning to recognize when it's time to hire is a crucial part of being a top producer.

When You'll Need Help

The easiest way to know when you'll need help is when you run out of time to PLAN. If you can manage all your files, run all your marketing, show houses to your buyers, and check all the paperwork yourself while still consistently generating and following up with new leads, you don't need help. Once you start to sell a consistent number of houses—say two a month—you'll realize you can't keep up with consistent lead generation and do all the work of a transaction. If you want to build a big business, you're better off hiring sooner rather than later.

It's important to understand there will always be a part of you that will say, "I don't need help yet" or "I can still do this on my own." That part isn't always lying either. Theoretically, you can do it all on your own if you work hard enough. Practically speaking, you can always work sixteen-hour days to get everything done. This is what your subconscious will tell you when you are nervous to hire someone. While technically it may be true, is it wise counsel? Are you actually going to work sixteen-hour days to do it all? My guess is no. You'll end up doing the things you like. The easy things.

Now, when I say "easy" things, I don't necessarily mean they are easy to do. I mean that psychologically speaking, there is a much stronger temptation to do them. The easy things are those things that don't require you to step outside of your comfort zone. They don't force you to face rejection. They don't require you to up your game, be creative, or talk to another human being. This is especially true if you're an introvert. Consider someone who hates running. Let's say they allot themselves twenty minutes a day to get in a run. Taking fifteen minutes of that twenty-minute time period to stretch would be the easy thing to do.

It's much easier to sit in my office and review paperwork, answer emails, and look up houses on the MLS than to talk to someone. I know this won't get me more business, but I often push that thought out of my head and focus on what's right in front of me. It is way, way too easy to tell myself, "I have to get this done." It's a convenient replacement for "I need to go find a new client."

Easy things can be your biggest threat to success in real estate sales. If success is a by-product of pushing yourself out of your comfort zone, easy things stand in direct opposition to success. One of the most important things you can do in your commitment to yourself to be successful is to remove the temptation to do the easy things. I accomplished this by hiring an assistant as soon as I made the commitment to go full-time into real estate sales.

Pressure to Create Success

When I hired Krista, I did more than just hire an assistant. I added a lot of pressure to my business, but this pressure made it *easier* for me to focus on the "not easy things." The perfect antidote to not working on the easy things was to make a decision that hurt me if I gave into that temptation. Hiring Krista helped me in the following ways.

1. Krista was dependent on me to get a paycheck. If I didn't put people in contract, she had no transactions to manage. If I didn't find leads, she had no one to follow up with and no appointments to schedule for me. If I didn't take new listings, she had nothing to put into the MLS. Her job was a natural extension of mine. Like a branch, she needed a trunk to attach to. This pressure made it easier for me to go find leads.

2. My business was dependent on getting my money's worth out of that check. Krista's job was to do the things that I was tempted to do—the "non-PLAN" activities. If I fell to temptation and did them instead, what was I paying her to do? Nobody likes to waste money, and I was no exception. Hiring an assistant put the thought into my head, "I'm already paying someone else to do this." I had this thought every time I was tempted to do something myself, and this made it much easier to say "no" to myself.

3. My income expectations were tougher to meet when a good chunk of my revenue went toward Krista's salary. I had been making $10,000 a month selling one home, but now I was only making $5,000 after paying her. This meant either I had to accept a lower salary for myself or sell more houses. Guess which route I took? The added pressure to improve my quality of life drove me to lead-generate harder. If you can add pressure to yourself to make more money, it only makes it easier for you to accomplish your goals.

4. Once I got used to someone else doing the administrative side of the job, I could focus on the sales side, and my business took off. When all you worry about are sales, you get much better at them. At a certain point, they actually become fun. There is when lead generation is no longer uncomfortable because you've done it so often that you can anticipate how to answer the things you didn't know how to answer before. When it's no longer uncomfortable, you'll start to get a rush from it. After a few years of having assistants handle the administrative part of the job, all I want to do every day is generate leads. I still put the occasional buyer or seller into contract, but other than that it's all lead gen all day. Now that I've tasted this life, I can't see myself ever going back.

5. When Krista left her former job to work with me, it wasn't just to have a new, cool boss. It was a career move. I could see how much trust she had put in me to grow this business into an opportunity for her to really thrive, and I felt pressure to make that happen. This pressure made lead generation and lead follow-up much easier because each new lead became a potential opportunity to grow the business into something bigger where Krista could thrive, grow, and lead.

As you can see, hiring someone to help in your business makes it much easier for you to focus on what top-producing agents are supposed to do. Simply having someone else to do the work you are tempted to do when you should be looking for new clients is a powerful way to avoid the temptation to hide from your responsibilities. A solid way to know it's time to hire someone new is when you find yourself giving in to the temptation to take the easy route and avoiding your highest and best use: finding clients.

Lead Bleed

The easiest way to know it's time to find help is when you physically cannot keep up with leads you've already generated, let alone find new ones. For many agents, this is the tipping point where they finally admit they need to hire new people. There is no worse feeling than a seller telling you they listed with someone else because you did not get back to them in time or they got the impression you were too busy. Losing a listing hurts, but it also hurts to lose a buyer. Really, losing any client will hurt.

I remember when this first happened to me. It was ten o'clock at night, and I was trying to schedule showings for the weekend. Realtors weren't answering their phone or their emails that late, and deep inside I knew I had already blown it. I then got a text from a client asking why his house was still not on the MLS. He had emailed me about it two days earlier, but I never saw it. At that moment, I realized I needed to hire someone to keep up with this administrative work before it was too late.

Once I had help, I realized my thoughts of "I can't afford help" had been completely off. It turns out that I had been bleeding buyers for a long time. It was only a matter of weeks after I'd hired someone (Krista) to catch emails, answer the phone, and set appointments that my calendar was completely filled with buyer appointments. However, these weren't from lead generating—these were all the buyer leads I had missed before I had help. These were from social media direct messages, emails, and texts that I hadn't responded to. They turned into inquiries that led to appointments. It turns out a lot of people don't text, "Hey I want to buy a house!" They start with asking how it's going and only asking about housing later, which was something I didn't understand.

Suffice it to say, the commissions I had been missing out on were much higher than the salary I hadn't wanted to pay an assistant.

Have you ever noticed that when we focus on the negative ("I don't want to pay money"), it's easy to justify not taking action? My question to you is: What if instead you focused on the positive? What if you're losing money now by *not* having an assistant? How much are your lost leads costing you every month?

Team Chemistry

Consider four years from now. As you put the principles of this book into practice and take the required actions, each year you will make more money and get more sales. Your confidence will increase, and with it your skill and the size of your business. Your assistant will need to grow *with* you as this happens. If you wait until you are in dire straits for highly skilled help, think about how much business you will lose by then.

The problem is exponential. Every day we don't grow, don't push ourselves, and don't improve in our craft is a day that we lose money. When compounded over time, these losses become substantial. Our assistants need time to grow and learn just as much as we do; sometimes even more. It's better to hire early and let them get their feet underneath them before we ask them to run at the incredibly fast pace we'll need them to when we are doing a large volume of deals.

Understand that assistants are not robots. You won't hire one that is just plug-and-play. There is another factor in play here, and that's the chemistry between you and your assistant. This will matter nearly as much as their skill in performing the required tasks. Assistants are extensions of you. If the chemistry isn't there, the result won't be either.

Think about a professional sports team. If running a successful franchise were as simple as just hiring the best players, the team with the most money would win. Many times it is not the team with the highest payroll, or even the most individual talent itself, that wins. The best teams have the best chemistry among the players. They complement each other, make fewer mistakes, and perform as a powerful cohesive unit. The more a team trains together, the faster they'll develop chemistry. This principle will be true in your business as well. The better understanding your assistants have for what you need to be successful, the more effective they'll be in their role.

If your assistants have to ask, or even wonder, if something is "their job" or "your job," it can lead to a lack of confidence on their part. The longer you work with them, and the more directly you communicate your expectations and needs, the faster they'll know when to run with any task and when they need to wait for your direction. There's no substitution or any way to rush this process. You have to give everyone time to learn what's expected of them.

When there isn't chemistry, clients pick up on this—and it can be very bad. Conflicting messages, information, or even energy can give an already nervous lead second thoughts about moving forward with you. Imagine being a nervous firefighter on day one of your job and getting ready to run into a burning building. That's how new home buyers feel. Now imagine you're following the most confident person on the crew into the home. You're scared, but you feel comfort in their confidence. Now imagine that just as you're about to rush in, another firefighter looks scared to death. They look almost as concerned as you. Do you still want to run in there?

That's how it can feel when team members don't share the same energy and confidence. You will lose clients over this. Giving yourself time to train everyone and help them adjust to the cultural dynamics of your style or business is crucial. This is why waiting too long to hire can negatively affect your opportunities to build chemistry.

The last piece of advice I'll give for when to hire an assistant has to do with your energy levels. It's not just time you're getting back when you hire someone else. It's also energy.

When I hired Krista and heard her talk on the phone with clients, I quickly realized how much more pleasant, kind, and patient she was than me. At one point I actually thought, "I would rather hear this news from Krista than from me." I knew then she could help me in major ways. I started looking for the tasks that drained me of energy and had Krista do them instead.

For me, all of this involves clear communication. Any time I had to call an agent to ask for just one piece of information or call a client to advise them of something, I would put it off. My brain loves solving problems and handling conflict/tough situations. It does not naturally like small talk or sharing emotions (although, as I mentioned earlier in the book,

I've learned to do it because it's part of the job). Any time I had to do something I didn't like, a small part of me would feel like it died inside. Too many of those in a day and I was pretty much depleted and useless.

Krista was a huge help to me when she took over things that drained me of energy. Calling clients to schedule things, reviewing inspection reports with them, deciding on which color of paint to use in the kitchen—these are all things an agent needs to do with their client. It just wasn't a great fit for *me* to be the one doing it. Krista was way better at it. When she took over that part of the job, it allowed me to preserve my energy for the parts she hated, which were sales, lead generation, reading the other side in a negotiation, and tracking numbers. Giving me back my energy allowed me to focus on growing the business.

How to Find Help

Admitting you need help is the first step. Knowing when is the second and knowing where to find it comes third. Finding, training, and keeping good help is not easy. Although I've found that leveraging other people to help grow my business has increased my success exponentially, it is also much harder to do than simply learning how to be a good agent myself. When you're learning to be a top producer, you are in complete control. You determine your habits, the skills you need, and the work pace required of you.

When we make progress in any new area of life, there comes a time when we must accept that we cannot continue to be who we were if we want to be successful in this new endeavor. Most people need to endure some level of pain before they are willing to do so, and some people make this change faster than others. The common element is this is a personal decision, and we control when we make it.

When you move from "me" to "us," you lose some control over when progress happens. Previously, it was completely in your hands. Now, you need those you have partnered with to make decisions. It is at this point when hard work is no longer enough to get by. You must add the skill of influence to your repertoire. If you want others to submit to the process of change, you have to make it easier for them to do so. This is much different than when you only had yourself in the equation.

Does this mean you should not try to scale? Absolutely not. Scaling is worth it. In the same way you realized making the jump to top-producer status was worth the sacrifice you made, learning to lead and provide opportunities for others will feel just as worthy. My point here is you should start preparing yourself now for a difficult road. If you expect hiring and managing people to be as easy as taking a listing, you'll be disappointed. Think about it more like the first time you ever tried to take a listing and were competing against other Realtors. Did you feel confident then? No. Real estate sales felt hard. This will too.

Until you learn it, of course. Then, just like everything else you've accomplished in life, you'll gain traction and confidence in your new skill set and reap the rewards for your hard work. When you learned sales, you weren't just learning how to sell a house. You were also learning how to find a lead, how to spot a motivated client, how to sell yourself (and by that, I mean paint a picture or cast a vision for what an end result can look like), and how to build and stick to a process or system. These translated into running a business.

Consider the following when putting together a game plan to build a team.

How to Spot Talent

In my office we have the following sign on the wall.

THE VALUE OF TALENT IN A ROLE	
Non-Talent	**Talent**
Brings you problems.	Finds solutions.
Doesn't fulfill your needs and ends up giving you back your job.	Shares your goals and fulfills your needs as a natural by-product of fulfilling their own.
Doesn't know what they want and isn't searching.	Knows what they want or is actively searching to know.
Requires pushing.	Pushes you.
May not know where the existing bar is set or even what bar you're talking about.	Is continually raising the bar.
Doesn't care who they spend time with and repels talent from them.	Demands to be associated with talent and attracts talent to them.
When they try to talk action and results, they can't back it up.	Talks the language of action and results.

The sign comes from the Keller Williams training curriculum and speaks to how to spot talent. In real estate sales, talent is not athletic ability, charm, or even IQ. In this world, talent is a mindset. It's not so much about whether you are talented or not. It's about if you act and think like talent does. I love this world because anyone can choose to be talent.

But not everyone will.

Most people you come across will not think like talent. In fact, you won't have to go much further than the first item on the list to find a reason to disqualify someone. Don't believe me? Just turn on the news or listen to people speaking around you. The majority of people are addicted to bringing problems rather than finding solutions. Almost every job you've had is full of people complaining about the problem. It's rare to find someone focused on bringing a solution.

You won't always recognize when someone is finding a solution as opposed to bringing a problem, at least not until you've trained yourself in this skill. But you'll learn to recognize the feeling you get when someone displays talent. They are the little feelings of hope, excitement, and optimism you get when in the presence of someone who wants to make sure they do the right thing and who shows they care about the role they play in the relationship you have with them.

The feeling is wonderful. It lifts you up and instantly attracts you to and bonds you to that person. When you get that feeling, pay close attention. Ask yourself if it's because they were acting like talent. If so, you've just spotted what you're looking for.

Talent is everywhere. The trick is to train yourself to know when you feel it.

How to Attract Talent

The sixth line down reads that talent "Demands to be associated with talent and attracts talent to them." This could be described as "like attracts like." I've stated this several times before as "rock stars know rock stars." When someone thinks in a positive, confident, talented manner, they find themselves drawn to others who do the same—and are repelled by those who don't.

The point is, when you develop a talent mindset, other talented people will find you. This won't look like someone knocking on your door and begging for a job. But if they do, you'll have to let them know what you're looking for. The good news is if you make your requests and expectations clear, many talented people will be excited at the thought of working for you.

Make it a habit in social media posts to comment that you are always looking for talented people to help you grow. When you meet someone and like their attitude, ask them if they've ever considered working in real estate. Plant those seeds, then give them the opportunity to see what it's like to be around you. Let your own talent shine.

When you see that restaurant server with the helpful attitude, try to befriend them. When the bank teller goes above and beyond for you, see if you can get their contact information. Be specific about bringing as much value as you can into these people's lives and then sit back and watch as the law of reciprocity works to return the favor to you. You can draw talent to you by making a focused, concerted effort to be more talented yourself.

Where to Look for Talent

Seek out people who set themselves apart by looking for solutions when others don't. You can do this anywhere: at a restaurant, at the movies, in the mall, at a theme park. People with the talent mindset are everywhere if you know what to look for. You may take the following examples for granted every day. Teach yourself to key in on them.

- The server at the restaurant who recommends something based on a comment you made or question you asked.
- The salesperson who makes sure the product you get is one that will really work for you or makes additional recommendations.
- The front desk worker who comes up with a creative solution to your problem.
- The supervisor in an office who values your time or wants to give you the best service possible.
- The loan officer who has ideas outside the box.
- The title officer who takes responsibility for finding ways to close the deal on time.

Most talented people have been noticed by peers or supervisors and are often in roles with more responsibility and possibly with more opportunities. This is a "cheat" code you can use to shorten your search. Look for the go-to person when something goes wrong, and that person is much more likely to be talent.

The key is to recognize when their current work world can't afford them the opportunity a talented mind wants and needs. For years I was the top waiter at the restaurants I worked in. I was constantly looking for more responsibility, more opportunity, more money. I always felt frustrated that I couldn't find it. It was only later in life when I realized the problem wasn't my boss. It was the restaurant world. There simply were not enough opportunities for me in that environment. I had already reached the top. I needed to find a new world.

I was hired by a sheriff's office, started at the police academy, and found the new world I was looking for. I often wonder what would have been different if a smart, top-producing agent had found me and offered me a job. How far could I have gotten with the right world to operate in?

As a top producer, you have that opportunity. You can change someone's life by having them work with you. Don't worry if they already have a supervisory position. Worry about if you can provide a better world for them.

How to Lead Talent

This part is usually the toughest because most of us can't even lead ourselves. That's why we aren't as successful as we should be. After we do learn to lead ourselves, learn to set a plan, and learn to stick to it, we find success isn't far behind. One of the most dangerous things we can do at that point is to get comfortable in that place and stop leading ourselves. A by-product of leading ourselves is success, but it's sad if that's the only person we ever lead well.

When you learn to lead yourself, you deserve the fruits of your labor (e.g., success, more money). But once you've tasted those fruits, wouldn't you want that for others too? There is a world of people out there who want to take the same journey you did. A journey full of pain, frustration, growth, and overcoming. And a journey with victory. Just like me waiting at that restaurant for someone to invite me into something more, there is a country full of people who want the same.

Leading others means helping them overcome the same things you had to overcome. They may not have the same problems or character flaws as you, but the process and the journey are the same. Once you've experienced victory over the parts of you that held you back (e.g., self-limiting beliefs, lack of discipline, fear), you now can help others to take on their challenges. When you help someone else find their potential, it's gratifying. In addition to that, it can be lucrative.

People have a strong sense of loyalty to those who help them in big ways. We see this in the movies all the time. Some reluctant hero saves the life of an important person. Then that important person pledges their life to the service of the one who saved them. This theme shows up in life too. Humans are wired to help those who look out for and help them. When you intervene in someone's life and bring them opportunity, they are much more likely to give back to you and your business for years to come. Again, it's the law of reciprocity.

Leading talent is also about providing direction. When I was waiting for someone to give me a chance, I felt like a Ferrari with an engine revving at 1500 rpm just *idling* for someone to put me in gear and let me out on the open road. I knew how to work hard, and I had a strong drive. There was just nowhere to go. Leaders provide the road their followers will walk (or hopefully, drive).

Leading talent means creating systems, structure, and defined roles for talent to operate in. This does take time, but so does everything else you're doing. Nothing says you have to do this in six months. Start slowly and build up from there. As you get better at finding talent, your business will start to grow and so will your revenue. Just like learning to become a top producer took time to figure out, so will this. The difference is that finding, attracting, and leading talent can take you from agent to top-producing agent to a rock star agent who makes millions of dollars a year while working only as much as you wish.

Win-Win Propositions

Hiring good people to partner with is important. So is keeping them. You don't want to find yourself on a never-ending cycle of searching for, finding, hiring, training, and managing talent—just to have them leave you because you could not lead them well or provide the opportunity they were looking for. There are several reasons a partner or employee will leave your business, and several reasons you'll have to let them go. The common element in all of these scenarios is when the outcome is not a "win–win" proposition.

Win–wins are twice as tough as a single win. Getting a win for even one person can be hard enough, so if you have to find a way for both sides to win, it's going to take a purposeful, concentrated, and carefully planned effort. If the deal is not a win for you, it's not a win for your partner either because eventually you will have to let them go. If the deal is a win for you but not for them, eventually you will lose as well because they will leave the partnership or lose motivation to stay productive. If the deal is not a win for both parties, it ends up being a loss for both parties.

How to Make Sure It's a Win for You

For the relationship to be a win for you, it must improve your business. This can happen in three ways.

1. You make more money.
2. You spend less time.
3. You spend less effort.

Let's go over the various ways a partner can help you in any of these three ways.

You Make More Money. Someone can make you more money in two ways:

1. They bring more revenue into the company.
2. They bring an asset or skill set into the business that allows *you* to make the company more money.

When you look at a new hire from this lens, you can make a quick determination if they are or aren't bringing revenue into your company. We only want to hire, partner with, and keep those who help make our business more profitable.

First let's look at those who bring more revenue into the company. Different positions in a company can help make the company money in different ways. Outside/inside sales agents help bring in new leads. Buyers/listing agents help bring in new leads and convert them to revenue. When you hire a salesperson, you are judging their performance based on how much revenue they directly produce. This is easily measured by tying closed sales to the agent or salesperson who produced it and reviewing these numbers at the end of every month.

Then there are those who bring an asset or skill into the business that allows you to make the company more money. When you hire support positions, you judge them based on how efficiently they handle the administrative tasks. Transaction coordinators, showing assistants, personal assistants, and other general administrative positions are supposed to take on tasks that allow the salespeople to focus on sales. As the primary salesperson in your company, you're looking for the same thing.

If a partnership is going to be a win for you, it has to allow you to make more money for your company. If your partner or hire does not make it easier for others to increase revenue, you have to let them go. This results in a loss for you in time, money, and energy spent on training them.

You Spend Less Time. A new hire or partner can benefit you and your company by saving you time. This time is then spent by you generating new business (i.e., leverage) or enjoying leisure time (i.e., luxury). This is the spirit behind the admin hire. Admins typically do not bring in new sales or revenue. Instead, they do the tasks required to collect the revenue a salesperson has created. The value they bring is in the time they save salespeople, who then focus on revenue-generating tasks.

For example, showing assistants save you time by showing homes for buyer's agents (i.e., the most time-consuming tasks of working with buyers). This allows buyer agents more time to prospect, follow up with leads, attend appointments, and negotiate deals (PLAN). When looking to partner with other agents to help with administrative tasks or to work with buyers, focus on finding people who can take the most time-intensive tasks off your plate, specifically those that do not produce revenue.

You Spend Less Effort. As just noted, you can make sure it's a win for you by hiring people to take over the tasks that drain you the most. Some tasks you want to keep may take more physical time to complete, but you enjoy them. These types of tasks aren't an effort. Instead, they can energize and invigorate you, making you more motivated to lead-generate and close deals. Consider the feeling of giving a new client their keys or dropping off a closing gift. Many agents love this moment because it juices them up, making them more likely to lead-generate for new clients to get that feeling again. This is an example of a task that takes time but that makes sense to do it yourself.

Other tasks may not take a lot of time to complete but they drain you. This could be calling home inspectors to ask questions about foundation concerns, uploading files into a database, or looking up comparable sales on the MLS. We all have tasks that are better suited for our personalities than others. By having others do these tasks, you can reserve that energy and redirect it into the parts of your business that bring in the most revenue.

Ask yourself: What tasks drain me the most? This isn't hard to figure out; you know exactly how you feel when you have to do them. Hire someone to do them for you ASAP. This is an easy way to make hiring someone a win–win for you and a new employee.

How to Make Sure It's a Win for Them

Those you hire need to feel like it's a win for them as well. If it's not, after you've trained and invested in them, they'll leave you. Learning how to make it a win for others is an important skill set to develop, and it takes time to get it right. The following three factors can help make it a win for those you hire into your business.

1. What they earn
2. What they learn
3. What skills they gain

What They Earn. The vast majority of people will be primarily concerned with what they earn. This is a by-product of the W-2 mindset most people have because it's all they've known. This does make it simple for you, as it's easy to say, "I will pay you X amount of money to do Y jobs." Paying someone enough will be an important part of making it a win for them.

You don't want to overpay them because it will stunt their desire to grow and improve in your business—something you'll no doubt want them to do. Finding the point where they make enough to pay their bills but not enough to have everything they want in life is the sweet spot. It creates the perfect mix of tension and safety that people need to get the most out of themselves.

What They Learn. What staff learn is actually a bigger component of how much money they'll make in the end. Showing houses and being paid per house is one way for an employee to earn money. It will pale in comparison, however, to how much money they can earn if they learn to work with and close buyers. Highlighting to hiring candidates what they will learn, and more specifically what you will teach them, is a powerful tool to show them how working for you will be a win for them.

In my company, I highlight a path where employees can grow with each task if they learn to do it as well I do it. Learning each of these tasks is usually accompanied by a pay raise, which keeps them motivated. But an even bigger value to them is that they are one step closer to taking over an entire arm of my business (say, working with a buyer directly) as well as growing in their own confidence and their ability to generate leads from their own sphere. A team member who can close my deals as well as generate a healthy number of leads on their own is on a path to a lucrative position in my company.

What Skills They Gain. In addition to the tasks they will learn, they'll also learn new skills. How to enter, run, and save a CMA is an example of a learned task. Learning how to *interpret* that CMA and how to secure a signed listing agreement is an example of a skill they've gained. Skills take more time, more practice, and more dedication to learn. Once learned, though, they have a much bigger impact on someone's bottom line.

In real estate sales, most skills are learned through experience. Presenting information to clients, interpreting market data, calming client fears, and selling yourself as the authority are all powerful skills to develop that lead to big money. It will take years before employees learn how to do this well, assuming they learn at all. But working with you will significantly increase their learning speed and learning curve. And that time and energy spent will benefit you when those skills are then used in your business and you receive a chunk of their revenue.

Real estate sales is different than almost any other job. It's not just knowing "what to do," like most jobs require. It's also knowing "how to do it" well. If you don't develop your skill sets in this industry, you will find yourself losing out to more skilled agents. Your ability as a leader to train, hone, and develop the skills of those working with you makes it a win–win for both you and your staff.

How to Ensure Mutual Growth

Win–Win Is Grow–Grow

The best way to ensure it is a win for both parties is to constantly incentivize those you hire to make more money and create a better life for themselves by growing along a path similar to the one you took. If your staff doesn't grow, you'll be stuck doing low-paying tasks in your own company. This makes you a slave to your business and stops you from achieving passive income status. In addition to that, if you keep growing but your staff does not, you'll bring in more leads than your company has the capacity to handle. This will leave you spread thin and unable to provide a high level of customer service because you've outgrown your staff's ability to handle new leads.

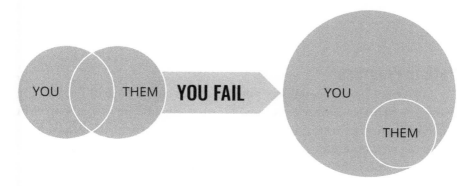

This will lead to your business failing as you personally crumble under the demands of your company and become a victim of your own success. While this is bad, the other alternative is even worse.

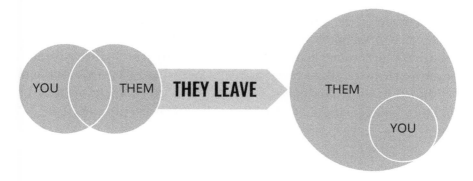

In this example, those you bring into your company outgrow you and the opportunity you can provide them.

If you don't continue to grow, you won't be able to provide them with new opportunities *as they grow.* When your showing assistants are ready to start working with buyers and putting them in contract, they'll leave you unless you have a steady stream of buyers. Then you'll be stuck hiring and training new showing assistants. Business leaders always have to be growing. If you don't, your employees will outgrow you—and eventually leave.

The ideal situation is one in which you push your staff to grow while they simultaneously empower you to do the same. The first way to make it a win–win is to ensure both parties are growing together. Win–win is grow–grow.

Path to Progress

To ensure win–win scenarios, you have to create a path of growth for those you bring into your company. This helps establish a steady stream of leaders gaining in skill and experience to help manage the issues your company will inevitably encounter. It will provide them a path to higher levels of responsibility—and higher levels of pay. Everyone likes clear directions on where they are going and how they can get there. If you can provide this, you'll create a sound value to your team members who are looking to make big money in real estate.

A path to progress should be shown to applicants. It includes the entry-level position for the new hire as well as the next steps in line. It can be a part of a bigger diagram, such as your overall organizational chart. You then zoom in on the individual steps needed to move up the ranks. The applicant will see the clear path to progress within your company and the required skill sets and expected results. This will draw high performers to you and help the others recognize right away that isn't the job for them. By showing this to candidates, you make your expectations quite clear, and they know their results determine their forward progress.

Organization Chart

My company's overall organizational chart currently looks like this.

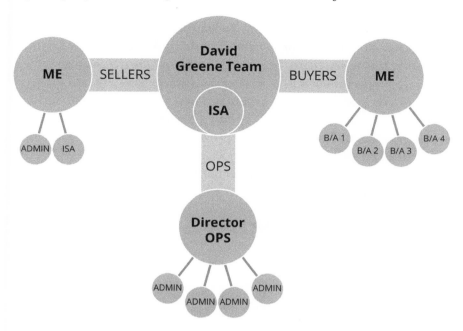

In the center is the company itself (David Greene Team). This is where the majority of leads are generated. It's the origin point for vision, leadership, and structure, and it is filled with agents who have become so successful that they have become directors in my company.

To the left are the listing agents. I manage them with the help of one admin and an ISA (Inside Sales Agent). My ISA contacts seller leads, fills out lead intake forms, runs a CMA, calls active and pending comparable properties to gather market data, and schedules and prepares me for listing appointments.

After a listing is signed, it's given to the OPS (Operations) department to prepare for market. On the bottom you see my Operations staff. The director of OPS is Krista, my senior hire, who oversees three admin positions (transaction coordinator/admin hybrids), who ensure contracts become closings. The transaction coordinator/admins also manage the client database, ensure legal compliance, and handle other administrative tasks.

To the right are the home buyers. Buying is more complicated than selling because the process has more moving parts. At the top is me (I currently still represent the buyers I bring in). Beneath me are four buyer agents (B/As). I give some an entire lead while others only help with communication, finding properties, inquiring about them, and setting appointments to see them. For the B/As who handle the majority of our clients, I support them with showing assistants.

Once you understand my organizational chart, the path to success becomes easier to understand. The entry-level positions assist the more senior positions, allowing them to grow in experience and skills until they can be promoted to a senior position themselves.

The following are the organizational charts broken down by individual paths to progress.

Showing Assistant to Buyer Agent

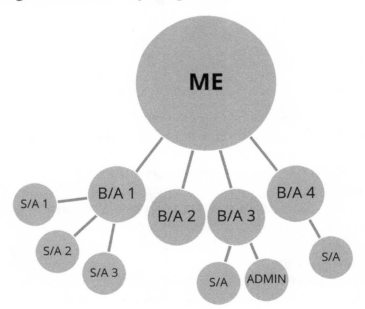

Showing assistants show homes to clients, attend inspections and walk-throughs, find comparable sales, and conduct other time-consuming tasks. Showing assistants allow B/As to work with a larger number of buyers. This position allows brand-new agents the opportunity to learn, grow, and develop their skill sets while also training under more experienced agents and earning some money doing so.

Showing assistants need repetition to develop their confidence and industry knowledge. When a new agent must find their own leads, it significantly slows down their learning process. It's a recipe for disaster when the only way you can learn is through experience, but you can't get experience because you can't find clients because you don't have experience.

My model allows showing agents to learn both from clients they show homes to and the more experienced buyer agents they are working with. Are you a new agent looking for a mentor? Here's the perfect arrangement to find one. My showing assistants get paid a portion of the commission when the deal closes. So do my buyer agents. I have created a system where my more experienced agents help the newer ones learn, and the newer agents help the more experienced ones earn more money. Want to know the best part? It's not all on *my* shoulders to train and manage everyone.

As S/As learn the industry and grow in confidence, they start getting more leads out of their own spheres and their own efforts. With success, they are eventually promoted to full-time B/As. After they have built up a decent volume for themselves, they earn the right to have their own showing assistants. This model allows the B/As to continually scale their business while teaching others the same things they were taught. Want to make sure your employees never leave you after they learn the job? Create an ecosystem like this.

Eventually buyer agents are promoted to the top of the food chain (as directors within the "Me" bubble) where they oversee several buyer agents of their own, who all have their own showing assistants.

Administration to Management

The most junior position in my organization chart is an intern. When someone approaches me who wants to work real estate sales but has no training, no experience, and no license, it usually means they have no value to offer either. While this isn't always the case, you should be leery about paying someone who can't bring an equal or greater value to your company. When this is the case, consider making them an intern and giving them the opportunity to earn themselves a job.

I primarily use this method with those who are studying to get their license and want to learn the business while they are waiting for the test. This is a win–win. Many people will pay a large sum of money to learn a trade. Offering an intern the chance to learn without having to pay anything is a definite win for them. And it's a win for me because I can train someone with relatively low financial risk and then see how they work before I give them a position on my team.

After an intern has obtained their license and shown they can help us reach our goals, they transition into the position of agent, showing assistant, or administrative staff. These are paid positions in which the employee supports the agents. Admin are encouraged, but not required, to bring in referrals and additional business. They are the backbone of the team and play a much larger role than most would think from the outside looking in.

Those who stand apart in the quality of their work and their leadership abilities are promoted to become a supervisor of a department. Krista, my director of operations, is one example of this. They earn more money than an admin because they are now recruiting, hiring, and training; or overseeing operations, revenue distribution, and bookkeeping; or other administratively important functions.

Buyer Agent to Seller Agent. For the buyer agents who have their own showing assistants and eventually their own buyer agents working under them, they now transition to listings (selling) and let those they supervise manage the buyer agents. The best seller agents are those who can look at a listing from a buyer's point of view and see what buyers will see. This makes it a natural progression. Buyer agents who have handled a large number of buyers tend to have developed a high level of emotional intelligence required to succeed in managing both people and listings.

The transition from buyer agent to seller agent isn't without difficulty. Seller agents have to be skilled with numbers and having difficult conversations with stubborn sellers. Buyer agents often succeed with buyers without much conflict, but this is different with seller agents working with sellers. For this reason, it's easier to transition to a seller agent after being a buyer agent with several B/As working under them. This helps thicken their skin and prepare them for the challenges and obstacles listing agents face.

Agent to Director. The ultimate path of progress is that from agent to director (the top position on the previous graphic). When an agent has so much success that they have ascended to the portion of my org chart in the middle (DGT), they are ready not only to work with clients but also to manage an entire business of employees, clients, and interns. When you recruit extremely talented people into your company, you shouldn't worry about them outshining or leaving you. Instead, you should worry about how you can create a world so big they never want to leave.

When agents show success in closing deals, managing those underneath them, and recruiting new talent to work in the company, it makes sense to offer them the opportunity to run a division of your company in a different area. If you don't need to grow in that way, you can consider promoting them to be the CEO of your current business and walking away to pursue other business opportunities or retire early. The path of agent to director is the toughest to accomplish. This makes it the most valuable step.

These paths to progress show candidates what they can expect as far as promotions go and my commitment to their growth in professionalism, skills, and earnings. They learn that they eventually help me recruit new talent to grow the business *and* that they aren't stuck forever in an entry-level position or won't be "taken advantage of."

If you are a top producer but have yet to hire your first help—or you are not yet a top producer but you are committed to being one—I challenge you to take a moment right now, fill out your future company's org chart, and post it on social media for me (and everyone else) to see. (Tag me @DavidGreene24.) This can be a powerful exercise in giving your subconscious something to strive toward, but there are practical benefits as well. A good organizational chart can double as an overview path to progress (as mine did here for you) and can create a detailed explanation of each role in the company.

People follow leaders, and leaders cast vision.

 # KEY POINTS

- If you hire too early, you might lose revenue. If you hire too late, you might lose potential revenue.
- The partnership hire splits up the tasks, and the partner is paid part of a commission rather than a salary.
- The paid hire involves more risk (paying salary), but is cheaper than the partner.
- The equity hire is similar to a partner, but they are paid a share of the company's profit.
- The time to find help is when you physically cannot keep up with your leads or generate new ones.
- Anything that is not PLAN should be leveraged to administrative support.

- Someone can make you more money in two ways: They bring in more revenue into the company or they bring in an asset or skill set that earns revenue.
- Give yourself time to train everyone and help them adjust to the cultural dynamics of your style, or business.
- Your business must continue to grow as your staff grows.
- A win–win is when both parties grow together.
- Show applicants your organizational chart.

CHAPTER TEN

LISTING LIKE A PRO

*"The path of mastering something is the combination of
not only doing the best you can do at it, but also doing it
the best it can be done."*

—GARY KELLER

In his wildly popular book *The Millionaire Real Estate Investor*, Gary Keller lays out the three pillars of a successful real estate business: leads, listings, and leverage. This chapter will cover how to use all three to help you reach and solidify yourself as a top producer.

Finding listings is the highest-dollar activity you conduct in real estate sales. Working with sellers takes less time than buyers, requires less emotional hand-holding, and does more for your marketing and advertising than working with buyers. A listing leads to a new listing or a new buyer much more than a buyer does. You can scale the listing side of your business exponentially faster and more easily than you can scale working with buyers. This is why many top producers choose to work only with sellers. Sellers take less time and generate more leads.

This isn't the only reason you want to prioritize working with sellers. Sellers give you more control over the process and more profitability than buyers. Buyer agents are beholden to accepting whatever commission the listing agent has already negotiated. (In my market, the standard is 2.5 percent—and oftentimes even less than that.) Listing agents have the luxury of negotiating their own salary in a deal. This control makes it much easier to run a profitable business than relying on the work of someone else to determine your pay.

A listing is easier to leverage. As a buyer's agent, leveraging help in the transaction is difficult, requires a lot of prep work, and depends on you finding talented and friendly people. In an escrow, the buyer's agent does most of the work. However, working with sellers relies more on research and administrative tasks, so it is easier to find help as they won't have as much contact with the clients themselves. You get more time back, and make more money, with sellers.

In addition to these factors, working with listings sharpens your trade skills. It is the listing agent who has to see things from the eyes of an appraiser when choosing the price to list the home. It's also the listing agent who has to consider making repairs on their listing before putting it up for sale. This forces them to understand the cost of repairs, what buyers want/care about, and how buyers will respond when they read the inspection reports. Working with listings forces you to tighten up your understanding of real estate. Your friendly, warm personality won't draw attention away from your lack of knowledge or experience.

Taking listings will:
- Make you more money.
- Be easier to scale.
- Take less of your time.
- Lead to new leads.
- Build your brand faster.
- Give you more control over your business.
- Be easier to leverage.
- Force you to learn more about the factors that affect a real estate market.
- Sharpen your skills with evaluating homes.
- Make it easier for you to build a team.

If you want a big business, you'll need to be good at taking listings and getting them sold.

The Skills You'll Need

Good listing agents make their clients feel like they are the right agent for the job. Most sellers will have a lot of questions, but they are really looking for a feeling. Sellers want to feel like you can sell their house quickly, easily, and for more money. Each seller requires a different approach to get that feeling, but they're all looking for the same thing. If you can give it to them, they'll hire you.

The tools we use to take listings and the process I've laid out here are designed to give the seller that feeling. If you want to make things easier for yourself, start with recognizing the necessary skills. As they become sharper, your success will come faster, more easily, and more frequently.

Confidence

All top producers need confidence, but it's an especially important trait when working with sellers. A seller is choosing a champion to go to war for them. They are expecting you to guide and prepare them through the process. More importantly, they want to know you'll fight for them. If they feel you're a pushover, unsure of yourself, or uncommitted to negotiating on their behalf (read: making them money), they won't choose you as their agent.

The confidence you show is how people will perceive you. When you contact a listing lead, be forward and confident. Take charge of the conversation, ask them the relevant questions you'll need to know, and set an appointment with them right away. When you arrive for the appointment, continue to display confidence. Make statements like "I can't wait to sell your home for you" and "I'm going to absolutely love selling this home." If they sense you want it, they will also sense you have the confidence to do the job. Nobody can display confidence if they have doubts about their skill sets.

Directness

A hallmark of confidence is directness. When someone is indirect, it's usually a sign they are unsure of their abilities. When you look someone right in the eye, answer questions honestly, and have a clear plan in place, it inspires confidence in your clients.

Listing leads will ask you questions related to their own fears. Direct answers will help quell those fears and make it easier for them to trust you. Consider the difference in the following responses:

Question: "Do you think my house will sell?"

Indirect answer: "Uh . . . that's the million-dollar question, right? I sure hope it does. It really just depends on the market, I guess. If we can find a good buyer, I think, yeah. It will probably sell."

Direct answer: "If I did not think your house would sell, I would not be committing my own time, energy, or money into it. Many sellers don't realize it, but agents invest quite a bit of money into every listing we take. If the property does not sell, I lose everything. I only take listings I firmly believe will sell, and I'm confident I'm going to sell this house for you. I'm actually very eager to get started."

Question: "How do I know we'll get the best price?"

Indirect answer: "Well, I can't really control what price the buyers give, but I sure hope we get a good one! I'll recommend to the buyers that they write their offers at their highest and best price. Then, we can look at all the offers and pick the one that's highest. If we don't get a good offer, we can always just wait longer."

Direct answer: "Because you have me negotiating for you, that's why. The reason you hire me is because I am very good at negotiating. I know the market, understand what buyers want, and will position your property to be just that for them. Before I even bring you an offer, I will already have negotiated it with the buyer's agent to get every last dollar I can. I will make you more negotiating for you than you'll be paying me to do the job."

It is difficult to create the feeling a seller needs to decide to list with you if you aren't direct with them. Indirect answers convey a desire for the agent to protect themselves from disappointing the client. They are given with their own best interest in mind, not the client's. If you can't be direct, it's likely you are unprepared for your appointment.

This applies to more than just your client. It also applies to the buyer agents you'll be negotiating with. When I represent a buyer and I call the listing agent, I listen intently to determine how confident that agent is that they will get a better offer than mine. If the agent is to the point, I interpret that as a position of strength and advise my client accordingly. If they are vague, it usually reveals a lack of promising interest in their listing. These are the times I advise my clients to write a much lower offer.

Conflict Resolution

Buyer agents tend to diffuse conflict or even avoid it. Listing agents don't have that luxury. When you are at a listing appointment, you will find yourself in direct conflict with the sellers several times until a resolution is reached. If you are uncomfortable in these types of situations, you will back down, and that will make your job more difficult. The issues of contention are:

- **Price.** The sellers will want to price higher, but you will want to price at a fair market value. If there is a range of fair market value, they will want to be on the high side, and you will want to be on the low side.
- **Commitment.** The seller won't want to commit to a long time to sell the house with you. They may not want to commit to using you at all. Conversely, you will want a longer period of time on the listing agreement to sell the home and an exclusive right to sell.
- **Control.** The seller will often tell you how to do your job. This will include how to market and describe their house and what to do to sell it. You will want to use your expertise.
- **Commission.** Your sellers will want to pay as little as possible, and you will want to make as much as possible.
- **Communication.** Your sellers will want instant access to you (read: whenever their emotions flare up). You, on the other hand, will want professional standards of communication and your personal boundaries respected.

These are just a few of the areas where your interests and your client's interests will not automatically align. Your job is to create a win–win compromise where you can do your job effectively and efficiently and they are satisfied with the result they get. You create this new environment by setting appropriate expectations, getting buy-in from the client, and establishing a plan to follow. You'll need conflict resolution skills to do this well.

Leadership

Leaders have vision; it's why people follow them. Listing agents are leaders. They are controlling a process, organizing a schedule, setting a price, and negotiating a deal. As a real estate agent, you are a fiduciary acting on your client's behalf, and they are paying you to do that. They won't be comfortable with that decision unless they trust your ability to lead them.

There are many ways to display leadership without being loud or forceful. Many leaders are soft-spoken and thoughtful, and when they do speak it's powerful. Being a leader is about creating a plan, believing in it, and being unafraid to follow it. If you display these characteristics to your seller leads, they'll become your seller clients.

Determining List Price

Choosing the list price for your property is one of the most difficult—but most important—skills for a listing agent to master. If you go too high, you set yourself up for failure. Most clients will blame you when the house doesn't sell. If you choose too low, you may lose out to another agent who gave them a higher price or cause the sellers to lose their confidence that you can make them as much money as possible. Agents are often considered lazy when they propose a price that is too low.

To choose the perfect price and keep your clients from questioning your decision-making abilities, create a CMA (explained in the next section) and then interpret it for your clients. When done correctly, this will impress your clients with your professionalism and skill, empower you as the leader in the relationship, and make it easier for your clients to trust your capability to lead them to a sale.

Have a list price in mind before your listing presentation with the seller. If you don't, you'll appear to be unprepared, not in control, and lacking an actionable plan.

Create a CMA

A CMA is a list of active, pending, and sold properties. You can typically create one using your local MLS search feature. Some MLSs have a CMA feature that automatically creates this search for you when you enter the property's address. The ideal CMA will have between ten and twenty-five properties. When putting one together, there are several key components to use to find comparable properties, including:

1. **Location (neighborhood).** When choosing the location for your CMA, you ideally want to keep it specific to the neighborhood of the subject property. When there are not enough available properties in this area, expand your search. When that doesn't work, use the entire city. Most MLSs have a "radius search" option. It will draw a radius around the subject property and only show properties that fall within this radius (you choose the size of the radius). This option is convenient but lacks accuracy. Sometimes this radius will cross over borders into different neighborhoods, and the properties that show up will not be good comparable properties.

   A better option is to physically draw on a map the area you want included in the search. This way you can eliminate areas with different school scores or those located on the wrong side of the freeway. Once you've determined the area, you can move on to the next component of the CMA.

2. **Size.** A good rule of thumb is to start your search looking for properties that are 10 percent bigger and 10 percent smaller than your subject property. This means that on a 2,000-square-foot house, your search would include all properties that are between 1,800 and 2,200 square feet (200 square feet each way, which is 10 percent of 2,000 square feet). If there are not enough properties that match these criteria, expand to 20 percent in each direction, then 30 percent, and so on until you reach the appropriate number of comparable properties.

3. **Amenities.** After the search has found the comparable properties, start to eliminate properties with amenities different than yours. If your home doesn't have a pool but other comparable properties on the CMA do, this may create a false impression to the sellers that their house is worth more than it is. The same is true for properties with views, workspaces, oversized lots, and other amenities.

   When your property has amenities that other properties don't, leave those properties in the CMA. This makes it easier for you to justify a higher price than the other homes on the list, and the sellers will never complain about that.

4. **Bedroom/Bathroom Count.** Try to eliminate properties that have more bedrooms or bathrooms than your property. While these factors don't necessarily affect the appraised value as much as most people think, they are still important to consider when buyers are creating their searches for properties. Most buyers base their search on the minimum number of bedrooms their family will need. If you have a three-bedroom home, those looking for a minimum of four bedrooms won't see it in their search.

Research/Due Diligence

Your next step is research. It's easy to run a CMA to show your prospective clients. It's also lazy. Before I go to my listing presentation, I call every agent with a pending or active listing as well as those who recently sold. I talk to the agents and put notes from my calls on my CMA to review with the seller. This demonstrates how much work I've already done as well as my level of dedication. Consider asking for the following information when speaking with the agents you call.

Active Listings. Ask the agents how many showings they are getting and what kind of feedback they are receiving. This is the only way to get a solid idea of how many buyers are looking at homes in a given market—buyers don't register anywhere to show they are looking. You have to find out this information with creative methods like this. I also ask the agents if they feel they priced the house appropriately or if they would change the price if they could go back in time. When agents tell me they feel they priced the home a little too high, it tells me they were overly optimistic. I don't want to make that same mistake. When they tell me they are getting a lot of showings/multiple offers and wish they had listed higher, I keep that in mind when considering the price I'll recommend to my seller.

Pending Listings. The most important piece of information you want about pending listings is the pending price. It's not difficult to anticipate what the answers will be. If their days on market (DOM) is shorter than other homes, they likely sold for more than asking price. If the DOM is longer than the rest of the market, they probably went into contract for less. If the agent will tell me how much they went into contract for, I notate that on the CMA. This is information not found anywhere online, and it shows my client I bring value they can't get elsewhere.

Recent Sales. When a sale is recent, I contact the agent and ask them how the experience was. I'm mainly looking to see how many showings they had, how many offers they received, and what kind of offers came in. If the offers were strong, it tells me there was high demand when they were selling the house. If the offers were not strong or they did not receive many, it tells me the opposite. I include these notes in the CMA as well.

I also include notes on the condition of the comparable properties. If they have amazing upgrades or are in inferior condition, I note that. I also note if they are a strong match. This allows the sellers to review these properties themselves if they doubt the accuracy of the information I present them.

Interpret the CMA

The skill in interpreting a CMA is how you separate the talented Realtors from the amateur ones. Anyone can put a CMA together. I've shown you exactly how. Almost anyone can take notes and do the research I just described. What sets you apart will be your ability to articulate and interpret this information for your sellers in a way they can understand and trust.

After you have the CMA and notes, you need to know how to interpret this information. I have details on how to do this in the next section (*Nailing the Presentation*). For now, consider the following metrics and how you should interpret them for yourself and your potential client.

Proportions of the CMA. The first thing to look for is the proportion of active, pending, and sold listings. Ideally, you want a relatively smaller number of active listings than pending listings. This indicates a market with a high level of buyer demand and quickly selling listings. When you see this, you can typically push your price to the higher side and do fewer improvements to the property before putting it on the market.

When you see more active listings than pending ones, it indicates the opposite: There is more supply than demand. This leads to properties sitting on the market longer, fewer showings, and more competition to get into contract. This is a buyer's market.

DOM. Days on Market is the metric that will explain the proportion of active to pending listings. When properties have a low DOM, there will usually be more pendings. When there is a higher DOM, this relationship reverses. Top-producing agents look to this number first before advising their clients what to expect. Also note that pending properties tend to have a lower DOM than the active properties. Reviewing the pending properties on the MLS will usually explain why this is. Look at the pictures to determine properties' conditions as well as the listing prices and where they are located.

A seller will always ask, "How long will it take my house to sell?" I recommend pointing to this metric to show how long it took others to sell and advising them they can most likely expect a similar timeline.

Market Trend Direction. By looking at sold homes and comparing them to the prices you received from agents with pending properties, you can see if prices are trending higher or lower. When pending homes are consistently under contract for more than the homes that sold over the last three months, your market is hot and on the rise. This is typically accompanied by low DOM and a higher sale price than list price.

List Price to Sale Price. I include this metric on my CMA under the "Sold" category. When I see a trend that houses are selling for more than they were listed for, it tells me a few things, such as:
1. Buyers are willing to pay over asking.
2. There is a better chance my clients can expect to receive over asking.
3. There is a shortage of inventory.
4. The DOM was likely low.
5. The sellers in this market may be *expecting* offers to be higher than list price.

I often use this metric when interpreting a market for my buyers, especially when they are averse to paying over asking price. It can also be useful when answering questions your sellers may have about their property. If homes were selling higher than list price but now there are more active homes than pending homes, there's been a cooling in the market. This is the easiest way to interpret and present this information so your prospective leads don't question your advice or your integrity after they hire you.

Hot Price Points. The pending category can show you what price points buyers are willing to pay for properties in a specific area. This makes the difficult task of convincing your sellers that their house is not worth as much as they thought much easier. If the active homes are sitting on the market with a high DOM and the pending homes have a low DOM, point out that the pending homes were likely priced lower than the active ones. This allows you to guide your clients away from pricing too high and having a home that doesn't sell.

Popular Features/Conditions. You can also see from recent sales and pending listings if there is a pattern in the conditions of the homes that buyers want. If the homes that show very well have neutral colors or updated kitchens, it helps you prepare your clients for what they can expect if they do not have similar upgrades or are unwilling to improve their property's condition. Examining the pictures of pending listings is a clear way to present this information and interpret it for the sellers.

Anticipate Objections

After you're prepared to interpret the CMA for the prospective clients, you'll want to anticipate their potential objections. Most objections are based on the following areas:

1. **Price.** Most sellers will want more for their house than it's reasonably worth. In today's environment, many people base this information on online portals like Zillow and Redfin. While we know these estimates are not always accurate, many of your leads will not know that. Assume they have looked at these numbers online and check to see if they are higher than the price you have come up with. If they are, prepare yourself to answer objections regarding why Zillow says their house is worth more than your estimate. Even the CEO of Zillow sold his own house for 40 percent less than the Zestimate.[9] This knowledge will highlight your point that online portals don't dictate value—CMAs do.

2. **Ability for Listing Agent to Influence the Buyers.** Many sellers will try to convince you why their home is better than the competition and make sure you communicate this to the buyers. You may have to

---

[9] Kurt Schlosser, "Zestimiss: Why did CEO Spencer Rascoff's home sell for 40% less than Zillow estimate of $1.75M?" GeekWire, May 23, 2016, https://www.geekwire.com/2016/zillow-ceo-spencer-rascoff-sold-home-40-less-zestimate-1-75-million/.

explain that you won't have contact with the buyers because they'll have their own agent. Use this as an opportunity to remind the sellers that to get top dollar for their property, they need to look at it through the eyes of the buyers. This is much wiser than trying to get the buyers to look at it from the seller's perspective, even if you could.

Be prepared that your seller clients will still want to list their home for too much money and expect you to miraculously get their price. Be ready to use the CMA to highlight the competition the sellers will be facing and remind them the buyers will be looking at all the homes on the market and comparing them to the seller's home. Nobody looks at just one home and decides to buy it when there are several options available.

3. **Commission.** Your buyer clients will want to pay you less commission than you are asking for, so be prepared to help them understand how paying less commission can cost them a lot of money. This is especially true in hot markets. Your job is not just to "sell their home." It's to net them as much money as possible. Using a discount agent may save them a small amount upfront, but they will lose much more because of what will be left on the table. Highlight yourself as a master negotiator who fights for every dollar. Use the homework you've done up to this point to drive home your value.

The Listing Process

One of the biggest surprises in this business is how many agents don't have a process for taking a listing. If you don't have a plan in place, you have no way to improve your closing percentage. You also leave your clients with the undesirable feeling that they have to come up with a plan. Without a process, you are just *hoping* the deal works out for you. When you have a process, you are *planning* on the deal working out. The process doesn't have to be complicated or difficult. I recommend a simple six-step process.

1. Lead
2. Appointment
3. Pre-Listing Process
4. Active Listing
5. Pending Listing
6. Sold Listing

Lead

The most important part of lead follow-up is having a system in place to reduce how many leads you lose. "Lead bleed" is real. It is likely the biggest expense your business has, and it's a silent one. My team uses a spreadsheet to track seller leads and work them along the funnel to get me a listing appointment. Once you have systemized this process, leveraging help becomes so much easier. While documenting the process is important, the most vital piece is literally putting the lead name somewhere that you won't forget it.

You can use a CRM, whiteboard, spreadsheet, or any other method that works for you. Just make sure you have somewhere to put the information. This will prevent you from forgetting about a client who wants to sell their house. It not only takes the pressure off the client to reach out to you, but it also puts you in the position of contacting them. My team's seller lead system looks like the following.

Name	John Smith
Property address	123 Main Street
Loan balance	$480,000
Client's estimated value	$650,000
Appraiser comps	yes
CMA	yes
Listing appointment set	yes
Listing agreement signed	yes
Entered in MLS	yes

The cells for *name, property address, loan balance*, and *client's estimated value* are self-explanatory. A "yes" in the *appraiser comps* cell means the assistant has ordered and received the comps from the appraiser. "Yes" in the other cells mean the *CMA* is complete; the assistant/agent has scheduled a *listing appointment*; the lead has signed the *listing agreement* and is now our client; and the property information has been *entered into the MLS* and is ready to be marked "active."

This information prepares the listing agent for the presentation, offers insight for the seller, and helps to resolve any conflicts that arise at the appointment. It also keeps everyone on track regarding what the "next step" is in the process.

Appointment

The primary goal of an appointment is to leave with a signed listing agreement that turns your Lead into your Client. The secondary goal is to set expectations at an appropriate level to ensure success in making the client happy. The tertiary goal is to collect the information you need to get the house ready for the market and a successful sale.

Pre-Listing Process

After you have a signed listing agreement, you start the pre-listing process. This is when you handle everything necessary to get the home ready for sale. Email the list of items your client needs to take care of and check in with them every few days to see how things are going.

While waiting for reports to be completed, start entering information into the MLS. Every MLS is different, but there is always a process for entering the home's information. It's better to start this early rather than wait until the last minute. You can schedule pictures of the home after the client has completed all the staging items you asked them to do. Make sure the property is clean and orderly before the photographer arrives.

During the pre-listing process, start your marketing campaign. Order a sign for the yard as quickly as possible. This will create more lead opportunities as people call to ask about the house. Post the pictures you took at the listing presentation onto your social media with information about the property. Tell people to direct message, email, or call you. Don't share so much information about the house that people feel they don't need to contact you. Your job is to find buyer leads, not to give other Realtors a heads-up about your listing.

Work out with your seller how showings will occur. I prefer to have buyer agents text my seller to set up the showings. One reason is to prevent me from playing middleman. Another is to protect my clients from buyer agents who show up without an appointment and say, "Oh, your agent told me to just come by." This does happen, and it will create bad blood between you and your client. If the client knows all appointments are scheduled through them, they won't fall for that line.

Once you have pictures, the house is clean, and the sellers are ready for showings, it's time to mark the property "active" in the MLS and start scheduling buyers to see it.

Active Listing

When you mark your listing as active in the MLS, you should quickly know if you priced it right. If your home is priced correctly and marketed well, you should immediately begin receiving requests for showings. Keep in mind that each market is different. If you know your market, you'll know if the number of requests you're receiving is more than, less than, or equal to the normal amount for a property like yours. The most accurate metric to determine this is the DOM. If the DOM for comparable properties is low, you should receive a large number of requests because there are more buyers than homes for sale in that market.

I recommend following up with each Realtor who shows your listing to ask the following two questions:

1. What did your clients think about the property, and is there any feedback you can share?
2. What did *you* think about the property, and is there any feedback you can share?

There are two reasons you want this information. The first is so you can share it with your clients. Your sellers are going to be nervous before their house goes into contract. During this period, you'll want to communicate more with them, and it helps to have something to share when you call them. I recommend having at least a weekly call to go over showing feedback and any market changes you feel are helpful to impart.

The second reason to obtain this feedback is so you can understand how your listing is being viewed. If you receive consistent feedback that the house shows well and it's on the top of the list for each buyer who sees it, you can confidently hold out for better and stronger offers. If you hear that your property is priced higher than the others they saw or doesn't show as well as the competition, it's a sign you should take an acceptable offer if it comes in, drop your price, or ask the sellers to improve the home's condition. This information is necessary for you to do your job of putting your property in a position to receive offers and get sold.

You'll also want to hear specific feedback regarding undesirable elements of the property. When I first started selling houses, I did not have a follow-up system to contact agents who showed the property. One bad experience with a house in Northern California forced me to make this a nonnegotiable element of our system in selling houses.

My listing was a split-level single-family home in a great school district on a hillside in Martinez. The property was priced near the top of its price range, but we had done some improvements to help the seller get top dollar. This included refinishing the floors, painting, landscaping, and more. When I put the property on the market, it immediately received a strong level of interest and many showings a week.

Despite these showings, no offers came in. When I would talk to the seller, I was forced to speculate as to why. This put a lot of pressure on me and made the experience less than enjoyable for both me and the client.

After several weeks, I had my assistant call the agents who showed the home and respectfully ask them to be as honest as possible about why their clients did not like the home. This ended up being a game changer. When we let the agents know how important it was to be honest with us, they shared the truth: The house had a very, very strong odor of dogs, particularly downstairs. The odor was so powerful that as soon as the buyers smelled it, they changed their mind about the house.

Each agent gave a similar story. The clients walked into the house, loved the location and condition, and had nothing but good things to say. As soon as they walked downstairs, everything went sideways. One agent even shared that her clients ran back upstairs holding their hands over their faces and exclaimed, "This is a hard no. Let's get out of here!"

The client had several dogs they had agreed to keep outside during the sale. It turns out this became inconvenient for the client, so they started bringing the dogs back inside while they were at work. The dogs had such a strong odor, and the downstairs unit was so self-contained and lacking air flow, that the smell became unbearable. This was the reason no one was writing offers.

When I presented this information to the seller, it took me out of a position of having to speculate (which sounded like making excuses) and put me in a position of strength. When I finally had solid feedback, we were empowered to make practical adjustments that put us in a position to get the house sold. The seller reluctantly agreed to keep the dogs outdoors, I put a plan in place to keep the area smelling better, and a few weeks later we received an offer we accepted.

Don't make the same mistake I did. There's no reason to waste that much time and strain your relationship with your client unnecessarily. If you make it a habit to receive feedback from showings, you'll empower yourself to do your job better.

When offers are received, you have two options:

1. Present offers as they are received and decide immediately.
2. Set an offer date and collect as many offers as possible before presenting them to the seller.

I prefer option No. 2 because it puts less pressure on the seller. When you receive an offer a few days after going active and present that to the seller, it puts them—and you—in a difficult situation. Even if you receive a full-price offer, the seller will say, "Should I take it or wait for a better one?" It's impossible for you to answer that question with any certainty. You don't know if any other offers will come in, so you can't honestly advise your client regarding that question.

Avoid this by setting an offer date for ten to fourteen days after the property goes live and present them all to the client at the same time. If only one offer comes in, it's an easy decision. If several come in, however, you can leverage them to negotiate prices and earn more money for your seller. You can also get buyers to write a better offer than they would have liked by leveraging the fact they can lock the house up immediately as opposed to waiting to see which other offers come along at the end date you had originally planned to review offers (known as a preemptive offer).

Pending Listing

After you've accepted the offer, you mark it pending in the MLS and start the escrow process. Since the majority of the work in an escrow is done by the buyer agent, you won't have as much to do at this point. However, on my team, we have a philosophy that we will always have to do both agents' jobs in an escrow. This means we continually check to make sure the buyer agent has ordered an inspection, ordered appraisals, made progress with their loan contingency, etc. I don't simply hope the other side does things well. We make sure they are on track, and if they are not, we know early.

I remind my clients that the close date on the contract is a best-case scenario and that they should not assume it will happen on that date.

There are often delays with an escrow closing. There can be title problems, signing delays, loan issues, inspection quotes, delayed appraisals, etc. Because escrow components are linked together, it is not uncommon for an issue in one part of the escrow to cause domino effects into other parts.

If your selling client is buying another home, keep them informed as much as possible. If they are buying the new home with a different agent, loop that agent into the communication as well. If they are buying another home with you, it's important to set solid expectations. Let them know you won't be looking for new homes until their current home is under contract, and you won't be writing offers on homes until the potential buyers of their current home have removed all their contingencies. This discussion is never fun, but it will save your clients tremendous stress because they won't be juggling twice as many moving pieces at the same time. Top-producing agents learn how to avoid these problems. It starts by not letting our inexperienced clients call the shots. That's our job, and we can save our clients from hardship when the relationship starts out on the right foot.

Sold Listing

After the property is sold, check in with your clients to make sure the money was wired to their account and to ask if they were happy with the process. When they are, use this as an opportunity to ask for a referral. It's always best to ask happy clients for a referral. If they are a raving fan, they will think hard to come up with people to refer to you.

You should also market your sold listing. Put it on social media for everyone to see and include pictures of your happy clients with the home. If you can use this sold listing to get you a new listing, you can string each listing into another (or several others) to have a never-ending supply of listings.

Remember to remove your sign from the yard and take all of your belongings from the house. (I've left iPads in homes that were there to display the home's features to buyers.) And don't forget to take your lockbox and any combo boxes you put on the property.

Make a note in your database to check in with the sellers twelve months later to congratulate them on the selling of their property. Use this as an opportunity to ask for a referral, if practical.

Nailing the Presentation

What to Bring

I bring the following items with me to every listing appointment:

- An iPad to deliver the listing presentation
- A folder branded with my logo that contains the following items:
  - A pad to take notes
  - A branded PopSocket for my client's phone
  - A branded pen
  - Listing agreement to be signed
  - Disclosure packet to be left to be filled out
  - The "Sellers Blueprint" marketing material
  - A copy of *Sell Your Home for Top Dollar* (a short book I wrote that describes the negotiating tricks and processes I use to sell homes)

I conduct the appointment in three phases.

Phase One: The Initial Walk-Through

Right after I arrive, I look for a place where I want to conduct Phase Two (the presentation) and leave my belongings there. It's usually a kitchen or dining room table. My goal is to sit with the seller next to me so I can share my iPad. By leaving my belongings there, I've set the stage for where the presentation will take place.

Next, I do a walk-through of the house with the seller. I take notes regarding anything I want to have changed or don't want to forget. These include pictures that have to be removed, cluttered décor that has to be cleaned up, or that awesome balcony off the master bedroom that might be missed. I continually express to the clients everything I like about the house.

"I love the floors. Did you put those in after moving in?"

"That backsplash really ties in the counters and cabinets. Did you choose it yourself?"

"Your backyard is incredible. Buyers are going to love this."

The primary reason for the initial walk-through is to put the seller at ease. They are most likely worried if their house is up to par, and it's difficult for them to focus on what you're saying when their "croc brain" is screaming at them. To make sure they hear you, start off by directly addressing their fears or concerns. That makes your voice louder in their mind than their croc brain. The secondary purpose is to take notes, and we'll talk about that later.

Never ever (ever) make any negative comments about the property until the listing agreement is signed.

Phase Two: The Presentation

You give your presentation right after your walk-through. Start off with the following line: "I have a presentation that covers everything I do to sell your home for top dollar. I think you're going to love it. Before I get started, are there any questions you'd like us to address up front?"

Write down all of their questions and don't answer any of them until they're done. Interrupting them makes it too difficult for them to remember what they wanted to ask if they're also listening to your answers. The result will be confusion on their part. They won't feel any smarter, but they won't know why. As they ask them, write them down, and say, "Great. What else can you think of?" Let them dump until their mind is clear. This will help them hear the information you're about to give.

Tell them many of their questions will be answered in the presentation. For anything that isn't, you'll address them when the presentation is complete. Begin your presentation. It should include who you are, what you do, and how your process will benefit the client (this is detailed in Chapter Three). The goal is to impress the client and make them feel like they are in capable hands. When done correctly, the client will feel comfortable turning control over to you and your staff and won't try to direct you in how to sell their house. It will also prepare them for what comes next.

Phase Three: The CMA

At the end of your presentation, include a slide that reads "What comes next." In my slideshow, it includes four bullet points:

- Review the CMA
- Complete the Agreement
- Choose the Start Date
- Marketing Takes Over

This lets the client know that I have a plan and a vision for their sale. I pull out the CMA, which has notes taken by my assistant or by me.

These highlight the following aspects of the houses on the CMA:

- The comparable properties and how they differ from this house, such as lot size, upgrades, pools, etc.
- The exceptional properties that aren't comparable because of unique features, such as water views.
- The homes in better/worse school districts than their property.
- The homes that went under contract or sold but in a different market (for instance, homes that went active right before the COVID-19 shelter-in-place mandate).
- The homes that are a good match, and why.

I use a script to explain the different categories on the CMA.

The CMA Script

This is a comparative market analysis. It is a list of all the active, pending, and sold homes that compare to yours. I've adjusted it to reflect the neighborhood, size, and other features of your home.

These are the active categories. These homes are our competition. There are three things that determine a home's value: price, condition, and location. Since we cannot change the location, we will focus on the first two.

When a buyer tours available homes, they will not just be looking at your home. This is a common misconception sellers make, which leads to the line of reasoning expressed in "If I add granite countertops, how much will that make my home worth?" This reasoning is flawed because it assumes buyers look at a home that way. They don't. Buyers are looking at every home on this list to choose the one they feel best fits their needs. If we are priced higher or if we are in inferior condition to our competition, they will skip over us. They'll choose another home. My job is to make sure we avoid that.

Next, we have the pending homes. This is actually the most important factor. It is a snapshot of all the "successful" sellers in a market at any given time. These are the homes that found a date to the dance. If we want to be successful, our best bet is to model what these sellers did. This category is a clear indication of what buyers in this market want and what they will pay for it. We're going to look at this carefully in a second. As you can see, I've already done some serious research and have useful info to share with you about the market.

Last is the sold category. These are homes that have sold. As you can see, I've included the date they were sold, how long they sat on the market, the price they listed at, and the price they sold at. This category is useful for the following two reasons.

1. Appraisers will use this category to determine a buyer's loan.
2. It shows us if market prices are trending upward, downward, or holding steady.

It's important to note that whoever buys your home will likely use a loan and thus will need an appraisal. Even if I sell your home well over fair market value (and I'll sure try to), the appraisal can stop that from happening. We need to keep these numbers in mind while pricing your home.

Let me show you the homes I feel compare most closely to yours. After that we can choose a price to list at and then I'll share what comes next.

I use this specific order because it prevents the sellers from thinking I'm the bad guy if the logical price for their home is less than what they want. In this case, the CMA (as a reflection of the market) is the bad guy. Not only does it prevent any conflict on the part of the seller toward me, but it also prevents me from having to answer question after question about how I priced the house. I've walked the seller through my process, so they are more likely to be on board with the price after seeing the process and the work that went into it.

I walk the seller through the active homes and point out those that have been sitting on the market for a long time. I carefully draw attention to the fact that they are either priced too high or don't show well. I want the potential sellers to clearly see the *downside* of any greed they're feeling. If you skip this step, they will likely want to list as high as possible and put pressure on you to sell the property at an unrealistic price. By showing them the horror stories of listings done incorrectly, they learn that no agent can make buyers want a home that is less desirable than the competition. Making this argument now will make your job much easier later.

After I explain the CMA, I ask the seller, "Based on what we are looking at here—and how buyers will be approaching their house hunt—which of these homes do you feel compares most closely to yours?" If the seller chooses the comps I agree with, I let them know. I say, "I agree completely. Those are the same properties I was looking at and the clear best choice is to list where they did and work for a similar result."

If the seller chooses more expensive comps, I again walk them through the differences. I ask them to explain their reasoning. When I hear their faulty thinking, I say something like, "That house has a pool and a three-car garage. I agree your interior is much nicer, but it's hard to argue that these houses are comparable." Work your way through these houses until an agreement is reached.

Conflict Resolution Scripts
If you find yourself with a particularly stubborn seller, use your conflict resolution techniques. When a seller wants to sell for an unreasonable amount, it's usually for one of two reasons.

1. They are greedy.
2. They need the money badly.

Ask them what they plan to use the money for. If they open up to you about financial difficulties, you'll need to address the root problem before you get deeper into the actual sale price. If they don't open up to you, you're likely dealing with greed.

The cure for greed is fear. When a seller is thinking purely about how much money they can get, they are *not* thinking about how much pain they'll be in if something goes wrong. This is where you can help them. Use your CMA to point out the houses that haven't sold. Use the following lines as examples of what you can say:

"This seller has been on the market for 150 days. What do you think that has done to their plans to move on into the next phase of their life?"

"This house has been on the market much longer than all the others. How do you think buyers will perceive that, even if they like the property?"

"This property has been sitting in the active category for a very long time. What do you think the seller needs to do to remedy that?"

These questions get the seller to think about what can go wrong if they list too high and stops their pie-in-the-sky hopes for an unrealistic sale price.

Phase Four: Get the Listing Presentation Signed

After a price has been reached, next work to have the sellers sign the listing agreement at this meeting. If the seller is hesitant to sign, remind them they are not obligated to sell the home just because they signed the agreement. Even if they list the house, they are *still* not obligated to sell the home. I remind clients that if we list the home and they don't receive an offer they like or they change their mind about selling, the agreement does not compel them to sell. It only spells out that if they do sell, I'll be the agent with the right to sell the home.

I then tell them I want to start a premarketing campaign (covered in my listing presentation) but can't until the listing agreement is signed. I also tell them that if the house doesn't sell, I will be the one who loses money, not them. I reassure them I'm taking the risks in this transaction and this agreement is just a required legal formality.

If the client still hesitates to sign, I ask the following questions to determine why:

"Is there something I've neglected to present that's important to you?"

"Is there something you think an agent can do for you that I haven't covered here?"

"Is there something about me you don't trust or aren't comfortable with that we can discuss?"

"Is there something I don't know about your situation that is causing you to feel uncomfortable working with me?"

As a top producer, you have to be comfortable making the lead uncomfortable. Remember, you'll have a fiduciary duty to your clients, but they won't with you. Leads can lie to you, deceive you, or use you for information. The listing agreement is your *only* legal protection. If your heart is in the right place and you know you'll do right by your potential client, there is nothing wrong with allowing them to feel pressure to sign the contract—especially when you've done the work up to this point.

After an agreement is signed, you can unleash the full power of your skills as a real estate agent. Obtaining a signed listing agreement is your No. 1 goal for this appointment. It should be the No. 1 goal for your business. If the client signs, congratulate yourself! A celebration is in order because you just took a huge step toward having a better year.

Phase Five: Do Another Walk-Through to Discuss Staging and Repairs

After the agreement is signed, take another walk-through of the property, making more notes on what needs to be fixed or changed or corrected before listing the property. This is where you discuss staging (including decluttering and cleaning) and making needed repairs. Make a list of the items the clients need to do to get the house ready to show and tell them you'll email this list to them when you get back in the office (and will keep track of their progress before officially putting the house on the market).

Recommend they pay for a home inspection, including pest and roof inspections, for the property. Doing this early will smooth out potential rough points in an escrow and make it less likely the house will drop out of contract later. It will also save your clients money because if a buyer reviews the report and then waives inspection contingencies, it will be very difficult for them to negotiate for credits or a reduced sales price. Issues in inspection reports are the primary reasons sellers pay credits to buyers in an escrow. That's why it's good to know the issues earlier in the selling process. Before leaving, take a few pictures of the best features of the property for your "Coming Soon!" marketing campaign.

After the inspection report comes back, make recommendations on which repairs you'd like the sellers to make and why.

Focus on Listings

It's not uncommon for the listing side of your business to take longer to develop than the buyer side, and that's okay. Buyers are easier to find, and it's easier to gain their trust. Many sellers feel comfortable only working with an experienced or top-producing agent, while buyers are likely to choose an agent based on their personality or the chemistry between them. It may take longer to start listing like a pro, but the payoff is worth it.

Listings are superior in the following ways.

Scale

The listing side of real estate is easier to scale than the buyer side because listings require less time and are much easier to systemize. The process of selling a home is largely the same for every single property, which is one big reason why I prefer this side of the business. The major differences among selling clients are the individual objections they'll have. The rest is standard, and you'll find the process I've outlined in this chapter is largely the same for each client. When the process is simple, repeatable, and easily leveraged, scaling becomes much easier.

Profit

Listings are more profitable because you negotiate your own salary. Listing agents determine the commissions for both the listing agents and buyer's agents. Your ability to show your value, inspire confidence in clients, and take control of relationships will dictate your paycheck, not what other seller agents have negotiated for you by letting them set the home price—which is what happens when working with buyers. Because listings require much less time, you can work on more of them at the same time. This has a big influence on your profit as well.

Leverage

Buyers can be leveraged, but not easily. One administrative person in my office can do most of the work for several sellers at a time. The majority of that work involves inputting data into the MLS, creating marketing information, disseminating that information, and completing legal compliance paperwork. These are all administrative tasks. Once you've hired good help, you'll find yourself needing to complete only a few things yourself, including:

1. Initial introduction/lead follow-up call
2. Listing appointment
3. Negotiating offers
4. Negotiating escrow conditions

Most top-producing agents continue to work their own listings deep into their careers. These are typically the last elements of your business you give up before you step out of sales.

Time

Listings take less time; buyer agents have far more to do than listing agents. Most of my work as a listing agent is performing due diligence. This means following up with the buyer agent to make sure their client isn't behind with paperwork. You won't be attending inspections, seeking appraisals, doing multiple walk-throughs, following up with lenders, and so on. You can use that time to lead-generate and get more business. Who can argue with that?

Additional Perks

Buyers usually bring only one thing to the table: a closing. Listings often bring more than just a closing: They bring more listings. With a sign in the yard and a clever marketing plan, you should be able to get one new listing for each one you have. Knocking on doors in the neighborhood, sending out flyers, and putting your listings out to your sphere is free marketing for you that can lead to new seller clients. Listings bring buyer clients too. Holding open houses and receiving "sign calls" (unrepresented buyers) are common ways to find buyers who need an agent to represent them based on nothing more than advertising your listing. This is much cheaper than buying leads.

Be disciplined in improving your listing procedure and you'll find your business growing faster every year.

➡ KEY POINTS

- Listings are the highest-dollar activity in real estate sales.
- Listing agents negotiate their own salary through setting the prices of the homes.
- Listing leads will ask you questions related to their fears; direct answers will quell those fears and make it easier for them to trust you.
- Have a list price in mind before your listing presentation or you'll appear to be unprepared and lack a plan to move forward.
- Before you do a listing presentation, call every agent with a pending, active, and recently sold listing. Ask about the number of showings and buyer feedback, and ask agents with pending listings the pending price. Mark this on the CMA.
- The skill in interpreting a CMA for a prospective client separates talented Realtors from amateur ones, as does preparing for potential objections during a presentation.
- Your job is to net your clients as much money as possible. Let them know that using a less expensive agent may save some money upfront, but they'll lose much more because of what will be left on the table.
- Have a system to reduce lead bleed.
- The primary goal of a listing appointment is to leave with a signed listing agreement; the secondary goal is to set appropriate expectations.
- The listing side of your business will take longer to develop than the buyer's side. That's okay.

CHAPTER ELEVEN

THE BUY/SELL COMBO

"A specialist is a barbarian whose ignorance is not
well-rounded."

—STANISLAW LEM

The best opportunity in real estate sales is the buy/sell combo. When you have one client (the result of lead generation) that leads to two different deals, it's a win–win for you. In the buy/sell combo, you eliminate the need to communicate with another agent (and avoid the inevitable conflicting advice). The more control you exercise in a transaction, the higher your odds of success.

Top-producing agents value efficiency. They know every deal matters, and they don't let opportunities go to waste. If you're lucky enough to find someone who needs to both sell their house and buy another—and your state allows it—do everything you can to get the sale and purchase combination. There are several reasons why this benefits you and the client, and the more you understand these reasons, the more likely you'll land the deal.

This chapter mostly relates to clients who object to you doing both sides or question if using the same Realtor for both is wise. Much of this material is directed toward helping you overcome those concerns. If your selling client acts like they simply expected you to do both sides of the combo, say nothing, come up with a plan, and start putting it into action.

Why You Want Both Sides

Volume

The first reason to want the buy/sell combo is the additional volume it brings your business. Two are always better than one. If you portray yourself as the best option to help your clients with both selling their home and finding a new one, you stand a good chance at getting both sides, or at least a first shot at it. There are several things you can do to improve your odds that I cover later in the chapter.

It's much easier to reach top-producer status when you double your volume. And as a top agent, it's much easier to convince your clients to let you do both sides of their transaction. It also makes it easier to get outside referrals from other agents. And all this work shows those in your sphere how successful you are. Improving your volume will improve your business, and that is reason enough to target the buy/sell combo.

Efficiency

Getting two deals from one client is about as efficient as it gets. Consider the work in lead generation to get just one deal. If it takes you one hundred phone calls to get one client, you can save yourself significant amounts of time and effort by getting two deals out of those same one hundred phone calls. Marketing yourself as a listing specialist or a buyer specialist has its drawbacks in these situations. If you want to do both sides, behave like it makes more sense for you to do both. The buy/sell combo is obviously a model of efficiency.

Convenience

Working in concert with another Realtor can be both difficult and counterproductive. There are many situations in which I've done the listing for a client moving out of state and had to coordinate my efforts with an out-of-state Realtor. These Realtors have one goal—get *their buyer* into contract. This can wreak havoc on my plans to sell *my seller's* home. Many times I'll want to pass on the first offer we get and wait for a better one, but the buyer agent will pressure our mutual client to take the deal. This conflicting advice makes my job harder and makes the client's experience worse.

The same can be true when I'm representing the client as the buyer and the listing agent has priced the home too high or failed to get our mutual client to improve its condition. While the client is pressuring me to take them to see homes or asking me copious amounts of questions about them, it can be difficult to hold them off for a significant amount of time if the listing agent isn't doing an effective job of getting their house under contract. When I do both sides, I can set expectations with the client about exactly when we will focus on buying the next house. When they come to me from another agent, I am at the mercy of whatever expectations that agent did or did not set.

The buy/sell combo makes it much easier to do my own job.

Advantages

You have advantages over your competition when you're not pigeon-holed as a "buyer agent" or a "listing agent." As a top producer, you want clients approaching you about every deal they have. This allows you the freedom to choose who you want to work with—and who you don't. When you market yourself as only one type of agent, not all types of clients will approach you.

If you hear your clients make statements such as "I didn't know you worked with buyers" or "I thought you only sold in the city," it's a clear indication you have mis-marketed yourself or you don't realize how you come across to clients. Your goal is to have clients think of you when they think "real estate," not when they hear "buy a home" or "sell a home." If they don't, you're missing out on listings—and missing out on buy/sell combos.

The Buy/Sell Pitch

Showing Your Value

The first step in landing a combo is to show the client why you're the best agent for both jobs. I start this at my initial presentation by acting like I assume I will be helping them with buying and selling. I do this to put the onus on them to deliver the bad news that they were planning on interviewing a different agent to handle either the purchase or the sale than to use me for both. Many clients won't actually deliver that news, and you'll pick up both sides simply for showing initiative.

The key to showing your value is not to say, "Let me show you my value." Instead, let your actions speak louder. Run the CMA numbers. Show the clients how you can improve their finances. In addition to that, use the following to demonstrate why letting you handle both sides is in their best interest.

Logistics

There are logistical difficulties involved in selling a home to buy another one. The biggest hurdles are:

The Money/Down Payment. Most clients will need the money from selling their home to purchase the next one. We'll discuss how to address this later in the chapter. For now, know this concern will be top of mind for your clients when they meet with you. Let them know that you have a plan for how to get the money from their current property and convert it into the down payment for the next property.

The Loan. Getting preapproved for the loan for their next house needs to be done before you list the current house. You don't want an upset client because they liked the house they just sold more than the one they were forced to buy at a lower price point because they didn't know their price range before they started looking. Make sure the lender knows *not* to include the monthly payment of their primary residence in their debt-to-income ratio. Obviously, they won't own their primary residence at the time they are looking to buy the next home.

Explain to your clients you can communicate these details to the lender on their behalf because you have the experience of doing this before, so you know the pitfalls to avoid.

The Move. The worst part of moving is the actual move. Coordinating when the first house will close, when the client must get all their stuff out of it, and when they can move into the next house is even more difficult when doing this with another agent. Help your clients see how much smoother this process will be when you coordinate all the details of both transactions. I explain that I will arrange the closings to happen on a timeline that works for them.

For instance, I tell them I will negotiate a rent-back from the buyer of their current home that will allow them to stay in the property after it closes. This will buy them the time they need to purchase the next house, and this means they only have to move once. Bringing up options like this one makes it easier for the client to trust you with both sides of the deal because you've already accounted for logistical complications they did not see coming.

Communication

When someone who has used you before calls you about new real estate needs, it's mostly likely because they enjoy the chemistry you share. When you are a referral to someone new, you have to develop some chemistry with the new person. In either situation, having an open line of communication is valuable and important. Use it to your advantage.

In the case of buy/sell opportunities, let the client know it's best for you to do both sides because there will be both fewer breakdowns in communication and opportunities for things to go wrong. The more people involved in a game of telephone, the easier it is to screw up the original message. You can answer questions about a property they want to buy and showings they had that week in the same phone call. You and the client simply need to know how the other prefers to receive communication.

Understanding Their Needs

When you meet with the client to find out why they're selling their property, you'll discover it's almost always because they want to buy something different. Very few people sell their homes and don't want another one. Start your conversation with the goal of understanding why they want to move in the first place.

Some people want to upgrade to a bigger home, better location, or nicer property. This often happens as a family grows. It is typically accompanied by raises at work or a stronger overall financial position. Although this frequently happens with younger people or young families, that's not always the case. If your client wants to upgrade, make sure you understand *why* they do. Once the seller knows you understand why they want to sell, they are more likely to let you help them buy the next house.

Some people want to downgrade to save money in retirement or are now on fixed incomes. Many of them are empty nesters who no longer need a large and expensive property. Others realize they must get their financial situation under control, so buying a cheaper home, house hacking, or a combination of the two makes more sense. With these folks, be sure to dig in deep to understand why they are downgrading. What do they hope to accomplish financially, and is there a timeline for the delayed gratification? If the sellers are younger, they may be planning to save money for a specific amount of time and then buy a better house later. If you don't completely understand the whys, it's easy for them to think you are not the right agent for the job.

Be very, very clear that you know what their needs are and that you are committed to helping them reach their goals. If they don't believe you understand, they may let you list their home but then hire a different agent to help them buy their next one.

Vision

Any agent can list a home or represent a buyer. What distinguishes you from your competition is your ability to cast a vision for the client. You do this with strong storytelling skills and effectively anticipating problems, avoiding snags, and communicating both the order of operations and how things should look as tasks are completed.

Leaders cast vision. They set the tone. Doing so makes it easy to inspire confidence because clients listen to those they trust. You may not feel like a natural leader in life, but if you're a fiduciary who has clients looking to you for guidance, in this relationship you are the de facto leader.

Running the Numbers

Knowing how to run the numbers on a combo deal is a mark of a true professional. Many agents can fill out forms, show homes, and hand out business cards. Understanding the financing involved in a home purchase will help set you apart from your competition. To run the numbers, do the following. Don't be intimidated by this process. It's not as hard as it sounds.

The Five-Step Process for Running the Numbers on a Combo Deal

Step 1: Determine How Much Is Left Over After the Sale of the Home.
Before your listing presentation, you will run a CMA and perform

preliminary research. This should give you a range of prices you believe the property will sell for. Have your preferred title company create a "net sheet" for the low end of the price range. The net sheet includes an estimate of all the fees associated with the transaction and who collects them. If you supply the prospective client with the lowest estimated sales price, they'll know the net after that sale.

Step 2: Look for Ways to Improve the Overall Financial Picture. In your business, always market yourself as someone who helps improve their clients' financial situation. Walk them through the best use of the equity in their current house and show them how you can save them money each month with a smaller home or how much a bigger home will help their family. Your ability to function as someone who helps clients make better financial decisions will help win over more clients than the traditional realtor pitch of being able to market, sell, and negotiate.

- Do Step 1.
- Determine the minimum down payment they'll need for their next property and how much equity they'll have left over if they sell their current home and pay all the expenses associated with that.
- Go over their current debt. If they don't know, the lender can access this via a credit report. Lenders use credit reports that are different from what the public can access on their own. Write down the loan balances for each form of debt and the interest rate associated with it.
- Determine the monthly payment associated with each form of debt.
- Identify the debt with the highest interest rate and determine how much they are spending a month on it. Determine the amount they can save each month if they pay off this high-interest debt.
- Determine the debts that make the most financial sense to pay off first. For example, if they have $40,000 saved and can pay off debt at 7 percent interest on a five-year loan, that will save them $792 a month.
- Run a comparison that shows the difference between taking some of their equity and paying off their debt with it as opposed to putting it down on the next house.
- If they pay off $40,000 of high-interest rate debt, they can save $792 a month. In order to do that, they'll have to borrow an additional $40,000 toward their next house (as opposed to using that same $40,000 as a down payment).
- If they borrow that additional $40,000 at 3.5 percent interest, their

payment would increase by $180 a month on a thirty-year loan.

- The difference between the $792 they save paying off high-interest-rate debt and the $180 they take on in additional mortgage debt is a net of $612 to the client.
- This is not an apples-to-apples comparison. The debt they paid off will be on a five-year schedule while their mortgage will be on a thirty-year schedule, but this shows them how to apply their equity more wisely toward their overall financial picture while still buying their next home. This also shows you have knowledge that other Realtors do not and will set you apart.

I use the following formula to show their monthly payments:

$$\textbf{Current mortgage payment} + \textbf{Current debt to be paid off} = \textbf{Current monthly payment}$$

If the new monthly payment is less than or close to their current monthly payment, they will likely move forward with a new property and oftentimes for a higher price than they originally thought they could spend.

Step 3: Determine How Much They'll Need to Put Down on the Next Home. I use a calculator (try the free Mortgage Calculator Plus app, which is easy to use) to determine what my client's payment will be if they put down the total remaining funds (after paying off the debt with the highest interest rate) from the sale of their original home on the new home. Be sure to include property taxes and insurance costs, as they will want to know the total amount after expenses. Caveat: Before having this conversation, speak with a lender to obtain the average interest rates available for primary residence homeowners and the average property tax base rate for the areas they want to buy in.

Using the calculator:
- Enter the estimated price of the new property.
- Subtract the payment.
- This is the estimated loan balance.
- Enter the estimated interest rate (go a little high as a precaution).
- Enter the assumed amortization period (usually thirty years).
- This is the estimated monthly payment for the new property.

Step 4: Determine How Much They Can Set Aside to Upgrade the New Home. Now, ask your clients if they'd like to use funds to put toward the rehab of their new property. I like to show fixer-upper properties at great prices and explain how the funds can be used to fix up that property to make it worth more. By showing how they can add $30,000 to $50,000 in value to the new property, I get them excited about appreciation. In the process, I make money too, as it takes them from talking about "saving" on commission to asking about how they can build the most wealth.

When it comes to properties that could use some upgrades, it's often in your client's best interest to set money aside they were going to use for the down payment and apply that toward fixing up the property. To help them determine the cost of this, add the amount of money the client is not putting down (say, $30,000) to the amount they'll be borrowing from the bank. Share the new monthly mortgage payment with the client and ensure it's an amount they can afford. If so, walk them through the upgrades they can make with that $30,000 in contrast with the slightly higher monthly payment to see which is more appealing to them.

Step 5. Review the Ways You Can Save Them Money. Tell the client that borrowing for the mortgage of a new house may be tax deductible (but first confirm this with a trusted CPA), which is one reason not to use the net funds from the sale toward the new property.

Next, review the expenses of their current property that won't carry over to the new house. This can be private mortgage insurance (PMI), home-owners association (HOA) fees, supplemental taxes, etc. You can also include expenses like a car payment or credit card debt they'll be paying off. Put this information into a table to review with them. It should look like this:

TOTAL DEBT	MONTHLY PAYMENT
Car payment: $15,000	$350
Visa card: $9,000	$115
American Express: $11,000	$137
PMI	$200
HOA	$175
Total	**$977**

The table illustrates money they are currently spending every month that they won't be spending once they sell their home and pay that debt off. There are several ways to present this information to highlight the benefits to your sellers.

- Use the mortgage calculator to determine how much more they can borrow for $977/month. At a 3.5 percent interest rate, this would be $217,500! Explain they can spend $217,500 more than their current mortgage balance yet pay the same monthly amount as their current mortgage.
- Show them that saving $977/month equals $11,724 a year. This money can instead be saved each year and put toward retirement, additional investment properties, improvements on the new house, and so on.
- Show them how paying off higher rate debt in exchange for lower rate debt (that is also often tax deductible) is financially responsible.
- Use this information to show them you're not just after a commission but are looking out for their financial interests. Real estate is a way to borrow cheaper debt than credit cards or car notes. You want to help save them as much as possible using the power of real estate.

The Roadmap

Step by Step

It makes people feel better when the steps in a complicated process are clearly laid out. They know what to expect. After I've run the numbers to show how the financial process works, I use a similar step-by-step explanation for the practical process.

1. We formally commit to the process.
2. They get preapproved for the loan on their new house.
3. They prepare their current home for the market before it is listed as active.
4. We review the list of potential homes that fall within their preapproval amount to ensure there are properties that meet their needs.
5. We determine how the transition from one home to the next will be made (more on that later).
6. I list their home and sell it.

7. When their current home is in contract and the buyers have removed their contingencies, we start looking for their next home.
8. We close on their current home, and they move into their next one.

I email all the steps to the client as soon as I get back to the office. This way, they can refer to it when the process starts.

Maintaining Control

With all these moving parts, it's incredibly important that you are the lead in this relationship and stay in control. It's natural for your clients to want to skip steps, but that complicates the process and hurts your chance of success at both ends of the buy/sell combo.

For instance, if your client starts looking for their next home without you and before they are preapproved for a loan, they may be disappointed when they see what's realistic in their price range. Or if a client pushes to put their second home in contract before the first one sells, they won't realize they will feel unnecessarily pressured to credit the buyers of their home out of fear of losing the second home. Maintaining control is incredibly important to avoid the pitfalls that will ruin your client's plans. We are the professionals in the relationship, so it falls on us to protect our clients from rushing steps in the plan.

The best way to maintain control is to start off in control. Let your client know you're in charge of each step. Let them know what comes next so they don't have to guess. Stay in close communication. Most clients will trust your leadership unless you give them reason to question it. That's why having a clearly defined roadmap is so crucial.

Staying Ahead of the Curves

In sports car racing, there are curves that could cause a driver to lose traction with the pavement and veer off course if they're not prepared for them. When a professional driver approaches curves, they slow enough to hit the curve at the right angle and on the right driving line. These drivers aren't surprised by curves. They know when they are coming and practice how to master them.

In our industry, these curves are usually transition points. The majority of these points involve a client needing to keep their emotions in check and delaying gratification. As the agent, it's your job to help them do that. These are the curves to prepare for:

Waiting for the Preapproval. Most buyers do not want to wait to be preapproved before they start looking at homes. They may not complete the preapproval process at all. It's not uncommon for lenders to receive partially filled-in applications or incomplete paperwork from borrowers and then not receive the missing information. You can help by reminding your clients they must complete the process before looking at homes. If you do this right, the "carrot" of looking at homes will motivate your client to avoid the "stick" of repeated reminders to complete their pre-approval paperwork.

Waiting to Buy the Second Home. As soon as the sellers have their home in contract, it's natural for them to want to start looking for the next home. At this point, in their mind they are buyers. There are several problems if this happens, though. For one, it's more difficult to get your now-buyer clients into contract if their offer is contingent on selling their current home. This is not a good thing from a financial or emotional standpoint. Having a client fall in love with a property but be unable to move forward because their current home hasn't sold can wear them out and cause them to lose steam. Be very careful because this *will* happen.

For another, it will put much more pressure on you as the listing agent if your clients want to move forward on their next home and their current home hasn't sold. You will find yourself quickly becoming the target of their frustration as they ask for frequent updates of what you're doing and eventually start giving you directions on how to do your job. Avoid all of this by being exceptionally clear upfront that their home search will not start until contingencies are waived on their current home.

Waiting for Contingencies to Be Removed. Many seller clients don't understand that an accepted offer is not the same thing as a completed sale. Sellers need to be told to avoid becoming emotionally connected to the idea their home has sold until, at minimum, the buyers have removed all their contingencies. It's easy to assume every deal will close but remind your clients that's not always the case.

Waiting for the Real Close of Escrow Date. Properties don't always close on time. Lending issues, appraisal hang-ups, inspection problems—there is no shortage of problems that delay the deal. Sometimes it has nothing to do with the property, such as when title companies need more time to clear certain conditions. Make it clear to your clients that the property will probably *not* close on time. That way if it does, they are pleasantly surprised and not irritated or blaming you.

The Four Methods of the Buy/Sell Combo

There are four ways to structure the process of selling a home to buy the next home. Most clients have the same concerns: They need the funds from their current home to buy their next home; they don't want to make two mortgage payments at the same time; and they don't want to move their possessions more than once.

COMFORT **PROFIT**

All four methods use the analogy of a spectrum, where one end is Comfort. For example, it's more comfortable to move possessions only once and it's more comfortable to identify their next house before they sell their current one. On the other end of the spectrum is Profit. For example, I can get them a better deal on their next house if we aren't rushed to find a place to put their possessions and if the offer isn't contingent on selling their current one. I can sell their current home for more if I don't have to make concessions to keep a deal alive because we put their next house under contract too early. Your clients need to understand that doing things the most comfortable way comes at the expense of profit. I use the following script to start the conversation.

Comfort versus Profit Script

Let's talk about how we can sell your home and buy the next one. There are four ways to do this. I want to highlight that each method has strengths and weaknesses. In all these methods, one end of the spectrum is comfort. Certain strategies will be more comfortable and you will naturally gravitate toward those. At the other end of this spectrum is profit. The less comfortable the strategy, the more profit you can make or money you save. To keep your finances the priority, I'd like to find out how far along this spectrum I can push you toward profitability without going so far that it's too uncomfortable for you to handle. Does that sound good to you?

I then explain the methods.

Method 1: Buy Contingent on Selling Current Property

The most comfortable way for a client to sell their home and purchase their next one is to find the home they want and write an offer that is contingent on selling their current home. This allows them to put their next home in contract and recoup their earnest money deposit if they are unable to sell their current home. Buyers like this method because (1) they don't have to worry about finding a home they like before they sell their current home; (2) they don't have to worry about moving their possessions twice because they set up the sale to close on their next home after they sell their current home; and (3) their earnest money deposit is safe in case their current home doesn't sell.

With this being the most comfortable option, your clients will usually want to start here. You'll need to show them why that's a bad idea. Buying a property contingent on selling their current one is not ideal because (1) sellers will not like this option since it's worse for them, which makes it harder to get your client the home they want; (2) to compensate for the uncertainty imposed on the seller of the second home, your client will usually have to pay more for the property; and (3) when your client is under contract on their purchase property, it puts more pressure on them to accept terms from the buyers of their current home they normally wouldn't take as there's the extra concern they can lose the purchase home. All of this means it's more difficult for you to negotiate for and guide them.

The best way to talk your clients out of looking for a property and writing an offer contingent on selling theirs is to share how much money they can lose. Remind them you are here to protect their finances. Unless money is no object, this is a poor strategy for your clients.

Method 2: Sell Contingent on Finding Replacement Property

This option is slightly less comfortable than the first option and thus slightly better from the profit perspective. When offers come in for your listing, most states allow you to accept the offer contingent on finding a replacement property. If your seller client can't find a replacement home, they can back out of the purchase contract and keep their current home. While this is better for your clients (less uncertainty), it is worse for potential buyers. Therein lies the rub.

Most buyers don't have the luxury of waiting to see if the property they put in contract is actually going to convey to them. Most will elect to skip writing an offer under these conditions and pursue properties with sellers more motivated to sell. When you decrease your buyer pool, you decrease your options and your ability to negotiate for top dollar.

After presenting this option, explain to your clients it will hinder your ability to get them as much profit as possible for their home. With this being the goal, you would prefer to focus on increasing their bottom line—even if that means more discomfort.

Method 3: Take HELOC Out of Current Property to Buy Next Property

A home equity line of credit (HELOC) is a loan given against the equity in a property. Most large banks offer these loans, and they are relatively inexpensive (oftentimes nothing more than the cost of an appraisal). This type of loan allows your seller to access a large chunk of the equity in their current home to be used as the down payment on their next property. Your client is accessing their equity without having to wait for their current home to close, which avoids unnecessary contingencies. Contingencies hurt your ability to make them money.

Two things need to be present to use this option: (1) the client must have enough equity in their home to pull out the down payment; and (2) your client's debt-to-income ratio must be strong enough to qualify them for their second home while still paying for their first. When these conditions are present, this is a great option that allows for the comfort of the first two options with a minimal impact on profit (the impact being two house payments for a short time and paying both for an appraisal for the HELOC and the interest on the money they borrow).

Method 4: Sell Current Home, Then Buy Next Home

The least comfortable option, but most profitable one, is to sell their current home, move somewhere else, then shop for the next home. If your client is willing to take things slowly and move their possessions more than once, it allows you as their agent to focus on selling their current home for as much profit as possible and negotiating their next home for as little as possible. This lets you maximize their profitability and your value to them as an agent. You need to do a little more work on the front end to help your clients with the logistics, but it will make your job much easier on the back end.

Synergy

Synergy is defined by Lexico as "the interaction or cooperation of two or more organizations, substances, or other agents to produce a combined effect greater than the sum of their separate effects." To become a top-producing agent, you want to focus on harnessing the power of synergy to make your job easier. When you can take one activity but benefit from it in several ways, you increase your productivity. When success in one area makes success in others easier to achieve, you increase your odds of building the momentum required to run a great business.

The following are ways you can use synergistic elements to increase your volume, improve your sales, and ramp up the efficiency in which you run your business.

One Action, Multiple Benefits

Real estate sales often involve a massive amount of effort for a small percentage of success. It often takes more than one hundred purposeful contacts to result in one successful sale. This is why it's important to capitalize on every opportunity with a client who is ready, willing, and able to sell their home. If 95 percent of the work is just getting in front of an eligible lead, it makes sense to give it everything you've got on that last 5 percent to land both the sell side and the buy side.

It's important to know that doing both transactions is not twice the work, at least not for you. When you consider the amount of work that goes into just generating a lead, servicing the client might be only 10 percent of your job. Don't you think it's worth an extra 10 percent of work to double your revenue?

Success in One Area Improves Success in Other Areas

Those at the top of their game often find doing well in one element of their craft makes it easier to do well in other areas. This principle is huge in your real estate sales business. For example, getting more listings helps you advertise yourself and leads to more buyers. Closing with more buyers makes you a better negotiator, and having better negotiating skills leads to more listings. Every deal you close makes it easier to close more deals in the future.

Create a Smooth-Running System

A turbocharger in an engine works by using the air pressure generated by the exhaust system to spin a turbine. This turbine creates horsepower that is redirected back into the vehicle's engine. The turbocharger uses synergistic qualities to create free horsepower for the vehicle. Your business can be adapted to function in the same way.

When you close more deals, you make more money. This additional revenue can be used to add components that make your business run smoother. As I noted earlier in the book, my team uses a CRM that costs $1,000 a month, but it eliminates administrator workload. This CRM allows us to generate leads from various sources, track timelines more easily, market our listings more broadly, and assign different tasks to different team members with the click of a button. These features allow us to do more volume with less work. This is an example of how synergy with software made my business work better.

The same is true for people. By closing more deals, you can hire more help. This help can come in the form of new administrative assistants, showing assistants, or buyer agents (as discussed in Chapter Nine). When you spend less time working on the daily activities of closing houses, you can spend more time working on the activities that contribute to more leads, more opportunities, and more revenue. As you increase the number of leads coming into the business, you hire more people to help you service them. This introduces more revenue and more time to generate more leads. Free horsepower.

Finding Clients for the Buy/Sell Combo

It's important to know how to find clients. The first way is to target buyers. Since most people sell their home to buy a new one, you will typically find combo leads by going to places where buyers start their new home search. Many of these methods spring from working the listings.

You can use the following ways to find combo leads via buyers.

- Hold open houses.

- Convert leads from sign calls.
- Knock on doors around your listing and talk to neighbors.
- Call/prospect the area around your listing.
- Send mailers to the area around your listing.
- Ask your seller for contact information of those in the neighborhood who may be interested in buying their house, selling their own, or both.
- Put out a "Coming Soon" yard sign and contact interested buyers.
- Post information on social media about neighborhood or area-specific businesses buyers would want to know about and respond to comments.
- Advertise your listing on sites like Craigslist.
- Use apps like Nextdoor to communicate with interested neighbors.
- Call your sphere to let them know about your listing and see if they have anyone interested in buying.

You can also look for leads by focusing on sellers. Many of the more driven clients will find the area they want to buy in on their own, then start shopping for a listing agent to help sell their house. Many clients still believe real estate agents are either a "buyer agent" or "listing agent." They have no idea they can use the same agent for both sides.

You can use the following methods to find combo leads via sellers.

- Create a landing page for your company that sellers will find online when searching for the value of their home.
- Place an advertisement with your information on a real estate portal (Zillow, Realtor.com, etc.).
- Tell someone who calls you about selling their home that you can also represent them on the buy side.
- Talk to the neighbor who attends your open house to inquire about the level of interest you are getting.
- Talk to the person who calls about one of your "For Sale" yard signs.
- Make friends with lenders as they may deal with buyers who have to sell their home first.
- Contact your sphere of influence.
- Respond to comments on your social media, your YouTube channel, and online profile/website. Social media posts about the state of the market trigger inquiries.

Finding ways to get both sides out of a single client is a smart business tactic, a powerful driver of your business, and a hallmark of a top producer. Keep a keen eye out for these opportunities.

➡ KEY POINTS

- The best opportunity in real estate sales is the buy/sell combo.
- Top-producing agents value efficiency and know every deal matters. They don't let opportunities go to waste.
- If you can portray yourself as the best agent to help your client with both selling their home and finding a new one, you stand a great chance at getting both sides.
- Most clients will trust your leadership unless you give them reason to question it.
- Take one activity and benefit from it in several ways to increase your productivity.
- Doing both transactions is not twice the work.
- Having more listings helps you advertise yourself and leads to more buyers.
- Many potential clients have no idea they can use the same agent for both sides.

CHAPTER ⟩ TWELVE

NEGOTIATION STRATEGIES

"Negotiation is not an act of battle; it's a process of discovery. The goal is to uncover as much information as possible."

—CHRIS VOSS

As a fiduciary to your clients' interests, you will spend a significant amount of time and energy doing everything within your power to help save or make them money and time. While this is your job, you'll quickly learn your clients don't often understand what you're trying to accomplish. Much of the time, their fears or worries get in the way of your work. Many agents make the big mistake of never realizing they aren't just negotiating for their clients—they are also often negotiating *with* their clients.

Don't assume winning in negotiation means destroying the other side. This is not accurate. True negotiating is helping your client get what they want and helping them feel good in the process. The best negotiators find a path that is agreeable to all parties so everyone feels good about the outcome. This chapter will provide you with the tools you'll need to help your clients realize what's most important to them.

249

The first thing to understand is that you'll often be negotiating for yourself. No one during the transaction will be concerned for your interests but you. This does *not* mean you are negotiating against your clients. As the professional in the relationship, you have to look for solutions that work for both you and your client. Your interests must be aligned. Agents who win for themselves at the expense of their clients don't last long in the industry.

The Power of Tension

In his best-selling book *Never Split the Difference,* former FBI hostage negotiator Chris Voss explains that "he who has learned to disagree without being disagreeable has discovered the most valuable secret of negotiation." This principle rings true in real estate sales, just like everywhere else.

There are two extremes you can fall into when negotiating. The first is to be seen as an adversary. To become unlikable or perceived as unreasonable will make you the enemy to the other side and cause them to put up walls and push back against you. The other extreme is to fail to stand your ground. To give in to the other side's demands—whether your clients or the other agent—in an effort to make them like you or develop goodwill toward you is to give them frame control. This fails to protect your client's interests (as well as your own). Both extremes result in a loss for you.

Rather than try to overpower the other side, I recommend the strategy of creating an emotional tension between yourself and the other party and then being willing to sit in that tension longer than the other side. If you can outlast your opponent (sometimes your client, sometimes the other agent), you will be successful without leaving the other side feeling beaten up. Your goal is to create an emotional tension that is very uncomfortable and to offer a solution that will allow them to escape that tension. This tension is created by you asking for what you want while being extremely likable and hard to say no to.

Human beings do not like pain or discomfort and will go to great lengths to avoid it. You can motivate someone by showing them that continuing with a certain behavior is not in their best interest. When someone is aware of pain, they are motivated to get away from it. You should never cause your clients pain. You should absolutely motivate them to move away from the pain they are already feeling.

Examples of pain your clients may be in without realizing it include:

- Paying someone else's mortgage and not their own.
- Being undisciplined in saving money and not building wealth.
- Watching the market continue to increase while they don't buy.
- Living in a home that does not suit them out of fear of selling.
- Missing out on the right home in pursuit of the "perfect" home.
- Looking at homes they cannot afford.
- Taking advice from those who are not experts in the subject matter.

Understand the importance of the tension you create. If you create tension but are afraid of making someone else feel uncomfortable or you want to be liked by them, you will subconsciously provide an escape valve for the very pressure you created.

Say you represent a buyer who has requested a credit of $3,000 to fix dry rot damage. You submit your request with the understanding your client may back out of the deal if the request is not met. The pressure created from your client possibly backing out of the deal is a necessary step for success as there is no other reason for a seller to agree to give away money. If you are too nice to the other agent or let them know your client will probably move forward with the deal even if the seller says no, the listing agent will advise their client to say no.

The Tension Formula

To make this formula work, you need three components: (1) a request; (2) a strong wall of likability; and (3) a strong wall of firmness.

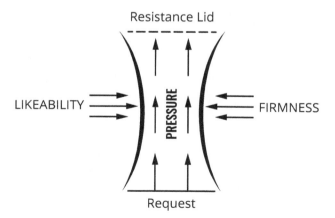

The tension formula is simple. Make a request of the other side that implicitly conveys their interests could be hurt if they don't agree. Create walls so that tension cannot escape through any means other than the acceptance of your terms. Continue to create this tension until their resistance cannot take the pressure and they give in.

Your request itself creates tension when it is delivered with a negative consequence, so that the tension will look for ways to escape. If you don't provide it anywhere to go, it will eventually burst through the resistance of the opponent's position, and your client gets what they want.

This is why maintaining both walls is so important. A breakdown in either wall will result in the same result: a loss of tension and a failed attempt. The key to success is maintaining the appropriate tension and waiting for the opposition to accept your request just to escape the discomfort you created.

If the tension you created escapes through the "firm" wall—you fail to hold your ground—there won't be enough pressure to blast through the seller's opposition. The result is a seller telling you no and you having to explain this to your client.

If your request is firm but you are not likable, the other side may find it easy to tell you no based purely on principle. Agents who make this mistake are those who take a hard line and show no empathy or understanding for the other side. They are often not very personable, not comfortable in conversation, and take a "by the numbers" approach.

Look for comments like these to recognize when you are being too firm.

- "You've got twenty-four hours to respond to our request before the seller sends a cancellation."
- "You have already been given as much grace as you will receive. My client expects an answer in writing by noon tomorrow."
- "I cannot understand how you still don't have the information you need. You've been given plenty of time. We are sending a notice to perform."
- "Please see the attached notice to perform" (delivered without explanation).
- Any communication delivered by yelling, screaming, cursing, or other unprofessional conduct.
- "It's been two days since we've made our request. My broker will be contacting you."

- "If you fail to agree to our request, we will be forced to take further action against your clients."

These types of agents usually know contract law very well and often prefer to communicate by email rather than over the phone, where the conversation has less leeway for tonality and charm and can be kept drier and to the point. The law of reciprocity works against them because you put up walls or look for ways to "reciprocate" the cold or harsh way you and/or your client were treated. Without realizing it, they set a confrontational tone and make their job unnecessarily harder.

Conversely, statements like these indicate you may be erring on the likable side.

- "We want to make this deal work and don't want to offend your seller. Please just see what you can do."
- "My client could really use the money and it would mean a lot to us if you could credit us something."
- "We don't want to ruin the deal, but my clients would be so grateful if you could give us this."
- "It doesn't hurt to ask!"
- "It's my client's first time and they are just really nervous. They would feel a lot better if they could get a credit."
- "We've already given you everything you've asked for. Could you please just give us this one thing?"

Requests made in this manner appeal to the goodwill of the other side. They may provide pressure on the seller to "do the right thing" but not on a seller's fear of losing the deal, losing money, or having their plans altered. This technique is largely ineffective for two reasons: (1) listing agents filter information and likely won't convey the emotion you intend, so your emotional appeal will not find its target; (2) appealing to someone's goodwill is unlikely to be a powerful motivator unless they know you. They must be given a reason to believe there will be a negative consequence if they don't give you what you want.

Agents Creating Win-Win Solutions

In any negotiation, each Realtor has two major concerns:
1. They don't want to let their client down or feel like the other side

"beat" them. This would mean they are not worth their commission and not good at their job.

2. They don't want the deal to fall apart and not be paid. This would mean they have wasted their time and have to start over, or possibly not get a sale from the client at all.

Both of the above results are unsatisfactory.

With that first concern, we want to "win," but so does the other agent. This creates a "win–lose" dynamic and leads to us seeing the other side as an adversary. If my client wins, theirs loses, and vice versa. When we take this perspective, we can easily become unlikable and offer solutions that work only for us. This escalates into both sides saying no, holding their ground, and jeopardizing the closing of the deal.

With the second concern, the Realtor doesn't want the deal to fall apart. "Beating" the other side only to not get the sale is a terrible outcome.

If you can focus on the fact that both agents want the deal to close and want to look for solutions that allow both of you to hand your client the "win," you can create a great working rapport with the other agent and actually close your deals.

When we fail to maintain a high degree of "likability," we make it easy for the other side to tell us no when they otherwise might not have. This hurts both our interests and our clients' interests. Because most of our communication is through nonverbal cues, such as tone of voice, we actually have a large degree of control over how our offers, requests, and solutions are perceived. This is true even when the request itself appears to be one-sided and hard to swallow.

Be Persuasive

In support of this point, Voss advises that "persuasion is not about how bright or smooth or forceful you are. It's about the other party convincing themselves that the solution you want is their own idea." When we take this approach, we invite the other side to focus on how we can work together to close the deal. This often leads to solutions whereby one side gives up something they don't really care about that is valuable to the other side.

The Persuasive Formula

There is a simple formula for how you deliver information in a way that makes it easier to receive.

1. Acknowledge the difficulty or negativity in the situation.
2. Empathize with the other side.
3. Align yourself with your opponent.
4. Propose your solution.
5. Use logic to support why you believe it's a win for all parties.

With this formula in mind, your requests should look like the following.

- I'm sure your sellers have made plans for their future, and I really want us to work together to arrive at a solution that works for everyone. How about you credit us $3,000 toward the worn-out AC unit and we'll drop the home warranty you're currently paying for? I can convince my clients they won't need the warranty if we already have the credit for the air conditioner.
- Thank you for your request for repairs. I'm sure your clients felt nervous when they reviewed the inspection report and realized the house wasn't without some issues in need of repair. I'm hoping you and I can be the voice of reason here. How about you ask your client to pick the three items they feel are most important out of the seven they mentioned, and I'll talk to my seller about fixing them? That way we can keep things moving without extending escrow. I can convince my clients much more easily this way than if it looks like their whole house is in disrepair.

Phrasing your requests as such creates a balance of firmness (clearly stating your need and solution) and likability (acknowledging the other side and empathizing with their feelings) but with enough tension necessary for you to succeed. When done correctly, the other side feels the discomfort of that tension and has no solution for escaping it other than to acquiesce to your request.

To sum things up, the best negotiating techniques include:

1. Making a request that is in your client's best interest but may not be for the other side. This is usually done by asking for credits, making a below-asking-price offer, asking for an extension of time, etc.
2. Forcing the other side to feel the effects of this pressure and not

letting them escape it. Be firm enough they can't ignore you or call your bluff.

3. Allowing things to stand until the other side comes to a solution. Look for ways to subtly bring up the pain of losing the escrow without making it obvious you're doing so.

4. Looking for ways to give them concessions that don't matter to your clients to help them feel better about giving in to your requests.

When it comes to No. 4, several tools can provide win–win solutions, such as:

- Giving rent back to the seller when your client doesn't need to leave their current dwelling.
- Increasing the purchase price on an offer to an amount equivalent to the closing costs your buyers need.
- Fixing the items in a request for repairs that your seller client can do without much difficulty.
- Giving away the appliances of a listing when the seller plans to move a long distance away and doesn't want to bring them.
- Paying for a home warranty to cover the possible replacement of an appliance that is in poor working order instead of replacing the entire appliance (e.g., furnace, HVAC unit)
- Shortening the escrow date to prevent the buyer from paying for an additional rate lock.

Getting Your Point Across Effectively

We are much more likely to have the other side in a negotiation *hear* us if they feel heard first. Relationship experts have given this advice for years. Those who try to make their point or share their perspective before disarming the other side will find themselves interrupting, out-arguing, or shouting over the other side. Instead, put your opponent in a situation where your words and solutions are more readily received.

I liken this to preparing the soil before you plant a seed. Your idea is the seed and your opponent's mind is the soil. Do you want your idea planted in rocky ground where it's very difficult to take root? If so, you may find yourself trying again and again as your frustration grows trying to be heard. Voss supports this theory in *Never Split the Difference* when he says: "Psychotherapy research shows that when individuals feel listened to, they tend to listen to themselves more carefully and to openly evaluate and clarify their own thoughts and feelings."

Consider that a professional boxer's goal is to knock out the opponent. If the boxer throws the right punch and it lands at the right angle, this goal is accomplished. The problem is that the opponent knows this too. If the boxer throws a flurry of punches and gives everything at the beginning of the fight, the opponent will see it coming. Trying to hit an opponent who is actively blocking is futile. If the boxer persists with this strategy, it will wear them out to the point of not being able to punch at all. This is the worst thing that can happen as it leaves the boxer vulnerable to being knocked out by the opponent.

In this analogy, as an agent, you work your opponent into punching themselves out while you block their attacks. Once they are exhausted, deliver your own punches. This is when you'll be heard.

To do this, let them communicate how they feel and let them make their points. Don't share your side of the story yet. Instead, ask clarifying questions and show empathy.

- What else is bothering you?
- What else should I know?
- Can you share more about that?
- How did that make you feel?
- How has that affected your relationship with your client?

Each of these will draw another punch out of your opponent. You don't need to fear these punches because you are in control. When they have nothing more to say and there is an extended silence, you are ready for the counterattack. This is when you share your side.

Baseline Adjustment

I define a "baseline" as a subconscious understanding of normal behaviors or expectations. We operate from various baselines every day. For example, people have different baselines for table manners, dietary restrictions, and social norms. When our expectations are exceeded, we are happy. If they are not, we are not. Many of us make up our mind about how we feel according to our baseline expectations.

To help your clients feel like they've "won," you need to understand what makes a human being feel like they've come out on top.

Think back to a time when you were proud of yourself for something you accomplished. Maybe it was graduating college with a higher grade point average than you expected, setting a personal record in the weight room, or receiving a compliment on something you never thought you would. If you look back at your proudest moments, you're likely to find one common underlying thread that connects each of them: You did something unexpected, or better than what you expected or believed you could.

Many situations in real estate involve scenarios in which we have little control. Consider when a seller believes their home is worth more than it is. Even if you sell it for more than fair market value, the seller will feel cheated if that dollar amount is lower than what they expected. You cannot change that much over fair market value, and you have little influence over a buyer's decision to pay a higher price. If you want happy clients, you have to adjust their baseline.

We do this during the listing presentation with a CMA which outlines what other properties in the neighborhood are selling for. By showing our clients these numbers, we adjust their hidden expectations to a more reasonable level and therefore make them happier. Learning to adjust your client's baseline expectations is a crucial part of negotiating well. It's the only thing you have control over.

Using the Spectrum

There are many times when your clients will push for something they believe is best for them when it's not. Consider a client who wants to write a weak offer on a popular property, or a seller who wants to sell their home for top dollar without improving its condition. If you're not careful, your client may end up blaming you for the poor result they experience. Adjusting their baseline can be difficult if you can't use a CMA for some reason.

When this happens, I use a tool I call the spectrum. The goal is to show my clients why they are hurting their own cause without looking like I'm the adversary. The concept is based on the fact that most people expect they can have their cake and eat it too. If you can show someone that in order to gain in one area they have to lose in another, they are more likely to follow this spectrum.

For example, we would all love to believe we can have six-pack abs while also eating cheeseburgers. A good personal trainer would point out that you can't eat whatever you want *and* look how you want. We have to choose which of those two things is more important to us.

When my client believes they can have everything in a deal, I start the conversation by drawing the following diagram.

COMFORT ◀━━━━━▶ PROFIT

On one end of this spectrum, I write out the word "comfort" (or "convenience"). On the other end I put "profit" (or "success"). I change them up as needed to make my point. I then deliver the following script.

```
I want to talk to you about your goals and how I can help
you with them. As in most things in life, real estate is
all about opposing desires. On one end of this spectrum
is the desire for comfort. There is a way of doing things
that is easier and more comfortable every time. On the
other end is profit. There is a way of doing things that
results in a better financial gain. What I'd like to do
here is find out which of these two opposing forces is
more important to you and then craft a strategy around
those wishes. Let's talk about that.
```

I then explain that the more comfortable way of doing things will hurt the bottom line. I provide specific examples to illustrate this. This helps the client understand how their desire for comfort or convenience works against their financial interests. When this is done correctly, the client will understand they need to change their expectations or the current plan, and they won't blame you for the result they get.

The spectrum can be used whenever a client needs to understand they're getting in their own way of making a profit.

Spectrum Example:

```
Real estate is useful for several purposes. Two of the
biggest are the comfort of owning a home you can cus-
tomize, as well as its ability to build wealth. While
real estate works great for each purpose, it rarely is
```

effective for both at the same time. The decisions someone makes for a property they want to live in are not
always financially prudent. Paying for nicer finishes,
taking down walls to make more of an open concept, and
investing money into the backyard are all fun options
that help build better memories. They are also poor
decisions from an ROI perspective. Conversely, creating additional spaces to rent out to tenants and using
durable, more basic finishes are typically more prudent
financial decisions.

I want to make sure I guide you into the decisions
that make the most sense for you. On one end of a spectrum, we have the comfort and convenience of finding a
property and customizing it to be a great home. On the
other end, we have a pure investment strategy meant
to maximize wealth. Most people land somewhere in the
middle. Based on your needs, how far toward the investment side do you think we can push this before it's too
uncomfortable for you to be happy?

The Triangle Theory

One powerful lesson I've learned in becoming a top-producing agent is
how important it is to never be in conflict with your client. While this
might sound obvious, you'll find yourself in these situations more often
than you might think. As a fiduciary, you'll be forced to do what's in your
client's best interest. This often means you have to be the bearer of bad
news, and sometimes even the crusher of their dreams. This is never fun,
but it is a necessary part of your job.

How you deliver the news to your client is oftentimes more important
than what you're delivering. The difference between a smooth delivery in
which the client receives bad news well and a rough delivery after which
they are left emotionally distraught can be the difference between a sale
and no sale. I created the triangle theory to help me deliver bad news in
a way that doesn't cause clients to automatically blame me or make me
their enemy.

It's human nature to look for someone or something to blame when
things don't go according to plan. We all do it. As the agent, your clients

may easily blame you when things go wrong, even when those things are outside of your control. Things like low appraisals, bad roof reports, buyers backing out of deals, and loans falling apart will often be put on your shoulders. Your goal is to prevent anything outside of your control from creating conflict between you and your client.

In essence, the triangle theory helps you shape your communication so there will always be something or someone else in your client relationship that can be the adversary.

In any situation where I have to deliver bad news—or really any news the client might not want to hear—I find some way to align myself with the client's side against our adversary (the third point in the triangle).

This solidifies my client's emotional alignment with me and reminds them I'm on their side. If you don't do this, the trust you have worked so hard to develop can be quickly eroded—making your job much harder. Even if you still close the deal, your client will be less likely to become a raving fan and send you referrals.

There are an infinite number of ways this theory can be applied. You don't even need to use a person to create the third point in the triangle. This works with interest rates, inspection reports, average rents, or the market itself. There is always a reason something is preventing your clients from getting what they want. The triangle theory can be used when a client is stressed or upset. The following examples are scenarios in which you can create a third party in a triangle to ensure your client is never in conflict with you.

SCENARIO	THIRD PARTY (ADVERSARY)	SCRIPT
Your client believes their house is worth an amount you can clearly see it is not going to sell for.	The market.	"I completely agree that your house is worth every dollar you do. The problem is that the market is clearly showing us buyers aren't ready to pay that yet. Not with the amount of comparable sales showing so much lower. I'd love to list your house at that price if I thought it would appraise. Can you find a comparable sale on this CMA that would support that?"
The buyer does not want to pay the original offer price when the house appraises lower.	The lender.	"You're right that it's unfair that an appraisal can affect the amount of money the buyer was willing to pay. They would have happily paid the price they agreed on if they could. The problem is the bank. Now that an appraiser has assessed the house where they did, they won't lend the money they said they would originally. The buyer can't buy the property if the bank won't lend them the money. They are still willing to pay what the appraiser considers "fair market value," and this new price won't affect your plans for your next home. Would you rather put your house back on the market and wait for a new buyer, knowing this might happen again?"
There are several other offers on the house your buyer wants.	Other buyers.	"I agree we have to pay more than we wanted to get this house. The problem is the other buyers. There are so many people out there desperate to get a property that if we won't pay the higher price, someone else will. We have to decide if we want the house more than they do. We know the top price offered was [$ amount]. Are you okay letting them get this house instead of you because they wanted it more?

The triangle theory isn't only useful for your clients. It's useful with anyone. When dealing with the other agent, you may need to align with them against your own client. Remember that as a fiduciary, everything you do is for the financial interests of your client.

Here are a few examples.

- "I know our offer was lower than you expected. I totally believe your listing is worth more. The problem is my buyers are preapproved at this amount, and I just can't get them any more. I wish there was more I could do. Do you think we can make this deal work and I'll make sure we write stronger terms in exchange for the lower price?"

- "I know your clients want us to credit them $10,000 to repair every single thing in the inspection report. The problem is this isn't a brand-new house. Of course, it will have some things wrong with it. I want to get my sellers to give your clients something, but you've got to work with me on this. Can you give me something reasonable I can present to my clients so they can agree to your request?"

- "Your clients didn't write the highest offer, but my clients liked them the most. I'd like to work with you since you seem to be the most professional Realtor who submitted an offer. Can you get your clients to keep their terms the same and increase their price to be where my other offer is so I can make the case to go with you?"

Prizing

Prizing is a way of shifting the value in a negotiation away from the other side and toward you. When used effectively, it not only removes their leverage but also leaves them wanting what you have instead. If you don't learn to prize what you bring to the table in a negotiation, you will constantly be on the defense. It's hard to move forward when you're always defending yourself.

A simple example of prizing in action is when a client asks you to reduce your commission because they have something of value: "David, I think you're a great agent and we want to have you represent us. Because we have a house to sell *and* a house to buy, we'd like you to give us 25 percent of your commission because you'll be getting both sides."

The seller has created a frame in which the commission is the prize. To get that prize, you have to give up something. Rather than argue about why you're worth the commission—which leaves you on the defense and allows them to continue to poke holes in your value—it's better to shift the prize away from the commission and on to something *you* possess. Your response could be:

> I can understand why that may seem logical from your perspective. I'm getting two commissions out of one client. My concern is I'm still doing twice as much work. In addition to that, there is more pressure on me to perform. And frankly, this is so important to me I'll be prioritizing this over other clients. There's too much at stake for you if this doesn't go well. I realize you may use two different Realtors to help you in this transaction, but in that case, you'll still have two different commissions involved and neither of them would give up 25 percent. Furthermore, you'd take the risk of neither side caring about helping the other as they only get paid for their own side. With me doing this, I can make sure the timing of both sides closing in sync happens smoothly and the result is seamless for you. You'd be hard-pressed to find a Realtor who can do what I do and as well as I can do it. A lot is riding on this. Are you sure you want to take the risk of working with two random agents just to save a small piece of this entire puzzle?

This reply subtly changes the prize from the commission to the risk they are avoiding by using only one Realtor—me. By highlighting everything that can go wrong if they use the alternative option, you establish yourself, your skills, and your guarantee of a good result as much more important prizes.

Look for ways to use prizing when you see the other side making comments that indicate you are in a position of disadvantage.

Prizing Scripts

> *Complaint:* I'm buying an expensive house and I want back part of the commission.

You say: It's true that commissions are based on sales prices and this home is more expensive than the average in the neighborhood, but candidly, the seller is paying me, not you. I'm compensated because I found a buyer for the seller's property. Although I'm your agent, you aren't paying me. My understanding is you wanted me to make sure I represented your interests in this transaction, and that's why you chose me. I know I'm good at doing this. Frankly, there are none better. Would you like to renegotiate our original agreement? Instead of negotiating for your interests with the seller, should I start negotiating for my own interests with you? The seller hasn't asked to pay me less than they agreed to, but you are. Let's back up a minute to get a clear understanding of how our partnership works and which roles we each play here.

Complaint: My client has a cash buyer and wants a deal on your listing.

You say: While it's true you represent a cash buyer, the other interested parties are paying in cash too—the bank's cash. I've spoken to the lenders involved for the other offers we received, and the borrowers look solid. I don't anticipate any problems with the financing of the other buyers, and I've communicated that with my sellers. Your client is avoiding closing costs and a mortgage payment by paying cash for the home. That makes this more affordable for them than the other buyers. Can you present an offer that is more competitive, not less, than the others? I'd love to work with you if you can.

Complaint: We have higher offers than yours.

You say: It may be true that other buyers wrote offers with a price higher than ours, but have you looked closely at them to make sure they can actually close? My buyer is fully underwritten with a very strong loan and a large down payment. In addition to that, they are agreeing to not ask for any credits after we go into contract and will take the house "as-is." Those other buyers may look good now, but we both know all that changes once the contract is signed. I can assure you a smooth escrow, a painless closing, and a more profitable end result for your seller. There are many houses on the market, but yours is our first pick. Let me know if we need to find a different seller who would like what we are offering. I hope that's not the case.

Complaint: You can represent me writing an offer on your listing, but I want half your commission. (In areas where it is permissible for the listing agent to represent the buyer and the seller.)

You say: I've had clients ask me this before, and I tell them the same thing. The reason you use me to represent you on this listing is because you improve your odds of getting the property. This is a hot market, and there are many buyers out there. In fact, the reason you are probably still looking for a house is because you've been outbid on those you have tried for. If you use me to write your offer, I can make sure you don't grossly overpay more than you had to, get the seller to credit you a reasonable amount for needed repairs, and prevent the egos of two different agents from ruining the deal. I am here to save you big money, not give you my money. If you aren't interested in that, then you're welcome to find another agent to represent you. I'm happy to tell my seller you asked for half of the commission. I'm sure the seller would prefer me to give it to them over you.

The Tier System

The tier system is a structure I designed to help address FOMO (fear of missing out) with clients who have trouble committing out of fear there is something better out there. This occurs most commonly with buyer clients who find a house that works for them but feel they might find a better one if they keep looking. Should they find a better one, the same problem occurs, and the cycle continues.

To overcome this, you need to create a framework in which the client understands there are no better options out there for them than the one they've found. In *Pitch Anything*, Oren Klaff describes how the midbrain receives information and evaluates it within a social construct (first discussed in Chapter Four). This part of the brain takes the information it receives and compares it to other information to decide if the stimulus is good or bad.

The tier system helps me satisfy my client's midbrain and FOMO concerns by eliminating unrealistic options. Every buyer starts off wanting the perfect house at the lowest price and in the best area. Only after seeing for themselves that these houses don't exist do buyers adjust their expectations to realistic levels. Amateur agents accomplish this by showing house after house until it finally sinks in for the buyer. Top producers accomplish this before they ever leave the office.

I start off by addressing the elephant in the room: I acknowledge that I understand the client's desires. I tell them:

```
I know what you'd really like is a fourplex in a Grade A
neighborhood. I want to say I'm absolutely going to try
and find that for you. In my experience, though, there
aren't many of these. And those that do hit the market
sell very fast and for a higher price than your current
preapproval. I also understand if we can't find a four-
plex, you'd like a triplex or a duplex in the same area.
I'm going to look at those too. In fact, I've compiled a
search of every available property that matches these
criteria. I'd like to show you that now.
```

Then I pull up the list of properties on the MLS highlighting the fact that everything is over their price range. I tell them:

As you can see, we would need to borrow significantly more money than we can currently afford to get one of these. Now, I'm going to commit to checking every week. In the meantime, can I show you some fantastic options that *are* in your price range and still meet your criteria to reduce your monthly payment by renting out part of the property?

At this point I show them the single-family homes that have accessory dwelling units, in-law units, or other ways to rent out part of the home. This allows my client to quiet the voice that says "there is more out there than this" because they can see for themselves there is not. It also gives their midbrain the ability to compare the best realistic options available, makes them feel good about their decisions, and helps them overcome FOMO.

 **KEY POINTS**

- Successful negotiation is the art of finding a path that is agreeable to all parties involved.
- Build solid walls of likability and firmness around tension, then maintain that tension until the opposition relieves it by giving you want you want.
- Show empathy by acknowledging the negative, aligning with the opponent, proposing a solution, and supporting your solution with logic.
- Draw out the "punches" from your opponent before punching back. Ask questions until they feel you've heard them. Only then speak.
- People travel the emotional spectrum from fear to greed. Learn how to help your client control those emotions to keep them closer to the center. This is where they think most clearly and make more reasonable decisions.
- Adjust your clients' baselines to adjust their expectations.
- Negative reinforcement is the strongest motivator. Use it to your benefit. Remind clients of their pain to make it easier for them to make the tough decisions.

- Use the comfort/profit spectrum to help clients see they can't have it all.
- Use the triangle theory to deliver bad news to clients so that they don't blame you. Create a third point between you and your clients to be the bad guy. It can be the other agent, the market, the appraiser, the lender, etc.
- The tier system helps satisfy clients' midbrain concerns and FOMO by eliminating unrealistic comparison options.

CHAPTER THIRTEEN

UNDERSTANDING FINANCING

"How many millionaires do you know who have become wealthy by investing in savings accounts? I rest my case."

—ROBERT G. ALLEN

Very few real estate agents also handle loans for their clients. In most states, this requires a broker's license, and in some states it is not allowed at all. Nevertheless, it's still important that you understand how they work. Loans and real estate sales work together to create the possibility of home ownership for the vast majority of buyers. Since most of your buyers will be using loans to purchase the property you're helping them with, you'll need to understand how that part of the process works to serve them best.

But buyers and sellers need help understanding financing. According to Realtor.com,[10] the No. 1 reason deals fall apart is buyer financing. This can happen for several reasons. If you want to protect the sale of your client's home, you'll need to verify that the buyer is approved for

---

[10] Margaret Heidenry, "How Long Does It Take to Close on a House?", Realtor.com, October 2, 2019, https://www.realtor.com/advice/buy/how-long-does-it-take-to-close-on-a-house/.

the financing needed and know how to troubleshoot financing problems when they do occur. This can save your clients thousands of dollars.

In 2019 I was representing a seller on a property in San Francisco. The buyers for the property were preapproved with one of the few lenders in the city that could underwrite this type of property. We were under contract for more than a million dollars and were halfway through the escrow period when the buyer's agent reported a problem.

The buyers had looked deeper into the details surrounding the property and realized they would have to pay each month for their water, sewer, garbage, and other expenses shared with the other owners in the property. These expenses were more per month than the buyers were expecting to pay. Their agent had failed to set an accurate baseline. As a result, the buyers requested a $95,000 drop in the purchase price. Their reasoning was the drop in price counterbalanced the higher shared expenses. The buyers threatened to back out of the deal if their request was not met.

I spoke with my clients, who didn't want to put the house back on the market. This put me in a tricky predicament. I knew they were losing a lot of money by not walking away from the deal. But not dropping the price meant the buyers could back out completely, and that's not what my clients wanted either. Neither option was in our favor. This was particularly frustrating because we had done nothing wrong.

I talked to the buyer's agent, and she was no help. She told me to reduce the price or they'd walk away. She didn't seem to have much control or influence over her client (a sign of a weak agent). As I pondered our options, I came up with the following solution.

I called the lender and asked how much it would cost if the buyers "bought down the rate" to make the monthly mortgage payments match the amount that reducing the purchase price by $95,000 would. "Buying down the rate" is when a buyer pays "points" (i.e., extra closing costs) upfront in exchange for a lower interest rate. The lender found it would cost approximately $22,000 to buy down the rate.

I brought this option to the buyer's agent and was very pleasant while firmly letting her know that if her clients really were concerned with their monthly payments, my clients would buy down their rate to get them the payment they claimed they wanted. I reminded her that the asset itself was not worth $95,000 *less* just because she had miscalculated her clients' payments. If they did not agree to this solution, then they weren't negotiating in good faith, and we would put the property back on the market.

This response didn't leave the other party with much choice. They accepted my solution, and I saved my clients around $73,000. My clients were thrilled that I was able to close on the property, and the buyers got what they wanted, so in the end everybody won.

This solution would never have happened if I hadn't been aware of how financing works in real estate. This example illustrates just how important your knowledge in this arena is. This chapter will teach you how lenders make money, what loan products are available for your clients, how they can put funds together for a down payment, and how to explain lending in general to your clients. You'll also learn some common pitfalls to avoid and some crafty hacks to get your buyers a better deal.

In addition to using this knowledge to service your clients, it'll help you grow your business. When you can clearly articulate the mortgage process to new leads at an open house, it helps you stand apart from the agents who don't have this knowledge. Buyers (especially those in the beginning stages of the process) will most certainly be concerned with the amount of loan they qualify for. In fact, this is all most buyers think about. Your ability to be a trusted guide with their finances will help you win their business and move them along your Sales Funnel from Lead to Client.

How the Mortgage Market Works

In legal terms, a mortgage is "the pledging of property to a creditor as security for the payment of a debt."[11] In practical terms, a mortgage typically refers to a loan that a home buyer receives to buy a house. If the homeowner fails to make their payment, the lender (or lien holder) can take the property back from the homeowner and sell it to someone else to recover their money. In simple terms, a mortgage is a loan in which a house functions as the collateral. The majority of the clients you work with as a real estate agent will be using a loan to purchase their property.

Origination Process

There are different routes to get a mortgage. Most mortgages are directly

---

11 Dave Roos, "How Debt Works," HowStuffWorks, December 11, 2007, https://money.howstuffworks.com/personal-finance/debt-management/debt.htm.

through banks. Mortgage companies, also known as mortgage brokers, will shop to find the bank with the most competitive interest rate and closing costs. Loan officers are licensed individuals who originate loans for the mortgage lender. The process of loan origination involves receiving an online application, collecting financial documents, verifying income and debt, and passing the loan information to an underwriter for final approval. When a loan is originated, the escrow is funded with the lender's money and the client's down payment. When the escrow closes, the funds transfer from the buyer to the seller and the title transfers from the seller to the buyer.

Loan originators are typically the following types of loan officers:

Mortgage Banker. A mortgage banker works directly for the lender (also called a direct lender) and originates loans for that bank's capital. These bankers are typically the people you see when you walk into a bank or credit union, but sometimes they work from home or in a satellite office. They can be compared to a real estate agent who works only for a new home builder and only sells that builder's inventory. A bank's mortgage department largely relies on walk-in business and doesn't always have the best pricing. The upside to mortgage bankers is that they often have direct access to underwriters and can therefore close loans faster and with fewer obstacles.

Mortgage Broker. A mortgage broker is a loan officer who originates a loan and then shops that loan to different banks or lenders to find the most competitive rate. Mortgage brokers are usually paid by the lender they've selected. The upside to mortgage brokers is that they can usually get a better rate for your clients. The downside is that they don't always have direct access to underwriters and therefore usually cannot close a loan as quickly as a bank and are likely to have more communication issues because there are more steps in the process between underwriter and borrower.

Hard Money Lender. Hard money lenders typically work for a fund or capital source and originate loans directly for that fund or source. These lenders are typically used for short-term loans (one year or less); they have less stringent loan requirements but higher rates and closing costs. Most borrowers use hard money loans for a short period and then refinance with more affordable loans. An example of this would be a client who purchases a property with a hard money loan until they qualify for conventional financing. Another example would be an investor who uses a hard money loan to purchase and rehab a property, and then refinances into a more traditional loan after the property is in better condition.

Aggregation Process

After a loan is originated and the title for the house is transferred, the agents are paid and the lender is left with a note. The note, which was agreed upon by the borrowers during the escrow process, spells out the terms of the loan. This is where the buyers agree to the interest rate, payment schedule, amortization period, and other details. Once a note is created, it can be kept by the originator or sold to someone else. When another entity buys a note, they are buying the right to collect the payment associated with it.

Most loan originators sell the bulk of their notes. Those who buy these notes are collectively referred to as the "secondary market," as they are the second owners of the notes originated by the lenders. Most notes are purchased in the secondary market after they've been grouped together in a process called aggregation. Aggregators may either group loans together to sell them or sell them individually. Most of the pooled loans are sold to:

1. Government-sponsored enterprises (GSEs) or
2. Mortgage-backed securities (MBSs)

A GSE is an organization chartered by Congress for the purpose of providing people with financial services. Two popular GSEs are the Federal National Mortgage Association ("Fannie Mae") and the Federal Home Loan Mortgage Corporation ("Freddie Mac"). These entities buy or insure mortgages originated by lenders throughout the country. By doing so, they increase the amount of liquidity available to lenders so they can lend to more borrowers and make it easier for Americans to get financing for homes.

Mortgage-backed securities are investments similar to bonds. They are made up of bundles of home loans that are packaged together, split into smaller pieces, and sold through the stock market. MBSs function similarly to GSEs in that they buy mortgages from those who aggregate them and then sell them to those who want to own a security in their financial portfolio. GSEs and MBSs help keep lenders funded to originate loans and keep the mortgage market satisfied.

Few borrowers realize the extent to which their mortgage is cut up into smaller pieces and packaged to be traded. In a matter of months, or sometimes even weeks, a mortgage can be originated and sold through several back-end buyers—ultimately ending up as a mortgage-backed security or part of a Fannie Mae or Freddie Mac portfolio in most cases. Because so many of today's loans end up purchased or ensured by GSEs, banks will underwrite most loans to the standards set by the GSEs. For entities that originate and sell loans, it pays to have them underwritten in a manner you know your end buyers are going to want.

These GSE guidelines are the standards that most lenders adhere to when originating loans for clients. Knowing this will help you explain to your clients why lenders ask for all that paperwork. Standard documentation that conforms to these standards are:

- Two years of tax returns
- Two years of W-2 statements
- Two most recent pay stubs
- Two most recent bank statements
- Credit report (the lender can run)
- Copy of most recent mortgage statement (if applicable)
- Two forms of ID

Lenders use this information for several reasons, but the biggest is to calculate a borrower's debt-to-income (DTI) ratio, which is a simple metric used to determine how much of a borrower's income is already allocated to paying off debt.

For the majority of GSE loans, the lender wants to see a DTI of 47 percent or less. This means no more than 47 percent of a borrower's income can be allocated to debt. This would include mortgage payments, taxes, and insurance on the property they want to buy. When a client's DTI exceeds the maximum allowable DTI, the borrower must pay off existing debts before qualifying for a mortgage.

Loan officers use the pay stubs, tax returns, and W-2 statements to gather information about the borrower's income. The credit report confirms the amount of debt in the borrower's credit history. This is also where they find the borrower's FICO score. After a lender knows how much income the borrower has left over after they service their debt, they calculate how much the borrower can afford and still remain below the 47 percent allowed. By using a mortgage calculator and current interest rates, the lender can provide a dollar amount that the applicant is allowed to borrow to buy a house. To determine the price point the applicant will be preapproved to borrow, lenders take the amount of the borrower's down payment and add it to the maximum amount they are eligible to borrow.

After this is determined, the lender issues a preapproval letter. Only then should you look for houses with your client at the appropriate price point.

Different Loan Products

Government Loans

Three federal agencies work with lenders to offer discounted rates and better loan terms to qualified borrowers. These large public/private entities were created by Congress to make mortgages available to more people with low and moderate incomes. The following agencies offer most of the home loans.

Federal Housing Administration (FHA). FHA loans are known for their characteristically low down payment (3.5 percent), flexible credit scores (currently 580), and competitive interest rates. FHA loans are offered by the government to help those who normally would not qualify for a mortgage become homeowners. The biggest downside to FHA loans is that they require a form of mortgage insurance called a mortgage insurance premium (MIP). Many loans require private mortgage insurance (PMI) if the down payment is less than 20 percent, but the PMI ends when the loan-to-value (LTV) ratio is 80 percent. However, MIP applies for the life of the FHA loan; it doesn't drop off, regardless of the LTV ratio of the property.

Veterans Administration (VA). VA loans are available to those who have served in any branch of the U.S. armed forces and are known for offering 0 percent down for the borrower, competitive interest rates, and the ability to borrow up to the maximum conforming limit determined by Fannie Mae/Freddie Mac for the area in which the home is located (conforming limits are discussed in this chapter under "Conventional

Loans"). Another benefit of VA loans is they don't require PMI. Those eligible for VA loans can:
- Buy a single-family home, up to four units.
- Buy a condo in a VA-approved project.
- Buy a fixer-upper.
- Buy a manufactured home or lot.
- Build a new home.
- Make changes or add new features (like solar power) to make the purchase more energy efficient.

VA loans aren't without their downsides. Many in the real estate industry believe the appraisals for these loans come in at lower valuations than conventional loans. There are also stipulations for the condition of the property itself that are not present in conventional loans (such as the handling of pest infestations). VA loans also have higher closing costs than conventional loans, and buyers may find their escrow periods are longer due to the extra requirements.

Rural Housing Service (RHS)/United States Department of Agriculture (USDA). If your client lives in a rural area or small town, they may qualify for a low interest loan through the RHS, which offers both guaranteed loans through approved lenders and direct loans that are government-funded. RHS/USDA loans are not made directly through the agency, but rather they insure loans that qualify under their guidelines made through approved mortgage lenders.

These loans are known for requiring o percent down and having low credit score requirements. They are only available in certain rural areas.[12]

Conventional Loans

A conventional mortgage is a loan that is not insured or issued by the federal government. They fall into two categories known as conforming and nonconforming loans. Conforming loans follow the guidelines set by Fannie Mae and Freddie Mac. The most well-known rule has to do with the size of the loan. Fannie Mae/Freddie Mac sets limits for home loan amounts that vary by location in the country. More expensive markets

---

[12] To learn more about these loans and which areas they service, visit https://www.rd.usda.gov/about-rd/agencies/rural-housing-service.

allow for higher loan limits than less expensive markets. Loans made for amounts higher than the conforming limit set for the area are called "jumbo loans."

These nonconforming jumbo loans are more difficult to sell because they cannot be purchased by GSEs on the secondary market, and MBSs do not value them as highly as loans within the loan limit standards. All this makes jumbo loans riskier and explains why they usually have higher interest rates, offer fewer low-down-payment options, require higher credit scores, and call for borrowers to have higher money reserves.

The benefit to conforming conventional financing loans is mainly that the PMI drops off when the LTV ratio for the home reaches 80 percent. This means when the amount of the principal on the home reaches 80 percent or less of the home's value, borrowers can request to have the PMI dropped from the loan without any refinancing. This is good because most refinancing adds the new closing costs to the loan's balance.

Preapproval Process

When you meet new buyer clients, the first thing to do is give them your presentation and get them signed up to work with you as their agent. You'll then immediately want to get them preapproved with a lender. This will let you know the price range of houses to look at as well as any potential hurdles in the process of obtaining financing.

Since a successful outcome for you and any buyer client—purchasing a house—is dependent on your clients obtaining financing, select a lender to refer business to that does an outstanding job with your clients *and* that makes you look like a rock star in the process. This is such an important piece of my business that I actually became a loan officer myself and started my own mortgage company, just to have more control over the end result and the experience my clients received. I can now service other Realtors' clients the way I service my own and make sure everything is done efficiently and to the highest standards. If you choose the wrong lender for preapprovals, it will negatively impact your own conversion rate.

The preapproval process comprises the following steps.

1. Filling out a mortgage application
2. Collecting supporting documents
3. Verifying income

4. Calculating a debt-to-income ratio
5. Determining an estimated interest rate
6. Running the file through "desktop underwriting" to scan for possible later red flags
7. Creating closing cost estimates
8. Issuing a preapproval letter

Most lenders will tell you that the process of issuing a preapproval letter—your goal in this scenario—mostly gets hung up while waiting for your clients to complete their mortgage application and submit the supporting documentation required to verify the information they provided. If you want to help your own cause, assist your preferred lender in collecting the information they need from your clients. This will get the process accomplished more quickly and get you showing homes sooner.

Keep in mind your client's perspective, though. They are being asked to share extremely personal financial information with someone they don't know and who was likely recommended by you or another person they don't know well either. This also means they have to do a decent amount of work gathering all the required documentation, including navigating unfamiliar websites, digging through old emails, and reaching out to their tax preparers or the Human Resources department of their workplace to get what is needed. This process is cumbersome, not fun, and the client usually doesn't understand why all this the paperwork is so important.

Use the influence you created during your presentation to motivate them to do what is necessary to collect the required documents. By helping the lender with the preapproval process, you're really helping yourself.

The purpose of a *preapproval* letter is to have the majority of the information an underwriter will need before they can *approve* a loan. We do this before we start looking at properties for several reasons.

1. We don't want to go in escrow on a home and then find out the borrower cannot get a loan.
2. We don't want our clients spending money on inspections and appraisals only to find out they can't buy the home.
3. We don't want our clients to pack up all their belongings and prepare their current home for sale—or even worse, sell their current home—before they know they can buy the next one.
4. We want to spare our clients the emotional pain of falling in love

with a new property, new location, or new financial situation only to find out it can't work out.

5. We want to spare ourselves the time it takes to find the right house for a buyer, and the money we spend to do it, if we aren't going to close on the new property.

After a client is preapproved and you find a property to put into escrow, you'll send the contract to the loan officer, who will forward it to the lender for the underwriting process. A few more items will need to be verified (the client's employment status, for instance), and as soon as the underwriter is satisfied with the conditions of the loan package meeting their specific standards, they will inform the loan officer that the loan is ready to fund the escrow.

Explaining the Costs of Borrowing to Your Clients

When you meet prospective home buyer leads, you'll notice the majority of their questions deal with the process of borrowing money. In my experience, they are primarily concerned with getting a low interest rate and are wildly ignorant of the other costs associated with getting a home loan. To protect their interests, save them money, and stand apart as a top-notch fiduciary, you must be able to explain the two components of borrowing money: (1) how the lender makes money on the loan; and (2) the various subcomponents that make up the loan itself.

Lenders make money (1) when they sell a loan to a secondary buyer, and (2) through the closing costs they charge the borrower.

The amount a lender makes on a loan they sell is determined largely by the spread of the interest rate. When a mortgage broker originates a loan, they use a pricing sheet that states the amount for which they can sell a loan to a secondary buyer. This pricing sheet is provided by the secondary buyer/investor who will buy the loan. There is a base rate at which the loan originator can sell for zero dollars. If they sell the loan for less than this rate, the loan originator will have to pay the secondary buyer to buy the loan. The higher the interest rate is above the base rate, the more the loan originator will be compensated for the loan.

When a loan originator can sell a loan with a higher interest rate, they can be paid more. When a loan originator sells a loan for less than the base rate, they will have to pay their own money to get someone to take the loan from them. In these cases, loan originators make up for that cost by charging the borrower increased closing costs.

This creates an inverse relationship between rates and fees (closing costs). In order to get a better rate, the borrower has to pay higher fees.

Comprehending this key principle will make it easier to help your clients understand their financing options, and this knowledge positions you as the trusted fiduciary to walk them through the process. Clients who plan to own a property for a long time and have enough capital in the bank are usually better served by higher closing costs and lower interest rates. For those clients who need to save more cash or who plan to own the property for a shorter period of time, paying less in closing costs but having higher interest rates makes more financial sense.

Understanding Closing Costs

As previously mentioned, closing costs are a large part of the cost of home ownership. While these costs vary from area to area, they can range from $5,000 to $20,000 (and higher). Clients must understand that this is money they will need in addition to their down payment. "Closing costs" is a general term that typically refers to several costs grouped into one amount that is due at "closing." These costs include:

- Origination fee
- Discount fee
- Processing fee
- Underwriting fee
- Wire transfer fee
- Credit report fee
- Tax service fee
- Flood certification fee
- Notary fee
- Title insurance fee
- Lender fees
- Courier fees
- Appraisal costs
- Recording fees
- First year's homeowners insurance premium (if needed)
- Property tax reserves for impound account
- Points
- Survey costs

As you can see, these costs really add up. Make sure your client is aware of the total. To receive an estimate of these costs to present to your client, you can request a "net sheet" from an escrow company that will highlight the anticipated amount the client will pay as well as a loan estimate from a lender that shows what the estimated loan fees will be.

Understanding the Loan

The following are loan terms and concepts useful for explaining the loan product to your clients and understanding it for yourself.

Amortization. The mortgage payment comprises two parts. One part goes toward the principal. This is the amount that is deducted from what the borrower owes the lender. The second part goes toward the interest owed. This is the amount the lender gets to keep. When these two amounts are combined, the result is the total monthly payment collected by the lender. This two-part system (principal and interest in the same monthly payment) is referred to as "amortization."

When a loan is amortized, the lender sets an amount of time for the borrower's use of the money and then calculates backward from the end date to create a payment schedule that will reach a zero balance on the last payment of the agreed-upon term. In common language, this is a "thirty-year loan," "fifteen-year loan," etc. The longer the length of the loan, the smaller the monthly payments are for the borrower.

The caveat to longer-length loans is that the borrower pays more of their monthly payment toward interest than principal. Shorter-term loans are more expensive, but a larger amount of the payment goes toward the principal each month. This means the borrower pays less interest over the length of the loan.

To check out what these schedules look like, download the free app I mentioned earlier in the book: Mortgage Calculator Plus. I use this tool frequently at open houses, during buyer presentations, and in other scenarios where I need to show my value to win a lead's business.

Monthly Payments. Four components—often referred to by the acronym PITI—make up a monthly payment.
- **Principal**: Deducted from the total amount the borrower owes the lender
- **Interest**: The amount the lender keeps

- **Taxes**: The property taxes collected on behalf of the borrower to be paid to the state
- **Insurance**: The homeowners insurance and any mortgage insurance required on the loan

A monthly payment consists of the mortgage payment (that is, the amount the borrower pays to the bank) and the impound accounts (that is, the amount the lender collects on behalf of the buyer to pay the PITI). The impound account usually comprises property taxes and homeowners insurance.

When discussing the monthly payments your clients will be paying after they close, I recommend giving them the total PITI amount, not just the principal and interest. This is a far more accurate reflection of the true cost of home ownership and will help prepare them for the responsibility they are taking on in becoming a homeowner.

Foreclosure Process

When a borrower defaults on making the payments they agreed to, the lender is legally allowed to begin the process of taking back the title to the collateral the borrower offered in exchange for the loan. In most cases, this is the property itself. Foreclosure is the legal process by which a lender takes possession of your client's home and sells it to get its money back. Lenders must follow a strict set of guidelines that vary from state to state. In general, though, there are five steps to a foreclosure.

1. The borrower defaults on the loan.
2. The lender issues a notice of default.
3. A Notice of Trustee's Sale is recorded in the county office.
4. The lender tries to sell the property at a public auction.
5. If the property doesn't sell at the auction, the lender becomes the owner.

Foreclosure proceedings can begin after a single missed payment, but this rarely happens. Most banks and lenders have a grace period for late payments that is usually accompanied by a fee or penalty. Once a borrower falls three months behind, things tend to get serious. This is the point at which most lenders will initiate the foreclosure process. All states allow for a judicial sale, while only twenty-nine states allow for a power of sale.

A judicial sale requires the foreclosure process to go through the court system and is therefore a more lengthy and laborious process.

Power of sale allows the process to be carried out entirely by the lender or mortgage holder. This type of foreclosure tends to happen faster because of fewer roadblocks or less red tape. If your state allows power of sale, the loan papers will usually have a clause stipulating that this method will be used. It is faster, easier, and less expensive for the lien holder.

The steps for these foreclosures are as follows.

Process for Judicial Sale

1. The mortgage lender files a suit with the court system.
2. The court issues a letter demanding payment.
3. The borrower typically has thirty days to respond with payment to avoid foreclosure.
4. If the borrower hasn't paid by the end of the payment period, a judgment will be entered in the court system and the lender can request sale of the property by auction.
5. The auction is carried out by the sheriff's office, usually on the courthouse steps several months after the judgment.
6. As soon as the property is sold, the previous owner is served with an eviction notice by the sheriff's office.

Process for Power of Sale

1. The mortgage lender serves your client papers demanding payment.
2. After an established waiting period, a deed of trust is drawn up that temporarily conveys the property to a trustee.
3. The trustee will sell the house at public auction for the lender.
4. Many times, these foreclosures are subject to judicial review to make sure everything was carried out legally.
5. There is usually a requirement for the lender to post a public notice of sale for the auction.

A common mistake made in real estate vernacular occurs when someone refers to a "foreclosure" when talking about a property the bank has already taken back title to. The best way to understand this phrasing is to recognize that "foreclosure" refers to the act of a bank or lender taking title. Once they have the title, the property is usually referred to as "REO" (real estate owned). REO is an accounting term that describes assets on a bank's balance sheet. While banks don't like to own the title to a property, they recognize that there are times when a borrower will default and they must hold the asset on their books until it can be resold. During this holding time, the asset is referred to as REO.

Most banks hire real estate agents to sell REO properties. Your clients will see these properties advertised on the MLS just like other listings. When a client wants to buy a foreclosure, this is referring to the auction on the courthouse steps before the bank has taken title completely. These sales are usually all cash, no contingencies, and made without title insurance or any of the other safety measures typically associated with the transfer of real estate title.

Common Pitfalls

As a top-producing agent, you'll want to serve each client well, but few areas will be as important as saving them money. You can show your value (and create raving fans while doing it) by helping clients understand the ways to save money on their loans and purchase transactions. Here are some of the hidden dangers that can easily trip up home buyers in the process of getting financing and completing their purchase. Study these so you can warn your clients about what to do and what to avoid to help save them money.

Not Understanding the Mortgage Interest Tax Deduction

One way to gain credibility as a professional and help your clients feel better about the stresses and fears of the buying process is to explain and highlight the benefits of the mortgage interest tax deduction that the federal government allows homeowners to currently claim.

As mentioned before, the mortgage payment is made of two parts: principal and interest. According to tax laws in place at the time this book was published, homeowners are allowed to add up the amount of the interest they pay on their mortgage payment and deduct that against their taxable income at the end of the year. This exception is meant to encourage home ownership and is a big incentive for those looking to buy a home. Consider the following amortization schedule.

MORTGAGE SCHEDULE

Payment (Principal & Interest Only) $1,133.86

	Date	Principal	Interest	Balance
1	5/2020	342.19	791.67	237,157.81
2	6/2020	343.34	790.53	236,814.47
3	7/2020	344.48	789.38	236,469.99
4	8/2020	345.63	788.23	236,124.36
5	9/2020	346.78	787.08	235,777.58
6	10/2020	347.94	785.93	235,429.65
7	11/2020	349.10	784.77	235,080.55
8	12/2020	350.26	783.60	234,730.29
9	1/2021	351.43	782.43	234,378.86
10	2/2021	352.60	781.26	234,026.27
11	3/2021	353.77	780.09	233,672.49
12	4/2021	354.95	778.91	233,317.54
13	5/2021	356.14	777.73	232,961.40
14	6/2021	357.32	776.54	232,604.08
15	7/2021	358.51	775.35	232,245.56
16	8/2021	359.71	774.15	231,885.85
17	9/2021	360.91	772.95	231,524.95
18	10/2021	362.11	771.75	231,162.83
19	11/2021	363.32	770.54	230,799.52
20	12/2021	364.53	769.33	230,434.99

This schedule reflects a home purchased for $250,000 with a 5 percent down payment, resulting in a loan balance of $237,500 at an interest rate of 4 percent over a thirty-year amortization period. This schedule reflects how much of the first payment of $1,133.86 goes toward the principal ($342.19) and how much goes toward the interest ($791.67). Obviously, your clients will not be thrilled about how much of the payment is going toward the interest. There are a few points you can highlight to help improve their outlook.

The first is that with each subsequent payment, a slightly higher amount goes toward the principal and slightly less goes toward the interest. With each additional payment the borrower makes, this structure moves slightly more in their favor.

The second is that the government will allow them to calculate the amount of interest paid in a year (in this case, the sum of the interest portion of payments one through twelve equals $9,423.88) and deduct that from their taxable income. Since income is taxed on a tiered system, this allows your clients to deduct this amount from the portion of their income that is taxed at the highest amount. For example, a client whose income is taxed at 20 percent would receive a deduction of $1,884.77 ($9,423.88 x 0.20). For mortgage balances of higher amounts or higher tax rates, this amount becomes even more significant.

You can explain it to your clients in one of two ways.

Script 1: The Yearly Savings

One great benefit to home ownership is the mortgage interest tax deduction. In this case, if you bought this property at a 4 percent rate, you would get back approximately $1,884.77. If you had almost $2,000 coming back to you at the end of the year, how do you think you could spend that money to improve your property? Let's talk about what you would fix or upgrade with it. [Discuss with your client.] These are fantastic ideas.

Now, how much is it costing you each year in tax savings to rent instead of own?

Script 2: The Monthly Savings

One great benefit to home ownership is the mortgage interest tax deduction. In this case, if you bought this property at a 4 percent rate, you would get back approximately $1,884.77. If we took that savings and divided it by twelve, we would see a $157.06 discount to your monthly expenses for housing. I know you were nervous about a payment of $1,800 a month, but when we factor in the tax savings, it's more like $1,650. Furthermore, as you make more money at your job and your income increases, the house will slowly become more affordable.

Can you see how owning real estate is so incredibly powerful for growing your net worth with all these systems working together to build your wealth?

If you continue to rent, and rent continues to go up while you miss out on a steady payment that never changes and the tax savings to go with it, how will that affect the biggest component of your budget—housing expenses—ten years from now?

Not Looking at Fees

Your clients can and should shop around and compare the fees of different lenders. The Real Estate Settlement Procedures Act requires lenders to provide clients with a good-faith estimate of closing costs after receiving an application. Because lenders make money from both the spread on interest rates and closing costs, advise your clients to ask about the interest rate *and* closing costs.

Since the true cost of borrowing involves both an interest rate and closing costs, a better metric to more accurately determine the costs your clients will pay is the annual percentage rate (APR). The APR is calculated by spreading out the amount of the closing costs over the life of the loan and recalculating the interest rate quoted to reflect the principal, interest, *and* closing costs. The APR is the average annual finance charge (which includes fees and other loan costs) divided by the amount borrowed.

APR is not a different way of saying "interest rate," although the two terms are often erroneously used interchangeably. It is a way of taking the interest rate and adding the amount of the closing costs over the life of the loan to determine the true cost the borrower pays. The APR will be slightly higher than the interest rate the lender is charging because it includes all (or most) of the other fees that the loan carries with it, such as the origination fee, points, and PMI premiums.

More simply put, the APR is a way of looking at both the interest rate and the closing costs being offered to determine the cheapest loan for the client. The federal Truth in Lending Act (1968) requires lenders to disclose certain elements regarding the act of borrowing money. The APR is one of those elements. When your client is considering several different lending options, have them look at APRs. This is one easy, simple, and fast way to provide value and establish your superior knowledge and ability to help guide them through the financial process.

Applying for Another Loan

A common mistake made by unwary buyers occurs when they unwittingly apply for another loan before the closing of the property. This happens most often with new cars, but it can also happen when they buy new furniture or pay for landscaping for the new house. If the borrowers open a new line of credit, the lender assumes the borrower will max the line out and be obligated to pay off these additional monthly payments. This affects your client's debt-to-income ratio. And it can absolutely affect their ability to obtain the financing they were previously approved for. Be sure to warn your clients not to open *any* new lines of credit until after the deal is closed.

Changing Jobs Too Soon

One of the criteria lenders use to determine a borrower's likelihood to repay a loan is the amount of income they earn at their place of employment. This means there are requirements for the length of time a borrower needs to have held their job. Your client changing jobs during an escrow process can destroy the deal. Be extra cautious when your client is moving from one location to another for work. Many of our clients approach us when they need help with a job-related move. Be sure to have the lender check what is required for the loan approval before your client makes the job change official.

Having Unexplained Fluctuations on Bank Statements

Major fluctuations on bank statements, whether they are large withdrawals or large deposits, can trigger red flags to lenders. Some loans require the lender to ensure the client isn't making payments on something that wasn't revealed during the credit check. If your client is receiving funds to buy the property from someone else, be sure the lender knows this and can "source" those funds according to lending guidelines. Tell your clients about this upfront so you don't run into any last-minute surprises.

Closing Existing Lines of Credit

This one may seem counterintuitive. While paying off credit card debt is a positive step, cancelling a card can remove years of good credit history from your client's history. This makes it harder for the loan officer to show the borrower's credit in the healthiest light possible. Rather than cancel existing lines of credit, tell your clients to keep them open but make sure the balances are low or paid off.

Not Understanding Adjustable-Rate Mortgages

While some mortgages are originated with a rate fixed for the entire amortization period, others are created with an interest rate that fluctuates. These mortgages are referred to as adjustable-rate mortgages (ARMs). ARMs earned a terrible reputation during the mortgage meltdown of 2009 to 2013, as many of them were originated unscrupulously and were intended to confuse and misdirect borrowers. This does not mean an ARM can't be used appropriately.

In short, ARMs work best for those buyers who can afford a potentially fluctuating payment and don't expect to own the property for a long period of time. Because ARMs usually start off with a lower interest rate than market rates but can potentially increase each year, they are a gamble the borrower takes in the hope that they will be rid of the loan before the rate adjusts upward.

Lenders prefer ARMs because the interest rate fluctuates based on an index the rate is tied to. This protects the lender from giving out a lower interest rate that is fixed for thirty years but then seeing interest rates increase. By marrying the interest rate to a financial index (e.g., the prime rate, LIBOR rate, treasuries) and adding a premium on top of that, the lender is protected when interest rates rise.

You will see ARMs expressed as, for example, "5/1 ARM" or "7/1 ARM." The first number (in this case the 5 or the 7) reflects the number of years the agreed-upon rate will be fixed (thus, five or seven years). The second number reflects how often the rate can adjust (in this case, every year after the initial locked period ends). Most ARM notes are originated with a set amount the interest rate can rise per year (often 1 percent a year). In most cases, this is an acceptable rate of increase and not a dangerous move for the borrower who is fiscally responsible.

Not all ARMs are designed this way, however, and borrowers should be very careful before agreeing to one. The upside for the borrower is they get a lower than market rate for a fixed period of time. After this period ends, the borrower is exposed to the possibility of their rate rising every year. Should there be a downturn in the market and your client is unable to sell or refinance their home, they can become stuck with an ever-increasing payment they may not be able to afford.

Finance Hacks

You can save buyer clients a remarkable amount of money by the way you structure the sale into contract. Below are some of the secrets top producers use to structure deals that save their clients money and make themselves stand out from their competition.

Offering Seller More Time in Exchange for Rent

When representing buyers on a property, it is easy to get caught up in their emotions and experience and lose perspective on what the seller's side is experiencing. Buyers are a cocktail of anxiety, excitement, nervousness, fear, and so on. When you keep a cool head and remember that there are two sides to every transaction, you can often find ways to structure a deal that costs your own clients very little but saves the other side quite a bit.

To a seller, packing and moving their possessions, finding a new place, storing their belongings, and other practical concerns dominate their thoughts. It's easy to forget sellers are experiencing stress over where their next home will be or when they'll be able move into it. You can ask the listing agent if this is the case and then offer structuring the deal to provide the sellers some flexibility around when they have to move out.

Many sellers need the money from the sale of their current home to buy their next one. This means there are few options when it comes to selling their house and then finding a new one, getting it under contract, and closing escrow on it before moving out of their current home. You can suggest an offer that allows the seller to stay in their home after it closes for a period of time that works for your buyer clients.

In multiple-offer situations, your buyer may need to give this rent-back agreement for free. In most other situations, you can write in your offer that the seller can stay in the property for a specified amount of time but must pay the buyer a rent equal to the buyer's PITI (thus an agreed-upon amount).

Not all buyers can offer this luxury to the previous owners of their home, but when they can, it gives your buyers a big advantage over other buyers. And in multiple-offer situations, it can mean not having to offer more on the purchase price.

Increasing the Credit Allowed by Buying Down the Interest Rate

In certain situations, you can negotiate a credit from the sellers that is greater than the amount of the *nonrecurring closing costs* your buyers are paying for the loan. This may happen when you get a pest report or home inspection report back that is much worse than either side anticipated.

It is illegal for your client to accept credit for more than their closing costs. This becomes a "lost credit." If the credit offer is higher, you must then find a way to increase your client's closing costs. The easiest way to do this is to ask the lender to add "points" to the loan, meaning your client is paying to bring down their interest rate. Remember, a lower interest rate means higher closing costs. This will allow your clients to receive the higher credit and get a lower interest rate in the process. All this is paid for by the seller's credits.

Higher Purchase Price, Better Terms

While, objectively speaking, all that should matter to the seller is how much they make from the net of the sale, this is rarely the case. Most sellers care more about the price their home sells for. This means they're not looking closely at the offer and who is paying for which of the associated closing costs.

If you keep in mind that the first thing the seller (and usually the listing agent) will look at when the offer comes in is the purchase price, you can structure your offer to give a great first impression. This is based on the psychology of how humans make decisions. An offer that comes in below asking price makes it easy for the seller and listing agent to view the rest of the deal negatively. When the offer comes in at the asking price or higher, it releases positive emotions, which allows them to look at the rest of the offer positively.

This is especially true at certain price points considered psychological "benchmarks." The million-dollar mark is the most obvious example. Writing an offer of $1 million for a property is much more appealing to the sellers than $995,000—even though the difference is only $5,000. You can easily get much more than that $5,000 back in better terms when the seller knows others will see that they sold their home for the million.

This benchmark also works at other large whole numbers, such as $500,000, $300,000, $200,000, etc.

Seller to Credit the Buyer's Closing Costs

This may seem obvious but hear me out. In many cases, a buyer saving money on closing costs is much more valuable to them than paying more for the house. Let me explain.

Tommy and Mary find a fixer-upper property with a huge lot in a hot location. The property is listed at $400,000 and has multiple offers in hand. Tommy and Mary only have 5 percent to put down and are barely able to make the down payment and still have money for closing costs. If they have to offer over asking price, they won't have enough money to handle the increased down payment.

The property has stained carpet, ugly cabinets, and old light fixtures, and is painted several different mismatching colors. You find comparable sales well over $475,000 for houses of the same size in the same area in superior condition.

The listing agent tells you she already has offers slightly over asking price but the terms aren't good. You ask her what is most important to the seller, and she tells you that the sellers prefer to net as much as possible. She says an offer of $410,000 would likely close the deal.

You tell Tommy and Mary the bad news and can hear the deflated tone in their voices. They can't offer over asking, but they also know not offering more means they won't get the property. You can offer a solution to this quagmire.

You propose that they offer $420,000 but ask for a credit back of $10,000 toward their closing costs. You explain that with the $10,000 they had planned on using toward closing costs, they'll have more than enough to cover the down payment on the extra $20,000—roughly $1,000 if they are putting 5 percent down—and have $9,000 toward fixing the house up. Your clients realize that by offering the sellers more on the purchase price but asking for a closing cost credit, their payment would go up by roughly $40 a month (to pay off $420,000 instead of $410,000), which is entirely manageable for them.

With the $9,000 they keep as a result of structuring the deal this way, they are thrilled to realize they can paint the walls, paint the cabinets, take down the wallpaper, and still have enough money left over to replace the hideous carpet. This will actually improve the property's value to be closer to the $475,000 of the comparable sales.

You call the listing agent and tell her you're sending an offer for $420,000 with a $10,000 closing cost credit, netting her clients the $410,000 they wanted, with the additional ego boost of a higher asking price and removing some of the embarrassment of selling a house for less than the higher sales in the neighborhood. The sellers accept your offer, and you end up with the following results:

- The seller nets what they wanted.
- The seller's ego is assuaged.
- Your clients get a home they love.
- Your clients save $9,000 they really needed.
- Your clients add approximately $45,000 in equity after fixing up the property with that $9,000.
- Your clients buy a property in their perfect location, and it is now upgraded.
- Your clients won a bidding war with a bad starting position (that is, not much cash, only 5 percent down).

The only downside? Your clients took on an additional $40/month in their monthly payment and they have a slightly higher loan balance. This is a good trade-off!

Multiple-Offer Pressure on Listing Agent

One of the worst things to experience as a buyer agent is putting in all the hard work of finding the perfect property for your client, watching them get so excited about it, and then realizing it has several offers and you can't be sure yours will be accepted.

When it comes to winning in a multiple-offer situation, there are two things an agent must do well to win:

1. Convince your client to write an offer the seller will accept.
2. Negotiate with the other agent to ensure your strong, solid offer is accepted.

There is a right way and a wrong way to handle this situation, and most agents choose the wrong way.

The wrong way is to get your clients to write an offer (strong or not) and submit it to the listing agent sounding as if you already have the upper hand. These offers are often submitted with a "love letter" from the buyers and a line from the agent that reads something like "My clients would love this house and I'll be great to work with!" or "Really hope we are the best offer, please counter me if you think we need to do better!" Statements like these do not create enough pressure on the other seller agent to get the result your client wants.

The right way is to submit a very strong offer and put proper pressure on the listing agent to accept it. Being polite, professional, and considerate allows you to apply substantial pressure without ruining your chances of losing the deal. Write your offer with an expiration date on it and call the listing agent. Talk to the agent directly. You can say:

Hey there, I've emailed you my client's offer, proof of funds, and preapproval letter. We have already reviewed the disclosures and are happy to sign and return those as well. I'm sure your clients will be thrilled at the extremely strong offer we've presented. My clients love your listing and I'm convinced it is the property for them. With this being the case, we've delivered an offer I don't believe will be beaten.

By the same token, I understand you have multiple other buyers interested and you may want to send out a seller counteroffer. If that's the road you choose, would you mind telling me first so my client can withdraw their offer? Part of why they wrote such a competitive offer was for the peace of mind that comes from knowing they won't be competing with any other buyers. If your clients decide to use the multiple-counteroffer route, please let me know so we can pursue other properties.

I would absolutely love to put this in contract with you today. Please note we've included an expiration date. Can you talk to your clients soon and let me know if they think we have a deal here? I'd really rather avoid having to show homes this weekend, but if we can't make this work today, I'll need to start scheduling showings soon.

Thank you so much, and please let me know when you can talk to your clients. I look forward to a smooth transaction with you!

Hold the listing agent to their word. If they tell you they will talk to their client in a few hours, start calling and texting in a few hours to find out how it went. If they said they will get back to you tonight, call them at night until they answer. Make sure they understand your urgency and make them fear losing your offer if they don't accept it soon. The more time you give them to make their decision, the more likely they are to take your offer to the other buyers who wrote offers and try to get them to increase their purchase price. This is called "shopping" your offer. If you don't pressure the listing agent, there is a very good chance this is what will happen.

80/10/10 Loans

80/10/10 loans are a creative way to structure financing that avoids PMI if the borrower does not have 20 percent to put down on the property. These loans are structured so that the borrower takes out a loan for 80 percent of the property's value on a first-position mortgage and a loan for 10 percent of the property's value on a second-position mortgage (often a HELOC or other line of credit), and puts 10 percent of their own money down.

The second-position loan often has a higher interest rate, but because it is only for 10 percent of the property's value, the increase in the overall payment is minimal. Because the loan balance is for a lower amount on the second loan, it is also easier for the borrower to make extra payments toward its principal to pay it off sooner. For clients who are facing a higher PMI number (due to lower credit or other issues), this can be a successful way to create a loan that will keep their payments lower.

Lender-Placed Mortgage Insurance

Another method to avoid PMI is lender-placed mortgage insurance (LPMI). When a lender structures a deal with LPMI, the loan typically has a slightly higher interest rate but avoids the PMI associated with conventional financing at less than 20 percent down. The benefits to this method are:

1. The higher LPMI rate usually still means lower payments per month than the PMI costs.
2. The higher LPMI rate means increased mortgage interest, but this mortgage interest is tax deductible and PMI costs are not.
3. Unlike PMI, the higher LPMI interest rate is not sensitive to the borrower's credit score.

Ask the lender your client is working with if they have LPMI options, especially if the client has a smaller down payment that would naturally equate to a higher PMI amount. Compare the PMI costs with the LMPI higher rate to help your client determine which is the better financial option for them.

Even though it's not necessarily your responsibility to handle your client's loan options, there are many scenarios in which you can use your knowledge of the financing side of real estate to directly benefit your clients. Top-producing agents know that they are a powerful resource for their clients and want to be involved in all aspects of their decision-making when it comes to buying a home. Set yourself up to be the person they can come to when they have questions, and you'll have way more leads than any other agents.

▶ KEY POINTS

- Understanding how financing works helps you save your clients money by structuring better deals, allows you to appear more professional, helps you turn leads into clients, and makes you a better fiduciary.
- Loans are originated through bankers or brokers, sold on the secondary market, and aggregated to be sold to GSEs or as MBSs on the stock market.
- Loan officers use a client's debt-to-income ratio to determine the amount of money the bank will lend them, and they collect the documentation underwriters need to expedite the lending process.
- FHA and VA loans are government loans known for their low down payment and credit requirements.
- The preapproval process includes submitting all the information an underwriter needs.
- Lenders make money in two ways: fees charged to the buyer at closing, and the spread on the interest rate they secure when they sell the loan on the secondary market.
- Mortgage payments comprise principal and interest, but monthly payments comprise PITI. Share with your clients the PITI amount for a full understanding of their costs.
- Use a mortgage calculator to calculate the payment on a hypothetical property.

- Foreclosure refers to the process of a lender taking back title to a property. REO refers to the title being held by a bank on a foreclosed property.
- LPMI is cheaper than traditional PMI.

CHAPTER ▶ FOURTEEN

WORKING WITH INVESTORS

"Real estate cannot be lost or stolen, nor can it be carried away. Purchased with common sense, paid for in full, and managed with reasonable care, it is about the safest investment in the world."

—FRANKLIN D. ROOSEVELT

The goal of becoming a top-producing Realtor is to reach the point at which your reputation precedes you. At a certain level of production, your name will become well known in the real estate community in which you work. Real estate investors and those serious about buying property will recognize your name and will eventually reach out to you. Anyone dedicated to building their wealth wants to work with those who have the ability to help them do it. If you're serious about working with real estate investors, consider the BiggerPockets investor-friendly agent directory. Investors use the BiggerPockets agent finder service to be matched with experienced real estate agents in their desired market who can keep investors' specific needs in mind. A feature on this directory could put you forward as a local expert and lead to great profits and recurring business.

Why Work with Investors

Investors will level up your business in several ways. They can teach you how to be more efficient in your business, how to spot deals (and recognize them for other clients), and how to interpret the numbers/math behind building wealth through real estate. You'll learn more from investors about the back-end process of owning real estate than from your standard clients. If you're lucky, you may even learn how to become a real estate investor and build big wealth for yourself. Real estate investors can help your business in several ways.

They Are Repeat Clients

Repeat clients are good for your business. Investors typically buy properties for one of two reasons:
1. They want to keep it as a rental property (buy and hold).
2. They want to fix it up and sell it for a quick profit (fix and flip).

Both of these methods make investors lots of money. The buy-and-hold method earns them money through monthly cash flow (the difference between the rent they collect and the cost of owning the property) and the long-term equity they create. The fix-and-flip method earns them faster, bigger chunks of cash. Most investors will fall into one of these two categories, with a few doing both.

When you find a client who flips homes, they are likely to continue buying more from you as long as you can find them properties and they have the money to purchase them. If you play your cards right, you can get the listing and sell the home for the investor as well. The same holds true for those who buy investment properties. As long as you keep finding the properties and they have funds to keep buying, you can close a lot of deals with them.

Making money for investors will mean they want to work with you. You make money for buyers by finding properties below market value. You make money for sellers by selling properties for more than your competition does.

They Refer Others in the Industry

Investor clients often make their living from real estate, so they know others in the industry. When you develop a good reputation with a strong investor, they'll tell their friends and others about you. Good agents are hard to find, and nobody knows this better than investors. When you find someone who has a strong circle of friends and their recommendations are highly respected, you'll have found the best referral partner you could ever hope for.

They Refer Useful Vendors

Investors are also highly valuable because of their connections. These are the best people to go to when you need a handyman to fix something to get a listing ready for market or a contractor to give a quote and do work on a fixer-upper your buyer client wants to purchase. They usually know qualified and trustworthy roofers, HVAC techs, and other vendors your clients will want your help in finding. I go first to my investor friends when I need help finding a lender who can do a special type of loan or a title officer who can fix a unique problem. Keep contact with these investors.

They Teach You How to Become an Investor Yourself

The most powerful thing you can do for your own wealth is to own real estate, not just sell it. Almost every person who made money investing in real estate had a mentor—someone who helped them get started and offered guidance along the way. If you make money for your investor clients, they are more likely to return the favor by helping you learn the process of investing, so you can make more money as well. The best way to find a mentor is to bring mutual value. Finding deals for those looking for them is a smart way to do that.

What Investors Want: ONFIRE Agents

Investors want great deals and spend obsessive amounts of time looking for them. Make helping investors find deals your top priority. To do that, you have to understand what a "deal" is for any particular investor.

In the book series *The Multifamily Millionaire*, best-selling authors and real estate investors Brandon Turner and Brian Murray spell out to future real estate investors what to look for in a real estate agent. Turner and Murray uses the acronym "ONFIRE" (organized, networked, focused on you, investor-friendly, responsive, experienced) to highlight the important qualities an agent should possess. Understanding what investors are looking for will give you a leg up in becoming an ONFIRE agent.

Organized

Organized agents don't miss calls, don't miss appointments, and don't miss opportunities. If you're not yet a top producer, you need to understand the importance of this statement. If you are a top producer, you already know it. Being organized is how you handle a large volume of clients and how you avoid making mistakes. Organized agents appear more thorough, more trustworthy, and more professional to those looking to hire them.

Networked

Investors know how important their network is to their success. Don't think they won't be expecting the same from you. Great agents have great networks. This allows them to bring more value to their clients and increases their ability to solve problems and close deals. If you really think about it, agents only exist because problems happen and clients need help navigating them. If your network allows you to solve more of these problems, you inherently have more value as an agent. Make sure you market yourself on social media and in conversations that you have a valuable network. Investors will notice.

In my book *Long-Distance Real Estate Investing*, I highlight the four people I need in any deal in any market (branded as my "Core Four"). These are:

1. Deal finder (agent)
2. Property manager
3. Contractor
4. Lender

Be the agent who can connect these Core Four members. Add these people to your network. Anyone who has read that book will know this. If you haven't read that book, you know now. These are essential people to have in your network.

Focused on You

It doesn't matter who the client is; they want to know that your focus is on them. All your clients will be looking to see if you care about their goals or if they are just another commission to you. I market the deals I've found for clients and point out the specifics that mattered to them. This shows that I care about the goal of the person I'm working with, not just my goal to sell a large number of houses. When you meet with investor leads, ask enough questions so they know that you want to make them money. If you can show that, they'll want to work with you.

Investor-Friendly

What exactly is an "investor-friendly agent"? Investors use this phrase to describe an agent who understands what they are looking for. Most newer agents won't have the capacity, knowledge, or ability to meet the heavier demands investor clients require. To reach this status, you'll have to meet the qualifications of being an investor-friendly agent. Recognizing these clients' goals, speaking their language, and seeing deals through their eyes will accomplish this.

Here are some fundamentals you'll need to know how to do.
- Calculate ROI
- Estimate rehab costs
- Analyze neighborhoods
- Determine market rent
- Determine after repair value (ARV)
- Negotiate
- Understand inspection reports
- Gather information from the other agent to advise on offer-writing
- Have Core Four connections

Responsive

This one is at the top of *everybody*'s list. According to a 2015 Redfin study,[13] 47 percent of buyers said they value responsiveness over professionalism. That's a big statement! If you're not responsive, you're going to have unhappy clients. Even worse than that, you're going to miss out on leads. When someone reaches out to an agent, they know how valuable their business is (they see us begging for it all over social media, trust me). If you don't respond quickly, it sends the message you're not interested. This isn't always fair, but it's still true.

This is a problem every agent needs to solve to become a top producer. On my team, we have a phone number that rings directly to one of my assistants' cell phones when we aren't in the office. I have a CRM that notifies us via text and email when a new lead reaches out and is

---

13 Alex Starace, Anshu Rustagi, and Suzanne Harrison, "Americans Want Change in Real Estate," Redfin, Updated October 6, 2020, https://www.redfin.com/blog/americans-want-change-in-real-estate/#. VRGhplyR081.

uploaded into it. I'm not perfect (my cell phone currently has 833 unread messages), but I do my best to put systems in place to remain responsive. It's important. Make it easy for clients to work with you.

Experienced

Clients want experienced agents to foresee potential problems and fix them as well as to articulate options for the situation at hand. We know how much we do as agents. Clients don't. In their mind, they just need an agent to find them a house, negotiate a deal, interpret what's going on in a transaction, and tell them what their options are. Experienced agents are better story-tellers. They explain options and describe scenarios in ways that soften any blows and keep their clients motivated and happy throughout the process.

You can show this to potential clients by improving your communication skills. When someone first meets you, there is no way they can know how much you know or don't know. This means they can't tell your experience level. Truth is, they probably won't even ask. What they will pay attention to is how you communicate with them and, more importantly, how they feel speaking with you. Do you inspire their confidence? Do you let them know you have a plan and have done this many times before? Experienced agents communicate better, and it shows in their Sales Funnel.

As with any other client, you have to make it abundantly clear to investor clients at the initial appointment that you can help them get what they want. The most important question to ask is: What does a deal look like to them? Not every investor is looking for the same thing, just like not every traditional home buyer is looking for the same thing. I'm now going to share with you the language investors speak so you can communicate with them in a way they understand.

The language of investors is based on their needs. Learning their vernacular will help you decipher what is important to them and empower you to find and deliver it. You'll also want to learn how to run numbers the same way they do. When you know what they are looking for, know how they speak, know how to run numbers, and know how to find what they want, you'll find yourself with a thriving business of repeat customers.

The Language of Investors

The language investors speak isn't just cool slang. Investors have phrases to describe the parts of a deal that matter to them. Learn what these words or phrases mean and, more importantly, learn *how to use them* to gain attention as the coveted "investor-friendly agent." Read the books investors read (look at anything published through BiggerPockets Publishing) and listen to the podcasts and watch the YouTube channels they do. All of this will teach you to look at deals through their eyes and help you build a much stronger bond with them and they with you. The following are investor terms you need to know and their acronyms.

Investor Terms

Return on Investment (ROI). This is a metric used to determine the percentage they will earn in a year on an investment. For example, a 7 percent ROI would mean they receive $70 annually on a $1,000 investment.

After Repair Value (ARV). This is the expected value of a property after repairs are made. This is important to those looking to buy distressed or fixer-upper properties.

Cash Flow. This is the amount left over after a property's expenses are deducted from the rent. If there is no money left over, this is called "negative cash flow" and would indicate a property is losing the owner money each month.

Rehab Costs. This is the anticipated amount of money required to rehabilitate a property to be in rent-ready or sellable condition.

Path of Progress. This is the general direction of increasing values in a specific market; it's also referred to as the "path of gentrification."

Buy and Hold. This is a strategy in which the owner intends to keep the property and collect rents for a significant period of time.

Fix and Flip. This is a strategy in which a house is bought, fixed up, and sold for an intended profit. Also referred to as a "flip."

BRRRR (Buy, Rehab, Rent, Refinance, Repeat). This is a strategy where an investor buys a fixer-upper property, improves its value, then refinances and keeps it as a rental. (See *Buy, Rehab, Rent, Refinance, Repeat,* my book on this concept.)

House Hack. This is a strategy in which an investor purchases a property to live in and also rents out a portion of the property to a tenant, thus combining primary residence and rental properties for an improved financial outcome. This can be done with two- to four-unit properties, with single-family properties with ADUs, or by renting out rooms.

Accessory Dwelling Unit (ADU). This is an additional unit, usually a smaller one, on a property with a separate entrance and living quarters. This is also referred to as a "granny flat," "mother-in-law unit," and "in-law quarters."

Single-Family Residential/Single-Family House (SFR/SFH). This is a classification of property that refers to a single, detached home.

Multifamily Residential/Multifamily Housing (MFR/MFH). A classification of property referring to duplex, triplexes, and fourplexes (two- to four-unit housing).

Appreciation. The act of a property increasing in value.

Depreciation. This is *not* the opposite of appreciation. Depreciation is a tax-related term that describes the benefits of writing off a portion of an investment property's value each year. For tax purposes, this can be used as an additional expense and subtracted from the income to decrease taxable income.

1031 Like-Kind Exchange. This is a provision of the Internal Revenue Service tax code that allows investors to defer paying capital gains taxes if they sell an asset and reinvest the money within specific guidelines.

Capital Gains. This is a tax levied against an investor who sells an investment or property. There are both long-term and short-term capital gain amounts.

Return on Equity (ROE). This is a metric determined by the profit a property generates yearly divided by the overall equity in the property to know how efficiently the equity is working.

Core Four. The four pieces an investor needs to invest in any market (discussed earlier).

Property Manager (PM). The person or company responsible for managing a property once you own it. Job duties include advertising the unit for rent, getting leases signed, collecting rent payments from tenants and sending them to owners, managing maintenance requests, and conducting walk-throughs to verify the condition of the property.

Seller Financing. This is when a seller holds all or a portion of the money owed to them by the buyer as a note, and the buyer pays the seller a monthly payment (that is, the seller is now the bank).

Amortization. This is the process of paying off debt through regular principal and interest payments.

Adjustable-Rate Mortgage (ARM). An ARM is an interest rate that can adjust over time. It is typically fixed for several years (say, the first three to five years) and can adjust once per year by a predetermined amount (often 1 percent) for the rest of the term of the loan. ARM loans reduce risk for the lender and put more risk on the borrower.

Fixed-Rate Mortgage. This is a fully amortizing mortgage loan (that is, the interest rate on the note remains the same through the term of the loan).

Real Estate Owned (REO). This is a foreclosure that has the title transferred back to the bank that gave the loan to initially buy it.

Holding Costs. This is the amount of money required to hold a property before it can be sold. It includes property taxes, homeowners insurance, HOA fees, the interest rate on a loan, and more.

Broker Price Opinion (BPO). This is a broker's opinion on the value of a property after completing a CMA.

Comparative Market Analysis (CMA). This is a snapshot of active, pending, and sold homes in a neighborhood or market that helps determine the value of a subject property.

Capital Expenditures (CapEx). This is money budgeted for and spent on "big-ticket" items that are assumed will need replacing in a property (e.g., roofs, HVAC systems, furnaces).

Cap Rate. This is a metric used in multifamily investing to determine the expected return on a property. For example, a "five cap" would indicate a 5 percent annual return if the property were purchased without financing. Cap rates are often combined with NOI to determine the value of a commercial property.

Cash-on-Cash (CoC). This is the ROI on a property.

General Partner (GP). This is the head or lead partner on a syndication deal; they have greater responsibility, control, and commitment over the investment.

Limited Partner (LP). This is a passive investor in a syndication deal with a limited role and fewer responsibilities and control over the investment.

Net Operating Income (NOI). This is the profit made on an investment (usually a larger multifamily or commercial property) after expenses are paid.

Triple Net Lease (NNN). This is a lease agreement on a property whereby the tenant or lessee promises to pay all the expenses of the property, including real estate taxes, building insurance, and maintenance.

Live-In Flip. This is a fixer-upper property purchased with a primary residence loan (usually for a smaller down payment than a traditional home loan) where the occupant improves the value of a property through rehabbing it and sells it when finished. This is less risky but slower than a traditional flip.

Turnkey. This is a rental property that needs no (or minimal) rehab work and can be rented out immediately after purchase. This is usually sold at a higher price than properties that need work.

Internal Rate of Return (IRR). This is a formula to capture the truest return on an investor's capital. It includes as many areas as possible where money can be made, including cash flow, principal paydown, reduction in expenses, and appreciation when a property sells. This is most often used in commercial property investments by syndicators looking to show value to potential investors.

Debt Service Coverage Ratio (DSCR). This is a percentage of gross monthly income that goes toward payments for rent, mortgages, credit cards, car payments, or any other debt the buyer has. Most lenders like to see a DSCR of 1.2 or higher (that is, meaning the property produces 20 percent more income than it costs to hold it).

As an additional resource, please review the glossary at www.bigger pockets.com/rei/glossary for an even more detailed list.

Running the Numbers

After learning the terms, you'll want to learn how to run the numbers to show just how valuable you are. The following are formulas and explanations on how to arrive at them.

Please note: If you absolutely hate math or don't want to understand how numbers are calculated by investors, skip this section and still get most of the same information using the calculators found at www.bigger pockets.com/calc. As a thank you for buying this book, use the discount code "books20" for 20 percent off a Pro or Premium membership to get unlimited access to them. You can even send your clients the PDFs they produce for you.

Cash Flow

This is the most commonly used metric. Cash flow determines if an investor will make or lose money on a deal. To determine cash flow, take the income (usually the rent) and subtract the expenses. The numbers are calculated on a monthly basis. The formula is:

Income − Expenses = Cash Flow

Income

Rent (two units at $1,100 each)	$2,200

Expenses

Mortgage	$1,400
Property Tax	$125
Homeowners Insurance	$50
Property Management Fee (8%)	$176
Repairs (5%)	$110
Vacancy (5%)	$110
Total	**$1,971**

In this case, the income ($2,200) minus expenses ($1,971) equals cash flow ($229). This would lead to a yearly profit of $2,748 ($229 x 12 months).

Capital Invested (Investment Basis)

This is the amount of money an investor will put into a deal. It typically consists of the down payment and the rehab budget combined.

Let's consider a hypothetical scenario in which an investor pays $200,000 for a duplex. The investor put 20 percent down on the property, has $5,000 in closing costs, and spends $5,000 in rehab costs to make the units rent ready. The investor purchases the property directly from another investor; in exchange for a lower purchase price, they use seller financing and have a high interest rate on the note.

Amount Invested

Down Payment $200,000 (purchase price) × 0.20 (20% down payment)	$40,000
Closing Costs	$5,000
Rehab	$5,000
Total	**$50,000**

Our total investment basis is $50,000.

ROI

The ROI is determined by taking the yearly cash flow and dividing it by the amount of capital invested (investment basis). The formula is:

Yearly Profit / Capital Invested = ROI

If we continue with the above example, we can easily determine the ROI by plugging in our yearly cash flow and our investment basis numbers.

$2,748 [Yearly Profit] / $50,000 [Capital Invested] = 0.0549 (5.5%)

In this example our investor can expect an ROI of 5.5 percent if they purchase the given duplex.

ROE

The ROE is determined much like the ROI in the example above. You would simply substitute the equity in the property for the capital invested and do your math the exact same way.

Let's assume our investor bought the duplex mentioned above, held it for five years, and is now considering selling it. During those five years, the rents increased as did the value of the property. The rents are now $1,350 per unit and the value of the property is $300,000.

Income	
Rent (two units at $1,350 each)	$2,700
Expenses	
Mortgage	$1,400
Property Tax	$125
Homeowners Insurance	$50
Property Management Fee (8%)	$216
Repairs (5%)	$135
Vacancy (5%)	$135
Total	**$2,061**

The monthly cash flow is now $639 ($2,700 – $2,061) and the yearly cash flow is now $7,668 ($639 x 12). The ROI on the initial capital invested is now 15 percent ($7,668 / $50,000 = 0.15).

While this ROI looks much better than the initial 5.5 percent the investor got on Year 1 (it always does with yearly rent increases), we still need to compare the ROI to the ROE to advise our client on whether they should sell or keep the property.

Yearly Profit / Equity – Selling Costs = ROE

$$\frac{\$7,668 \text{ [Yearly Profit]}}{\$300,000} - \frac{\$160,000}{\text{[amount still owed] [Equity]}} - \frac{\$24,000}{\text{[Selling Costs]}} = \frac{0.066}{(6.6\%)}$$

The ROE in this case is 6.6 percent.

Even though the ROI on our client's initial investment ($50,000) has increased from 5.5 percent to 15 percent, the ROE has barely improved, increasing from 5.5 percent to only 6.6 percent.

How did this happen? When a property's equity increases (based on appreciation) at a rate faster than its cash flow (based on increasing rents), you can easily be deceived into believing the property is performing well if you look only at ROI. In this case, we can clearly see the client should sell the property if they can beat the 6.6 percent return they are currently receiving on their equity and reinvest the money.

Now, do you know any good agents who can help them get top dollar for that house and buy a new one? These numbers will be important after you master the buy/sell combo.

House Hacking

House hacking is a phrase used to describe when someone rents out a portion of the house they are living in to help generate income and therefore cover the housing expenses. This can reduce or eliminate monthly expenses, and in some cases actually earn the house hacker money. Each market is different, so the numbers will vary by region. Additionally, there are several different ways to house hack. When you combine the different markets with the different methods, you get infinite possibilities.

Your job as an agent is to come up with a strategy that works for your client and then create a plan to bring it to life. The better picture you paint, the more buy-in you'll get from the client. You'll do this more successfully after you have a better understanding of house hacking yourself.

I like to think of house hacking on a spectrum, similar to the one used earlier in the book. On one end is the most comfortable way for the client. On the other is the most profitable way. The client needs to understand that earning the most money and having it be the most comfortable aren't compatible. I discuss this with the client with the following dialogue.

You can best understand house hacking by considering a spectrum. On one end of the spectrum is comfort. The simplest way to do this is to buy a two- to four-unit property, live in one unit, and rent out the others. This will give you your own living space and require little or no rehab work to make happen. The tough part is there are fewer properties like this and more competition to get them, and they are often in the worse parts of town.

At the other end of this spectrum is profit. We buy a big house with as many bedrooms as possible, add more bedrooms if we can, and rent them all out. While this will typically earn you more income, it will also be less comfortable, as you'll be sharing your living space with other people.

There are several options in the middle of this spectrum. These include buying a single-family with an ADU, a finished basement with a separate entrance, or putting up walls to create two units out of one. My job is to find how far along this spectrum I can move you toward the profit side while still having it be comfortable enough for you. Based on what I've said so far, tell me what sounds most appealing to you.

House hacking can be done numerous ways and is my personal favorite investing strategy. It is particularly effective in areas with high housing expenses, and these areas are usually also accompanied by high wages. When you combine high wages with reduced housing expenses, it can mean big savings for those living there. If you want to run the numbers for a house-hack client, it's simple. You start with their normal housing expenses and then subtract what they can collect in rent.

As long as this number is less than what they are currently paying for either their rent or their mortgage, it makes financial sense to move forward. When you can clearly make this case to the client, it's tough for them not to buy with you. This of course assumes they are interested in saving money each month and that's the concern that prompted the house-hack conversation.

House hacking takes the sting out of investing in several ways.

1. You get a better interest rate when you buy a property as a primary residence.
2. You have lower down payment options when you buy a property as a primary residence.
3. When you put less money down, you can buy more properties.
4. When you put less money down, you don't have to refinance to take it out, reducing the need to BRRRR.
5. You're already paying a housing expense to someone (the bank if you own or a landlord if you rent). Removing this expense is a benefit you get when you buy a house hack that you don't get when you buy a traditional rental property.
6. It allows someone to buy in a nicer area without having to pay the full price.
7. It's scalable. Someone can repeat this process ten times using Fannie Mae/Freddie Mac loans.
8. It's compatible with the FIRE (Financially Independent, Retire Early) movement.
9. It destroys the argument that renting is cheaper than owning.
10. It allows people to take advantage of current tax incentives for home ownership.

I propose house hacking as a solution to anyone who has objections to buying real estate, such as:

- Renting is cheaper.
- I can't afford it.
- This market is too expensive.
- I'm worried prices will drop, meaning I can save money if I wait.
- I don't want to be house poor.
- I can't afford to live in the areas I really want.

- I want to buy a rental property, but I don't have 20 percent to put down.
- I don't want to spend all my money on one property.
- I want to BRRRR, but I can't find anything.

At minimum, house hacking is a terrific marketing technique to get people in the door and to share the financial benefits of home ownership, not just the practical or comfortable ones. After you have the conversation, people may still want to a buy but decide house hacking is not for them. This is still a win for you as you can now go find them a traditional house. Investor principles will work on more than just investors!

Pitfalls of Working with Investors

Now that you know some of the advantages of working with investors, I'm going to share some disadvantages. Not everyone who calls themselves an "investor" really is. If you want to protect your time and maximize your business, you have to be as delicate as a dove but as shrewd as a serpent. Keep an eye out for the following ways investors can waste your time or be tough to work with.

They Don't Know What They Want

Some people call themselves investors because they own property. Others use that word to describe their desire to build wealth through real estate. Not all are equal. When you meet someone who gives you crystal-clear criteria on what they want, it's a positive sign they are a legit investor who will act to close deals. When someone gives you criteria that are broad or unspecific, that's often a sign they are an amateur investor.

Be leery of the following red flags:

- "I'm always open to a great deal!"
- "I don't want to miss out on anything!"
- "Can we use X to negotiate the seller down on their price?" (before even seeing the home)
- "I won't pay over asking price."
- "I want to write fifty offers a week, and you'll be okay with that, right?
- "Let's put it in contract, then renegotiate after the inspection report."

These phrases are not deal breakers per se, but they do warrant you digging deeper to find out the motivation behind them. When you're working with an investor, you want to make sure they have integrity and will do what they say. You can quickly tarnish your own reputation in the market playing fast and loose writing offers you don't intend to honor. Many of these types of clients won't care about or consider your reputation at all. Before you work with any client, make sure they know what they want. Investors are no exception.

They Care More About Getting Your Money Than Making Their Own

Oh, how I wish this one were not true! As an investor myself, I really hate when I see this. Any client can ask you for a portion of your commission, but it does seem to happen more often with investors. Investors tend to be more concerned with the financial aspect of real estate than the emotional side. If they don't understand the value of relationships, they will be more likely to ask for a cut of your buyer-side commission on the deal. If you are representing them with selling too, this is even more likely to happen.

Be prepared to stand your ground or even push back when they ask you for your money. If you give in even once, they will expect it every time you work together. What's more, they'll tell those they refer to you about it. This will leave you feeling pressured to discount your commission for *everybody*. Investors take more work than traditional buyers. It's not an enviable position to be doing more work for less money every time. Consider the following counters when an investor asks for a cut of your buyer-side commission.

- "I'm already free for you. Why are you asking me for money you don't even have to pay?"
- "I understand you'd like a cut of my commission. I'm open to that. Which parts of the job are you going to do in exchange for the pay?"
- "Let's say for some reason I did that. Does it seem smart to you to incentivize me to bring the best deals to someone else who is going to get me paid more? Maybe we need to talk about what kind of a bonus you'll pay me for what I bring you."
- "That would make sense if you brought me more clients. How about if we revisit this when you've sent me some referrals?"
- "Do you want me to focus on giving you my money, or making you money on the deal?"

They Propose Value on Future Deals, Not on the Current Deal

Many investors will ask you for a discount in exchange for the deals they say they are going to do. This rarely works out well for you. I don't care what someone tells me they are going to do. I only care what they have done or are currently doing. I see this same argument when you are going to sell someone's home and help them buy a new one (the buy/sell combo). The client will often ask you to reduce your commission selling their home because they will be buying their next home with you.

The answer to this is if a commission is to be reduced, it will be on the house they buy, not the house they sell. This will save you a lot of money because many clients will sell their house and then decide not to buy a new one. You will have discounted your commission for no reason and there's no way to get that money back. This philosophy holds true with investors as well.

When an investor tells you they will be buying more houses with you in the future and asks you to credit your commission, tell them you will consider that in the future, after more houses have been bought. This way they can't argue with you, and you won't discount your wages based on a promise that may never happen.

They Want You to Take Unreasonable Steps in Helping Them

Sometimes an investor will say they want to work with you, and you get excited. This can be lovely at first, but it quickly turns sour when you realize what they are actually asking for is a full education in how to buy, manage, and make money with real estate. It's a blurry line agents walk between bringing value to a client and working for free. Investors often take advantage of this line. If you're not extra careful with where you draw your own lines, this can easily happen to you.

When an investor wants you to show them how to run numbers on a property, spend large amounts of time finding them lenders to qualify them, have you run lots of comps on houses they don't offer on, or have you look for vendors (e.g., property managers), it's a sign they may not know what they are doing and are looking for a free education at your expense.

It's important to tell clients upfront what they can and cannot expect from you. This rule applies to investors asking you to do things that do not fall within your normal scope of work and for which you won't be compensated. The safest thing to do is to have that conversation early in the relationship and make sure you avoid falling into this rabbit hole of work without pay.

They Want the Credit of Being an Investor without Taking the Risk

Let's face it. There's something cool about calling yourself a real estate investor. It's trendy, it sounds entrepreneurial, and nobody really knows how much wealth you may or not may have. One look at Instagram accounts related to real estate will tell you everything you need to know about how appealing it is to brand oneself that way. Labeling yourself as a real estate investor can seem appealing, but it should come with a price.

Authentic real estate investors take risks. They understand risk is an ingredient in the recipe for their success, and they have learned to account for and work around it. Genuine investors see risk as something to be mitigated but never entirely avoided. If you're working with someone who does all their due diligence but is then afraid to commit to moving forward, it may be a sign you found a poser.

Keep an eye out for the moment in a transaction when a commitment and the risk associated with it is required. See how the client acts. This typically comes when it's time to sign a buyer representation agreement, write an offer, accept a reasonable counter, or waive a contingency. If the person you are working with is looking for the glory without the risk, it will likely show up here.

They Want You to Represent Them on Off-Market Deals Where You Won't Be Paid

If your client doesn't care that you get paid, you're not in a two-way relationship. As a fiduciary, you're legally required to do what's in your client's best interest. Your client is not legally required to do the same. Since you don't have any protection here, it's important you protect yourself! Working with a client who doesn't care if you are compensated is simply foolish.

When someone asks me to represent them on a deal in which I won't be paid, I first ask them if they're aware I won't be paid a commission. If they still want me to help them with the deal, I politely tell them that we are a bad fit to work together, I only work in mutually beneficial relationships, and they should find another agent to help them. It's rare when a client is told by an agent they don't want to work together. This often makes them think.

Off-market deals can be better for the client, but they come with more challenges. An investor who wants to use you to navigate those challenges hasn't accepted, or doesn't understand, the nature of off-market deals and isn't ready to be pursuing them. Working with someone like this will cost you time and energy and not make you any money.

Leveraging Your Real Estate Investment Knowledge to Close More Deals

Most clients want to work with someone they know, like, and trust. We've talked about how to make yourself more known and how becoming more likable never hurts. But how do you build trust as an agent? You do it through your knowledge about how real estate works.

Consider a car salesperson. They may be well known. They are probably highly likable. But do you trust them? If you're like most people, that's a hard no. Why don't we trust car salespeople? Because their major incentive in offering advice is to make money off us. We don't know if they own the type of cars they are trying to sell us. How do we know we can trust their advice when so much money is on the line, but we don't know if they truly understand the car they're selling? This is the inherent problem in many sales positions.

As real estate salespeople, we face the same problem. There's a lot of money on the line. If we don't own real estate ourselves, it's tougher to build the credibility we need to represent others. If we aren't investors ourselves, it's harder to convince an investor to choose us over an agent who is one. I'm not saying only people who own real estate can be agents. The good news is, even if you don't own real estate, you can make up for that by having more knowledge about how real estate works than the average agent who does own a home.

Understanding the language of real estate investing and how to run numbers will definitely help you work with more investors. It will also help you work with more traditional buyers and sellers.

When you can talk about adding value, increasing ARV, or calculating ROI, investment buyers will take notice. This is a fast, powerful way to build trust with someone you don't know and quickly show the value you can bring. The more you understand how to work with investors, the more traditional buyers you will also be able to attract and work with. This is a big reason why this chapter is so important. As a top-producing agent, you want to close as many deals as possible. Working with investors can do that, but applying what you learn here to more standard conversations with new leads will be effective as well.

I recommend sharing your knowledge during lead generation activities such as open houses or phone calls with people you are reconnecting with. When someone does a walk-through at an open house that needs some updating, describe the contractor your other client is using to do the work on their flip. It sends a strong signal to the lead that you might be the best person to help them accomplish their goals. It also shows you're more likely to know your stuff. Everyone wants to work with an accomplished, credible, knowledgeable agent. It's just so hard to know who actually fits that bill. Conversations like this will establish yourself in this way.

You can also share this information in conversations with your sphere. Casually mentioning the rental property you helped someone buy or sharing about the investor who's receiving a 15 percent cash-on-cash return on the duplex you just closed is a powerful, attention-grabbing line that will open up dialogue and get you some serious street cred when it comes to your reputation as an agent.

Everyone is interested in real estate investing. Talking shop with people makes them feel like they are in the loop, and it takes some of the fear out of asking the questions they're bound to have. It can even jump-start conversations about buying their next property. Ask if they've heard of house hacking. If not, this is an excellent way to start the conversation and perhaps get them interested in buying. Who doesn't want to call themselves a real estate investor? Take advantage of this desire and show them the way to that dream.

Build Your Wealth through Real Estate Ownership

The last reason I'll share with you on why you should pursue working with investors is it brings you one step closer to owning real estate yourself in case you don't already. I know many real estate agents and many investors. I don't know anyone who would say that selling real estate will build wealth as fast as owning it. Even titans of the real estate industry, like Gary Keller and Jay Papasan, share this sentiment. Selling homes will make you money. Owning homes will build you wealth.

As a real estate agent, you sit in the perfect position to spot and land the best deals. Working in this industry every day and seeing the inventory available sets us firmly in the crow's nest of opportunity. If you work in real estate, you're much more likely to recognize a solid deal when you see it. There really aren't many excuses for why real estate agents shouldn't also buy and own property.

One easy way to land deals occurs when you are contacted about a listing in which the seller needs a fast and easy sale, or when the property is so distressed you know it will be very difficult to sell through traditional means. In these situations, consider telling the seller you'd like to buy it yourself and make them an "as-is" offer. If they say no, you can still take the listing. But if they say yes, you likely just made yourself much more money than you would have if you were only selling it.

Another method of finding great deals is incorporating searches into your lead generation. We all know to ask our sphere of influence to tell us if they hear of anyone looking to buy or sell a home, so don't hesitate to also ask them to let you know if they hear of anyone who needs a fast sale or has a fixer-upper property they need to unload. By telling people what you're on the lookout for, you increase your odds that someone is eventually going to bring you something you can buy yourself.

If you're not currently house hacking, I recommend you start there. House hacking is a fantastic way to learn the fundamentals of real estate investing without taking huge risks. The low down payment, coupled with the need to pay a housing expense, creates a great opportunity to learn investing with training wheels. Even if it takes you a long time to get good at managing tenants and collecting rent, you'll still be getting paid money to live in a house you would be paying for by yourself anyway, and you're getting some important real estate training in the process.

I love being an agent because of the synergy it creates with my own investment portfolio. The more investment properties I buy, the more credibility I have with my sphere. The more credibility I have, the more people approach me about buying a house. The more houses I sell, the more money I have to invest. This beautiful cycle benefits me in two ways: I make more money selling homes, and I build more wealth buying them for myself. With the cash flow that I receive on top of my commissions, I have diversified my income stream and make money while I sleep— instead of just while I work.

Wise business owners diversify their income streams. As a real estate salesperson, you're a businessperson. As you begin making money in this industry, be disciplined about saving it. Keeping a portion of your income set aside for investing will ensure you are able to buy a good deal when the time is right. After you get the first deal under your belt, each subsequent deal will become easier and easier. Soon enough, you'll be just as passionate about owning real estate as you are about selling it. Maybe even more so.

Here are some good rules of thumb to consider if you're new to real estate investing and want to make prudent decisions with what you buy.

1. Look for properties that meet the "1 percent rule." These are deals in which the rent you collect monthly is close to 1 percent of what you paid for the home. On a $100,000 home, you would be looking to collect a rent somewhere around $800 to 1,000 a month.

2. The amount derived from the 1 percent rule becomes increasingly less important the higher the price point. That is, you have more slack on a home worth more than $200,000; but on a $50,000 home, it's very important to hit that number.

3. The 1 percent rule is a general guideline, not a hard-and-fast rule.

4. The 1 percent rule is sensitive to interest rates. Lower rates give you more flexibility with this guideline.

5. Multifamily properties make easier cash flow than single-family homes.

6. The only thing you cannot change about a property is its location. Do not be lulled into buying a property in a bad area because the numbers look good on a spreadsheet.

7. Don't be afraid to use a professional property manager for your first few properties. I use them for all my properties.

8. It's wise to buy in the part of town you see improvement headed (the "path of progress").

9. Starter homes are always easier to sell than step-up or luxury homes.

10. Condos include HOA fees and more restrictions than single-family homes.

11. HOA communities may limit your ability to have tenants.

12. A house hack can become a rental property when you move out of it.

13. Don't wait to buy real estate. Buy real estate and wait!

➡ KEY POINTS

- Anyone intent on building wealth wants to work with an agent who can help them do it.
- Investors typically buy properties for one of two reasons: to buy and hold or to fix and flip.
- Someone with credibility and a strong circle of friends who recommends you is the best referral partner.
- Being organized is a huge component to handling a large volume of clients and not making mistakes.
- When you set your initial appointment with an investor client, make it abundantly clear you can help them get what they want.
- Learn the words investors use and how to use them to gain immediate attention as the coveted "investor-friendly agent."
- Your job as an agent is to come up with a strategy that works for your client and then create a plan to bring it to life.
- If your client doesn't care that you get paid, you're not in a two-way relationship.
- It's important to tell clients upfront what they can and cannot expect from you.
- The most powerful thing you can do for your own wealth is to own real estate, not just sell it.
- As a real estate agent, you can land the best deals for yourself.

CHAPTER ⟩ FIFTEEN
MOMENTUM

"People who succeed have momentum. The more they succeed, the more they want to succeed, and the more they find a way to succeed. Similarly, when someone is failing, the tendency is to get on a downward spiral that can even become a self-fulfilling prophecy."

—TONY ROBBINS

Who among us doesn't want to be like the "big dogs"? We all want plenty of leads flowing to us with the supreme confidence we can convert them into escrows. Put simply, momentum in business will change your life. But looking at individuals several steps ahead of us on the path we've chosen is often as discouraging as it is inspiring. Why?

We see the relative ease at which they navigate terrain, take ground, and overcome obstacles. From our place back on the path, it seems like they can accomplish in a week what may take us years. If you feel this way without understanding momentum, you may become too discouraged to continue at all.

We shouldn't compare a car traveling at 90 mph to a skateboard we're learning to ride. Those who are several steps ahead of us aren't using the same resources as us. They have way more. It's important to understand that the speed you'll be moving at in six months will be faster. The key to success is to build momentum so things move faster in your funnel. This chapter explains how top producers take advantage of momentum and how you can start developing your own momentum to replicate their results.

I'll start by discussing the different ways we make progress in life.

Progression Models

In Gary Keller and Jay Papasan's best-selling business book *The ONE Thing*, they deliver a compelling argument for focusing hard on your goals. They cover the concept of "geometric progression," which says that growth can start off slowly but then quickly scale to massive success. This is in opposition to linear growth, which is steadier and more predictable.

Linear Progression

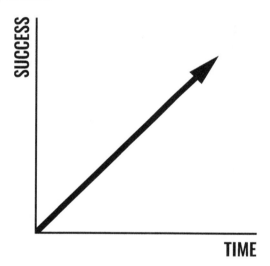

Most of us are used to linear growth in our lives and our jobs. An hourly or salary wage is akin to linear growth. As more time is spent, more income is made. Linear progression is more closely associated with entrepreneurship and skill-based jobs. Large amounts of time can pass until a certain "tipping point," which is when one (or more) skill has developed to become highly effective. This spike in productivity creates a massive growth in success.

Geometric Progression

Geometric progression is exponential growth. It typically starts off much slower than linear progression but reaches a tipping point faster. This is typically how we learn a new skill. To grow your business to top-producer status, you must harness the power of geometric progression.

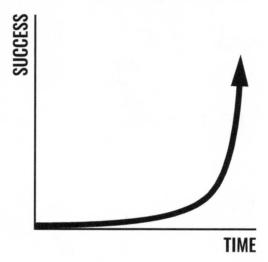

Shift in Results

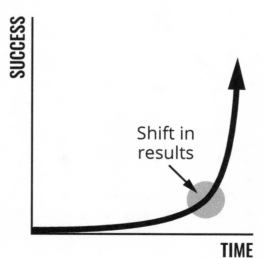

The point at which success comes faster and in larger spurts is represented in the graph with the circle labeled "shift in results." This is your target. The core goal of your business plan should be understanding what it will take to reach geometric progression and to work backward to achieve it. That is how you grow your business.

Domino Theory

Mastering new concepts or skill sets is complex. Before you can be successful at any new undertaking, you have to spend a significant amount of time and effort before reaching mastery. Nevertheless, geometric progression is possible throughout life.

For an analogy of geometric progression, *The ONE Thing* uses dominoes. Keller and Papasan explain how one domino can knock down another domino that's 50 percent bigger. For example, a 1-inch domino can knock down another domino that is 2.5 inches, which can then knock down a 3.75-inch domino, and so on. By the eighteenth domino, that first one—at only 1-inch tall—started a chain reaction capable of knocking down a domino the height of the Leaning Tower of Pisa. By the fifty-first domino, the chain can take down a domino as tall as Mount Everest.

Their domino theory clearly explains just how powerful building momentum can be for creating huge results, and real estate sales is no exception. This theory is prevalent in every top producer's business. Consider the following scenario.

New Agent Nora

New Agent Nora goes door-knocking in a specific neighborhood to "farm" it. After six months of work, she gets three listings. All three sell. During the sales process, Nora continues to work the neighborhood and meets 70 percent of the neighbors. Using the listings as a jumping-off point to start conversations, she puts all information about the people she's met into her database and maintains consistent contact. This results in a new listing every month from that same neighborhood. As she skillfully works her marketing and open houses, she picks up one buyer a month as well. As Nora's sales grow, so does her confidence, and with it her ability to convert new leads. This makes her the top agent in her office and gets her several walk-in deals a year from leads asking for the top agent. She has a large database and is known throughout town. More and more sellers contact her for help selling their houses.

Nora's Zillow reviews skyrocket, and more online leads find their way to her inbox. When she is no longer able to handle all the buyer leads, she hires buyer agents and splits commissions 50/50 with them. Soon she hires listing coordinators and marketing specialists to handle the high volume of listings she generates, and she hires showing assistants for her own top-buyer agents. At a certain point, every new agent knows that working on her team means they're on the fast-track to learning the business.

Nora can cherry-pick the top talent to work for her, and she makes enough money to increase her advertising to include billboards and radio ads. Several years down the road, she is dominating her local market as well as the talent pool of new Realtors. She now buys her own brokerage and rebrands the office with her name.

Nora is on podcasts and at big Realtor events to share her story. This increases her visibility and reputation even more and makes recruiting even easier. Nora opens several new offices and hires additional staff. She retires comfortably and lives off the passive income her massive momentum provided her.

Rules of Momentum

Success like this isn't easy but it's not impossible. The secret is in how you handle your dominoes and geometric progression. Here are the rules I've learned concerning momentum and success.

Rule 1: Never Let a Domino Fall without Knocking over Another Domino

Don't waste your dominoes! If you push a domino over (e.g., get a listing, close on a deal), capitalize on it in any way you can. This is how you build momentum. Every listing you take makes the next one that much easier to get, and every open house you hold should net you buyer leads. Don't let any success go unadvertised to those in your circle and always build on what you've started. Consider the following successes and how to capitalize on them.

First Success	Follow-Up Opportunities
Taking a listing	Door-knock in the neighborhood, post on social media for free marketing, tell your friends, hold open houses
Closing a deal	Get a testimonial, ask for online reviews, ask for referrals, throw a housewarming party to meet new leads
Receiving multiple offers on your property	Tell nearby homeowners you have a list of buyers who want to buy in their neighborhood, ask if they are interested in selling (double-ending the new deal, if legal in your state)
Winning an award	Advertise it on social media, tell other Realtors about it, tell your current clients about it
Saving your clients' money through negotiation	Ask them for referrals, tell other leads about it, share the information as a strategy with potential clients

In the context of real estate sales, pushing down a domino is hard work, especially at the beginning. Look for creative ways to use your current momentum to make future success more likely—then follow that up with even more success. Momentum is an extremely powerful force that makes someone a Realtor juggernaut. While it's fabulous once it gets going, momentum is notoriously difficult to build at first.

Rule 2: Don't Knock over Dominoes That Are the Same Size—Go 50 Percent Bigger

This rule has to do with never selling yourself short. While it's possible to line up a whole bunch of same-sized dominoes, why not go big? There is still some inherent value in the momentum of the past domino helping you knock over the next same-sized domino, but you're leaving a lot of money on the table if you don't aim for a bigger domino. Taking one listing and turning it into another is great—but why not shoot for a bigger listing? Or two more listings?

In general, you want to consistently grow your goals, with each one being slightly scarier than the one before. Shoot for bigger goals than you previously believed you could reach but also keep your milestones manageable. This cycle of big goals made by smaller milestones is a very effective way to achieve enormous success.

Rule 3: Don't Knock over Random Dominoes Hoping They Knock over Others

Most people have a rudimentary understanding of momentum and domino theory, even if they don't realize they do. To the amateur, it makes sense to push over every domino in the hope that something will eventually fall over, and that this random act will result in more random success as new dominoes are accidentally toppled. This will still create some measure of success, but it will be far less than if you are strategic. Falling into the seductive excuse of "it's all a numbers game" will result in the sporadic and inefficient waste of energy, like a lumberjack in the woods who chops wildly at whatever tree is found.

When you find yourself hoping that the action you took or the success you accomplished will result in future success, it's time to stop and reevaluate. Top producers do not "hope" for success. They plan, study, and strategically prepare for it. Before knocking a domino over, look to see what else is reasonably positioned to fall and be prepared for that before it happens.

Rule 4: Start at the End Goal and Line Up Your Dominoes Backward from There

The true professional Realtor understands this rule and how it applies to real estate sales. By beginning with the end in mind, we give ourselves the highest possible degree of success. If you want to make sure you never waste a domino and always get the most momentum out of each one, start at the end goal. In fact, if you get this rule correct, you'll end up following every other rule as well.

Consider the story of Nora and how she could retire and live off the passive income of her brokerage business. In her story, it appeared she ended up in this position accidentally by knocking on doors for six months. I told the story that way for a reason—as a newer or average Realtor, you likely aren't sure where you want to end up, but it's important for you to recognize that your career can take you to incredible places if you believe and follow the steps in this book.

What will it look like if you get there on purpose? Had Nora mapped out her entire journey by setting goals and creating smaller milestones, she would have gotten there much sooner. Nora could have written out her entire destiny, lined up her dominoes, traced them back to where she was in that present moment, and put all her effort toward pushing that first one over. Had she started with the end in mind and set her goals up backward from there, her plan would have looked something like this.

Last Domino/Ultimate Goal:
- Retire from sales with $60,000 each month in passive income.

Preceding Dominoes:
- Own three brokerages, each netting $20,000 in monthly profit.
- Recruit one hundred agents into each brokerage.
- Get featured on twenty-four real estate podcasts each year.
- Speak at four large real estate conferences each year.
- Become my region's top producer.
- Have a team of four buyer agents, one listing agent, and three full-time administrative assistants.
- Net $50,000 per monthly profit from sales to afford salaries.
- Close twenty-five deals each month (ten listings, fifteen buyers).
- Hold fifteen listing presentations each month.
- Have my team hold fifteen open houses each month.
- Speak to ten people each day to ask for business.
- Grow the database by ten people each week.
- Budget three hours each day for lead generation.
- Calendar priorities and stick to schedule.
- Hire assistant to handle all productive activities not related to revenue.
- Interview twenty assistant candidates.
- Net $10,000 each month in income to afford assistant.
- Become current office's top agent.
- Hire a productivity coach.
- Enter entire database into a CRM and create high-touch sphere campaign.
- Give listing and buyer presentations to three people each week (leads or friends/family to practice).
- Show homes for other agents in office to gain experience.

- Practice CMAs on friends' homes.
- Review hot sheets daily to understand local market.
- Arrive at office before 9 a.m. every day.

This is an example of how to start with an end goal and work backward to create a roadmap for yourself. During your journey, you will add or remove dominoes as needed, but the important thing is that you give yourself a path to follow. The mind does not like to move or act when it doesn't know where it's going. Creating a path like this can make reaching success much easier. Focus on the milestones so you don't become overwhelmed by the size of the next objective and the ultimate goal itself!

Vicious and Virtuous Cycles

When I was a police officer, I saw many lives ruined by the use of illegal drugs. When I would talk to the users, it was always a different variation of the same story. Familiar patterns always emerged. Someone would hit hard times. These hard times would often be of the same nature as what many experience in life. The caveat for the future drug addict was that when the hard time hit them, they often lacked the resources, support system, or inner strength to fight back. Worn down emotionally and feeling hopeless, the addict would look for a quick solution to their pain. Drugs and other substances would provide that—with a cost.

You know the cycle from here. Each hit gave less of a high than the previous one, and addiction slowly began to form. At a certain point, the scales tipped past the point where the addict could hold it all together. They lost their job, hid their problem from the world, and began to steal or commit other crimes to support the habit. They lost their self-respect, and they turned to their animal nature. Their relationships were destroyed, they became isolated, and one bad decision made the next one even easier. With each cycle of poor decision and poor response to this decision, the addict picked up momentum on their downward spiral. It was typically at this point where they entered my world. At the bottom of this spiral was incarceration, sickness, or death.

This series of events where one poor decision makes the next one easier and momentum heads in a negative direction is referred to as a vicious cycle. Momentum is an incredibly powerful force of nature—but it doesn't have to lead to death and destruction. The story of the drug addict is one in which the individual cannot control momentum; rather, it controls them. But this does not have to be the case for you. You can learn to control that same power, make it work for you, and use it to help you reach your goals. This is your responsibility as a human being who wants to do good in the world. Top producers have learned to harness this power.

The story of New Agent Nora is one in which she harnessed her momentum—even if it wasn't carefully planned—to create a series of events in which each new success was capitalized on to make the next step easier to accomplish. When momentum leads upward and is harnessed to make every step easier, we call it a virtuous cycle.

It's important to acknowledge that nothing in life is stagnant. Ever. Living things are always growing; when they stop growing, they die. Even dead things do not remain in their present form because they decompose. You are always moving in some way. One of the many gifts of life is that we are blessed with a will that lets us choose that direction. We can use momentum to create a virtuous cycle or fall prey to it and be swept away in a vicious cycle.

To complicate matters, it's entirely possible to live in a virtuous cycle in one area of our lives but in a vicious cycle in another. We see this in the example of the successful businessman who loses his family after having ignored them for too long. Ideally, we need to strive for virtuous cycles in all aspects of our lives.

The above example of the domino theory includes the practical steps of a virtuous cycle you can use to build momentum for your own real estate sales business. Putting these steps into practice will help you build the momentum you need to become and stay a top producer and eventually transition from salesperson to CEO. They will keep you continually striving for bigger, better, and more impactful results and accomplishments. Harnessing the power of momentum will allow you to change your life. Failing to do so will leave you a victim of the subtle gravitational "hooks" of the vicious cycle.

Flows and Cycles

Steven Kotler, in his best-selling book *The Rise of Superman*, provides a unique perspective on one specific way that successful people have learned to harness the power of momentum. Kotler cites research on the chemicals that are produced when a human being reaches a heightened state of awareness, which he refers to as "flow."

When in a flow state, dopamine and serotonin are released into the human brain. Neurotransmitters send signals to create an experience in which things slow down and the right decision in the moment becomes clear. This chemical mixture creates a heightened state of acuity and ability to focus.

Kotler explains the science behind flow's genesis. The prefrontal cortex is where "thinking happens," but thinking produces complexity and confusion (this assertion is supported by Oren Klaff's research in *Pitch Anything*, referred to earlier). Thinking is, in fact, the opposite of flow state. In a state of flow, the mind shuts down thinking and overanalyzing. It reacts to what is in front of it much more rapidly. It "feels" the right decision to make.

This flow experience is frequently described by extreme athletes such as professional skateboarder Danny Way, who jumped the Great Wall of China on a fractured ankle and torn ACL. Living in a flow state is how athletes reach their highest potential and produce their best results. This experience is often reported as occurring in the most dangerous or high-stakes arenas, because it's only in such environments that they feel a natural desire to be at their very best. And in the case of professional athletes, their very lives may depend on it.

But what if you could access this flow state without actually risking your life? What if your Big Why was so big that your success felt like a matter of life and death? What if you could let go of the belief that you have to know everything first? What if you could shut down your prefrontal cortex to instead feel the right answer? What if tapping into your client's emotions and feeling their mix of fears and excitement felt as exhilarating as catching a big wave in the ocean, forcing you to respond the same way surfer Laird Hamilton does in Hawaii?

You can access the same parts of your brain that professional athletes do to experience the same sense of clarity and confidence in the moment.

The reality is, no two clients need the exact same advice, and they definitely don't need it delivered in the exact same way. Using your flow state will help you in your individual interactions with people and do wonders for building your confidence and your momentum. Tapping into this state on a regular basis will take your business to levels you can't possibly anticipate or even imagine today. The flow state will take the dominoes you've lined up—your virtuous cycle—and knock them all down, and it will feel both fun and effortless.

Kotler explains that "every action, every decision, leads effortlessly, fluidly, seamlessly to the next. It's high-speed problem solving; it's being swept away by the river of ultimate performance." This describes exactly how an agent can harness momentum to build business and stack one success on top of another. Entering your flow state is imperative for creating your momentum.

Skill Set Bleed-Over and Momentum

Another way to create momentum in your business is to look for ways that build experience, proficiency, and skills in one area of your business that are likely to lead to greater success in others. I refer to this concept as "skill set bleed-over." It recognizes that improving yourself for one purpose/in one area will often have a positive impact in other areas. For example, a basketball player who improves her form in shooting three-pointers will most likely see an improvement in her shooting percentage and free throw percentage. Building your leadership skills in one area doesn't just benefit you in that area but also in every situation in which you are called upon to lead. Improvement in one concentrated area bleeds over to have a positive impact on multiple other areas of your life or business.

Keller and Papasan pose the question: "What is the one thing that so doing will make everything else easier or unnecessary?" They are referring to this same principle. What is one thing I can do that will bleed over into everything else to make me more successful? Skill set bleed-over contributes to building momentum in big ways. What you learn by knocking down the first domino helps you more easily knock down the second one. You build better form and muscles in the process, and you learn what worked and what didn't. Combined together, this makes the act of knocking down your next domino that much easier.

Plus you have the weight of the domino itself working for you.

Repetition develops mastery. You should learn something new with each new obstacle you overcome and apply that to the next challenge. Soon, you'll have plenty of experience and knowledge to draw from when facing obstacles. The muscles you've built in the past will serve you in the present. Skill set bleed-over contributes to your geometric progression and momentum.

Practical ways to build skills in one area of real estate sales mastery will help you in others. For example:

Areas of Skill Set Development	Additional Areas that Will Benefit
Negotiating with sellers to take listings	Negotiating with other agents to get what is best for your clients; negotiating with your own clients to guide them; negotiating with lenders to get better rates for your clients
Remaining steadfast but pleasant to close deals	Causing sellers to like you (so as to get more listings); preventing buyers from asking for part of your commission; getting home inspectors to prioritize your inspections; getting appraisers to adjust their reports; convincing agents to join your team; paying less for software that is contractually negotiated
Being bold in asking for referrals	Putting pressure on listing agents to take your offer; helping buyers feel more comfortable writing stronger offers; refusing a request for repairs; door-knocking conversion rates; winning the lead over several agents in the running
Tracking your numbers monthly	Looking closely at your profit and loss numbers; setting and hitting financial goals; ensuring accurate commission demands and broker splits; helping new agents track their finances; budgeting for your business
Learning how the lending industry works	Being more knowledgeable during open houses; helping your clients understand their rate sheet; negotiating closing cost credits for your clients; recognizing who are the better lenders to work with; helping your clients with refinancing; explaining the difference in monthly payments between two houses
Learning how the construction industry works	Interpreting and explaining inspection reports better; negotiating more credits for repairs; being more knowledgeable when showing homes; delivering stronger listing presentations; discussing what repairs sellers should or shouldn't make
Learning how to calculate mortgage payment amounts	Giving strong buyer presentations related to full monthly payments; talking sellers into selling their current house and buying a new one with you; helping clients feel comfortable writing stronger offers; being able to explain the difference in monthly payment between two houses
Articulating the real estate process to clients	Articulating why you get paid your commission; explaining your offer to other agents; explaining how contingencies work to clients; explaining your team structure to new agents who want to work with you; explaining changing market conditions during a shift; getting sellers to agree to a price reduction

Momentum and Business Growth

Momentum will provide you with opportunities to expand your skill sets and thus your future business. As you move more and more clients through your Sales Funnel, you'll get better and more efficient at doing so. This will lead to higher conversion rates and consequently more income. As clients close and you market the closings correctly, you'll get even more leads making their way into your funnel. With your improved sales skills, you'll close more of them too.

As you continue on this virtuous cycle, your company dollar will start to increase. This will open up new opportunities. You can use your increased income to start buying marketing, advertising, and even leads. More important is that you can use this income to hire leverage; that is, hire staff to take things off your plate and keep you focused on the main thing: acquiring new clients and putting them in contract. Ways to scale are covered in detail in Chapter 9.

As a reminder, your first hire should be an administrative assistant. The right person will help drive your business to new levels and take away much of what you don't like to do. This will not only make you happier but also make you more productive and focused on the big picture. When you can take a step back from the busy work, you'll recognize new leads, follow up with them more quickly, and improve your conversion rates.

When you hire the right people, you'll see a major increase in your own productivity and thus in your sales and revenue. This momentum will open doors. You can hire a second assistant, a showing assistant, a buyer agent, and so on. Eventually you can open expansion offices. The skills you built learning to sell houses can be used to train other agents to do the same.

Investing in Real Estate to Improve Your Business

Increased income means more opportunities to invest in your business and in real estate for yourself. Owning real estate is typically much, much more effective for building your personal wealth than just selling it. In fact, 90 percent of millionaires in the United States became so through owning real estate. If you want to build big wealth for yourself, start by owning the asset class you make money selling. Investing in real estate can do wonders for your net worth, but your balance sheet isn't the only place it will show.

There is a virtuous cycle when representing clients and owning real estate yourself. When you generate a healthy income selling homes, you can be approved for financing and apply disposable income toward owning investment property. When you own rentals and/or flip houses, you gain a new appreciation and respect for—not to mention knowledge of—elements of real estate you normally would not experience as an agent. This is skill set bleed-over in action. As you learn more about owning real estate, you have more knowledge to help you sell it.

Your increased sales will help you buy more rentals, which in turn will help you sell more real estate. This is powerful momentum. If that weren't enough incentive, you gain more than just knowledge when you own real estate yourself. You also gain credibility.

There's a big difference between running numbers for a client to recommend they buy a property and running numbers and sharing that the deal looks good enough that you would buy it. When you own the asset class you're selling, clients are more likely to take your advice and follow your instructions. And they should. You're much more qualified to share advice with them when it's advice you follow yourself.

Buying properties for yourself also gives you the opportunity to share your new purchases on social media. This new, unique, and fresh marketing perspective gives your sphere of influence something to look at that's different from your usual posts and pulls them into your world with a stronger attraction. When you can talk about the numbers of real estate and not just the contract terms, you're more likely to present a compelling argument that will help you close more deals and win more leads.

In short, buying investment property earns you credibility with leads and wins you more business. Selling more houses earns you more money and allows you to buy more investment property. Doing both of these things at higher volumes gives you more content to post on social media, more content to discuss on phone calls with your sphere, and increased power to your lead generation. Buying real estate for yourself harnesses the power of momentum to build the net worth of both you and your business.

Buyer/Listing Skill Set Bleed-Over

One major skill set with bleed-over is market listings, because you get better at it after working with so many buyers. Many agents believe you should work with only buyers or only sellers, and that you can't be good at working with both. While there is some merit to this thinking (buyers and sellers do require completely different skill sets), there is also something lost when an agent focuses entirely on buyers or sellers at the expense of the other.

One key component to selling a house is improving its condition before bringing it to market. The tricky part of this is that most sellers believe their house is already the best-looking house on the block and are hesitant to spend any time or money fixing it up before putting it on the market. The fastest way you'll lose a listing is by bringing this up with sellers too early in the process. Never tell a seller anything negative about their property until after the listing agreement has been signed.

When you walk houses every week with different buyers, you develop a sixth sense for what they like and what they don't. Buying a home is an emotional decision, and buyers may not always be able to articulate how they feel when they walk through a home, but they will feel it nonetheless. Being an astute observer will allow you to notice things that turn off buyers as you walk the property with them. When you point out the reason why they felt turned off, you can address the issue immediately (often it's something minor) and help them see past it. This skill will help you put buyers into contract. It will also help you prepare your listings for the market.

Consider the agent who regularly works with buyers and is now preparing a listing for sale. As the agent prepares the listing, their trained eye immediately notices things a less experienced agent would miss. Many of these less-than-fashionable components are relatively inexpensive to change or remove but leaving them in place could cost the sellers quite a bit of money. It may seem petty, but the following items can have a large negative impact on today's buyers.

- Brass fixtures
- Kitchens separated from the living spaces
- White tile countertops with brown grout
- Oak-colored cabinets
- Wallpaper
- Popcorn ceilings
- Carpet in common areas
- Carpet in bathrooms
- Leaning or deteriorating fencing
- Yards without landscaping

- Nonworking vehicles on the property
- Rooms painted different colors
- Old-fashioned light covers
- Linoleum
- Brown spots on chipped bathtub and sink porcelain
- Water discoloration stains
- Family portraits on the walls
- Cluttered properties
- Several different flooring types
- Unfinished garage interiors

When an agent regularly works with buyers, they notice things like this before their seller clients do. This is a big advantage to have when preparing listings for sale. Your property may be priced at the best value on the block—on paper. But buyers don't make decisions based on how things look on paper. They make decisions based on their emotions. If you want your listing to sell for top dollar, it's imperative you look at it from the eyes of the buyer.

Conversely, understanding how to price and sell listings can give you a big advantage when working with buyers. When you regularly sell houses, you get a feel for how long most homes sit on the market, how quickly they get offers, if it's standard for offers to be over asking price and if so by how much, etc. Your sixth sense allows you to understand how your seller is on an emotional roller coaster. You sense when greed overrides fear. You feel when sellers start to doubt if their house will really sell, and you intuitively know the right time to bring an offer with rock-solid terms but a low purchase price. This knowledge and intuition gives you a huge advantage over agents who work only with buyers and don't understand the timing of selling a house.

Being both a listing and buying agent also gives you an advantage when it comes to understanding how homes are priced and comparable sales are viewed. When a house is priced below market rate and your clients want to offer asking price, it's highly unlikely that their offer will be accepted. The ability to look at comparable sales and explain why your clients should write a stronger offer is an incredibly useful skill when trying to put buyers in contract. Working with sellers will help you develop this skill.

The ability to interpret a listing agent's actions and tone are helpful when determining how motivated they are to sell. You don't want to write a low offer if the house has a lot of interest, but you also don't want to write too high an offer if no one else is interested. Of course, listing agents will never tell you when they don't have any interest. You have to learn to read this for yourself.

When you list and sell homes, you develop an understanding of a listing agent's emotions. When there's a lot of interest about your listing, you'll receive nuisance phone calls and inquiries from buyer agents that are irritating to you. When you're worried that your listing won't sell, an interested party becomes the best part of your day and you're more than happy to talk to them for as long as they like. You hope that your enthusiasm will be passed to their clients and they'll write an offer.

The secret to reading listing agents is to ignore their words and focus on their tone and actions. An agent who is excited to speak to you and spend time on the phone is usually a sign of weakness on their part. When you sense this weakness, exploit it. Get the listing agent to talk to you about their seller's situation as much as possible. Do the sellers have another home in contract and need to sell this one soon before they lose the other? Is the listing getting close to expiring? If so, a low offer might be a great tactic. The listing agent is conveying their client's weak position.

Conversely, if the listing agent won't call you back, it may be a sign that they have several offers in hand already. The more listings you sell, the better sense you'll develop for these types of interactions. Working with sellers gives you an advantage with buyers and working with buyers gives you an advantage with sellers. The skill set bleed-over between the two sides is powerful.

Momentum is key to success in life, and real estate sales is no exception. There are so many opportunities to build on your successes and turn them into more successes. If you begin your career with this in mind, you will experience the benefits of geometric progression for yourself.

➡ KEY POINTS

- Geometric progression takes more time but there's a rapid increase in productivity. Linear progression is more predictable and closer to how we get paid in most jobs. If you want to grow your business, learn to harness geometric progression.

- A significant period of time and effort is needed before you reach mastery.
- Use the domino theory to build your real estate business. Never let a domino fall without knocking over another domino. Don't knock over random dominoes but be strategic.
- There are four rules to the domino theory.
- Start with your end goal in mind and line up your dominoes backward to help you get there faster.
- Vicious cycles increase in speed as bad decisions lead to worse ones; virtuous cycles work in the opposite way.
- The flow state creates momentum.
- Skill set bleed-over occurs when you increase your skills in one area that will help you in other areas.
- Investing in real estate builds your credibility as an agent.
- Working with buyers can give you a better understanding of how to stage your listings. Selling more listings can help you understand how to write stronger offers or target better deals.
- Working with buyers and sellers will help you develop your sixth sense to guide your clients.

CONCLUSION

At the end of *SOLD*, I explained that a new agent's job is to create a database of people they serve. This is similar to how a farmer plants and grows seeds. The more seeds that are planted and cared for with watering, weeding, fertilizing, and so on, the stronger the crop.

SKILL takes that concept and expands on it further by focusing on creating great farmers (that is, Realtors), not just great crops (that is, databases). In this book, *you,* not your database, are the focus. These concepts will allow you to harvest much more of your database with less wasted time and energy so you can build a better real estate business. Running an incredible business and having an incredible reputation will bring you an incredible lifestyle, and that's the reason you got into real estate sales in the first place, isn't it? None of us study to get our license and then hope for a mediocre career.

As your skills improve, your business will grow and so will your income. For those not yet producing big numbers, what I'm describing may sound like the pipe dream: big money, big clients, and big smiles from happy customers. I encourage you to pursue this dream by following the advice in this book, but I also want to share two facts as follows:

1. When you achieve this high volume, you will be faced with a whole new set of problems. Rather than a lack of money, it'll be a lack of time to enjoy it.

2. I have anticipated this problem for you and provided you solutions. In *SCALE*, the third book in this series, I will help you tackle those challenges head-on.

Don't be discouraged if it seems like agents have to make a never-ending series of adjustments to grow their business. This is how everything in life works. This pattern of striving, accomplishing, leveling up, then starting over but at a higher level is a natural progression. It is, at least, for those always aiming to be their best. My opinion is that my clients deserve the best representation possible from me and my team, so it is our responsibility to always be improving.

Mastering the concepts in this book should leave you feeling confident. There should be a little swagger added to your step. Listing appointments should feel more exciting than scary, as should negotiating with the other agent or even your own client. It is exhilarating to flip the real estate script from scared to victorious.

That being said, it's not just about you leveling up. New agents need to learn the same knowledge you were once lacking. New agents need the same opportunities to work with buyers that you once needed. New agents must cultivate the clarity, direction, and support that you once had to cultivate. If you continue to grow your business, help more clients, and increase your income, you'll hit a point where you've grown the skills detailed in this book. This is the point of diminishing returns in skill development. When that happens, it's time to focus on systems, processes, and people. This is what you learn to do in *SCALE*.

This third book in the series focuses on turning your brand into a business. You will pass along the skills you have mastered to others, creating a small army of skilled, charismatic, service-oriented agents who represent your clients with the same standards as you. Their collective efforts will grow your business, increase your income, and—most importantly—give you back your time.

This team model improves everyone's experiences, including your own. In fact, *the success of our entire industry depends on those who are the best agents passing on their knowledge and skills to new people.* If you don't guide, lead, and direct others, it's not only your own business that suffers. The entire industry depends on teaching new agents correctly to prevent thousands of clients from having bad experiences at the hands of untrained, unskilled real estate agents.

Without question, the most rewarding experience you'll have in this industry is when you help more clients and more agents by sharing your skills.

If you enjoyed this book, I highly encourage you to read *SCALE* and begin planting the seeds for the next phase of your business. While you may not be quite ready to turn your business into passive income, you should still begin looking for your next business stage and considering how to steer in that direction.

As amazing as it is to make a great income, it loses much of its luster when you're unable to enjoy it. Getting off the "hamster wheel" is a huge part of the BiggerPockets ethos. It only makes sense that you will eventually turn your active business income into passive business income so you can help more people *and* live your best leisure life.

I want to thank you for reading this book, and I send deep gratitude to those who purchase a copy for a friend or loved one who is struggling in their real estate business. We can improve our industry's reputation, better guide our clients to find or sell their homes, find our niche in the space, and aid our fellow agents when we share our knowledge.

Become a **BiggerPockets Featured Agent—TODAY**

The best way to fuel your pipeline with high-intent leads

- **Stand out in the largest network of real estate investors**

- **Instantly match with buyers interested in your market**

- **Save time and sell more with better leads**

"...BiggerPockets is our best performing lead source. The clients that reach out through BiggerPockets are already well educated in the buying process and many are already pre-approved and ready to go."

—Jonathan Bombaci of Boston

"The program is fantastic. I've received so many qualified leads that I'm expanding my team to handle the increase in volume."

—Peter Stewart of Indianapolis

How It Works

❶ Pick your top markets

❷ Get featured when investors search for agents in your markets

❸ Receive instant text alerts when investors want to connect

Get started now
at **www.biggerpockets.com/ featured-agent/skill** or scan the QR code!

More from
BiggerPockets Publishing

The Book on Negotiating Real Estate

When the real estate market gets hot, it's the investors who know the ins-and-outs of negotiating who will get the deal. J Scott, Mark Ferguson, and Carol Scott combine real-world experience and the science of negotiation in order to cover all aspects of the negotiation process and maximize your chances of reaching a profitable deal.

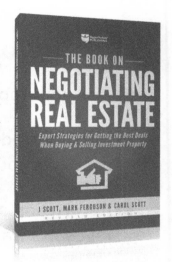

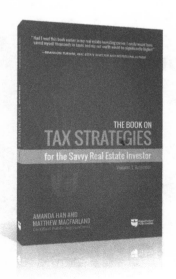

The Book on Tax Strategies for the Savvy Real Estate Investor

Taxes! Boring and irritating, right? Perhaps. But if you want to succeed in real estate, your tax strategy will play a huge role in how fast you grow. A great tax strategy can save you thousands of dollars a year. A bad strategy could land you in legal trouble. With *The Book on Tax Strategies for the Savvy Real Estate Investor*, you'll find ways to deduct more, invest smarter, and pay far less to the IRS!

If you enjoyed this book, we hope you'll take a moment to check out some of the other great material BiggerPockets offers. BiggerPockets is the real estate investing social network, marketplace, and information hub designed to help make you a smarter real estate investor through podcasts, books, blog posts, videos, forums, and more. Sign up today—it's free! **Visit www.BiggerPockets.com.**

SOLD: Every Real Estate Agent's Guide to Building a Profitable Business

Most agents lack the necessary mentorship, guidance, and training to succeed in the competitive and independent world of real estate. *SOLD* provides a much-needed look at how successful real estate agents build their business, close deals, and generate commissions. Best-selling author and expert real estate agent David Greene shares everything he wishes someone had shared with him—including the exact processes he used to become rookie of the year and top agent in his office.

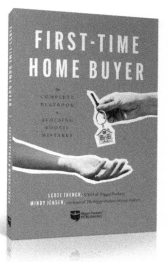

First-Time Home Buyer: The Complete Playbook to Avoiding Rookie Mistakes

Everything you need to buy your first home, from initial decisions all the way to the closing table! Scott Trench and Mindy Jensen of the *BiggerPockets Money Podcast* have been buying and selling houses for a collective thirty years. In this book, they'll give you a comprehensive overview of the home-buying process so you can consider all of your options and avoid pitfalls while jumping into the big, bad role of homeowner.

CONNECT WITH BIGGERPOCKETS

and Become Successful in Your Real Estate Business Today!

Facebook
/BiggerPockets

Instagram
@BiggerPockets

Twitter
@BiggerPockets

LinkedIn
/company/Bigger
Pockets

Website
BiggerPockets.com

CPSIA information can be obtained
at www.ICGtesting.com
Printed in the USA
JSHW031332290522
26440JS00002B/2